ID0947470

THE HATTERASMAN

THE

HATTERASMAN

by Ben Dixon MacNeill

illustrated by Claude Howell

FIFTIETH ANNIVERSARY EDITION

edited by John F. Loonam, Jr.

with new introduction by Philip Gerard

THE
PUBLISHING
LABORATORY
UNIVERSITY OF NORTH CAROLINA **WILMINGTON**

2008

The Hatterasman by Ben Dixon MacNeill, Fiftieth Anniversary edition
edited by John F. Loonam, Jr., with new introduction by Philip Gerard
© 2008 University of North Carolina Wilmington

All rights reserved. No material in this book may be copied or reproduced
in any manner without the express written consent of the publisher.

First edition John F. Blair, Publisher, 1958
Original illustrations by Claude Howell

Fiftieth Anniversary edition by The Publishing Laboratory, May 2008
Second printing, August 2010
Book design and illustration reproduction by John F. Loonam, Jr.
Publishing Laboratory faculty: Barbara Brannon, Emily Louise Smith, Robert Siegel
FRONT COVER: From the title page illustrations by Claude Howell

Printed in the United States of America
ISBN 978-0-9791403-4-1

LIBRARY OF CONGRESS CATALOGING-IN-PUBLICATION-DATA

MacNeill, Ben Dixon, 1889–1960.
  The Hatterasman / by Ben Dixon MacNeill ; illustrated by Claude Howell ; edited by
John F. Loonam, Jr. ; with new introduction by Philip Gerard. — Fiftieth anniversary ed.
     p. cm. — (Lives in place)
  Originally published: Winston-Salem : J.F. Blair, 1958.
  ISBN-13: 978-0-9791403-4-1 (alk. paper)
  1. Hatteras Island (N.C.)—Social life and customs. 2. Ocracoke Island (N.C.)—Social life
and customs. 3. Hatteras, Cape (N.C.)—Social life and customs. 4. Hatteras Island (N.C.)—
Biography. 5. Ocracoke Island (N.C.)—Biography. 6. Hatteras, Cape (N.C.)—Biography.
7. Hatteras Island (N.C.)—Description and travel. 8. Ocracoke Island (N.C.)—Description
and travel. 9. Hatteras, Cape (N.C.)—Description and travel. I. Loonam, John F. II. Title.
  F262.A19M3 2008
  975.6'175--DC22

                              2008011787

THE
PUBLISHING
LABORATORY
UNIVERSITY OF NORTH CAROLINA WILMINGTON

Published by The Publishing Laboratory
Department of Creative Writing
University of North Carolina Wilmington
601 South College Road
Wilmington, North Carolina 28403
www.uncw.edu/writers

For

Flora MacKinnon MacNeill

and

Angus Benjamin MacNeill

I started making the trip as a teenager in the company of a neighbor family, the Coopers—Harry and Ruth, and their daughters Susan, Sally, and Sandy. I was their paperboy. Harry was teaching English literature at the local high school. He had an ear for a good story, loved to fish in the surf, and cooked the best outdoor breakfasts I've ever eaten, concocted from a special chuckbox he had built and stocked for his Hatteras camping trips. Ruth and the girls were equally hardy campers who seemed to love the lore of the island as much as the physical place. It was they who introduced me to Ben Dixon MacNeill's wonderful book *The Hatterasman*. They loaned me a copy, and I was so entranced by it that I bought my own hardback edition at the lighthouse store— for $6.95.

The language of the book is oddly timeless—archaic and colloquial at the same time, a chronicle of nested stories you might hear from a salty old-timer at the bait shack. You don't quite believe them, except you do. They hold the appeal of both history and myth—the larger shape of our beliefs personified in distinctive, sometimes heroic characters, from explorers like Amerigo Vespucci to surfmen like Rasmus Midgett.

As I fell under the spell of that lovely low coast, *The Hatterasman* became my companion—a voice to revisit every winter during the gloomy indoor days of sleet and rain. After a brutal senior year of high school, I hitchhiked down to Cape Hatteras to hide out for the summer, with *The Hatterasman* tucked away in my backpack, and lived for months in a small A-frame tent, and it was probably then that the island got inside of me for good.

When my life landed me in the Arizona desert, my imagination still lived at least part of the time on that windswept island. I found myself dreaming it alive in the pages of what would become my first novel—*Hatteras Light*—the story of families and a community caught up in a war. I think a writer can capture a place best when he is far away from it, since he must then create it all over again in memory and invention. The Hatteras Island of my book was a place that existed only in my head, not in history, and yet the novel was also a valentine to a place that had formed me.

And *The Hatterasman* clearly shaped the vision of the novel in profound ways that became apparent only in retrospect. MacNeill writes about the real-life surfmen and keepers of the United States Life-Saving Service—later part of the U.S. Coast Guard—who for the better part of a century launched wooden boats into the breakers and rowed out to ships in distress, driven onto the Diamond Shoals by storms or torpedoed by U-boats, rescuing their crews and passengers at great personal risk. They went out in the worst weather, often at night, using only muscle power and courage—iron men in wooden boats.

The surfmen became the heroes of my novel. I simply could not imagine a greater test of courage against fear, of human striving against implacable forces. MacNeill taught me about these men—about Captain Benjamin Dailey, keeper of the Hatteras Light, who took his crew out in a December sleet storm in 1884, the temperature well below freezing, and brought off six crewmen from the foundering schooner *Ephraim Williams*, a ten-mile round trip that left his hands so frozen and bloody that he could not enter the events into the station log for nine days. He became one facet of my own composite hero, Malcolm Royal.

Likewise, MacNeill writes of a Hatterasman who builds exquisite ship models, and one day during the writing, a character of mine, the storekeeper Ham Fetterman, began shaping a model under his hands, a model of a strange new ship, before the ship ever appears on the horizon—a German submarine. The U-boat makes a cameo appearance in MacNeill's book, lobbing off a few shells at the telephone wires, and that was all I needed to set my plot in motion.

MacNeill captures the stoic humor, the foibles, the strong-willed women, the superstitions, and especially the landscape—a landscape in constant motion, sand moved by water and wind into ever-shifting configurations: an accurate metaphor for the world of our lives, which never stands still but challenges us to know it fresh after every storm. And in that way he shaped the landscape in my novel. Partly my Hatteras is a landscape built from memories of living outdoors in the actual place—cooked by the sun and scoured by the constant wind, swept by violent storms, blessed by sweet breezy evenings—and partly it is the place in the pages of MacNeill's book—an island as magical as Atlantis, a once-upon-a-time land of stories almost too good to be true, peopled by sea captains and castaways, life-savers and scoundrels, all of them larger than life.

I did not even realize until recently that the illustrations in *The Hatterasman* were the work of Wilmington artist Claude Howell—despite that fact that I knew him for years and broadcast alongside him during fund-raising drives for WHQR public radio, for which we both wrote commentaries. His were charming and funny tales of life in old Wilmington, alternating with adventure stories of traveling the world, told in a mellifluous, somewhat theatrical Southern drawl. But my first and lasting impression of Claude, before I ever met him, before I ever connected the dapper raconteur with the book I had read every summer for a dozen youthful years, was that this man knew how to draw wind—in a few clean pen strokes, Claude makes the air move, the world on the page come alive with swirling, restless motion.

He is the perfect illustrator for a book that captures the ephemeral breath of oral history, the story of an island people whose lives are never more than a few feet above the reach of the sea.

Philip Gerard
Whiskey Creek
May 2007

A PUBLISHER'S NOTE
ON THE FIFTIETH ANNIVERSARY EDITION

WHEN THE PUBLISHING LABORATORY, the book publishing imprint of the University of North Carolina Wilmington's Department of Creative Writing, set about to establish its "Lives in Place" series, featuring titles of literary and cultural significance to our region, bringing Ben Dixon MacNeill's *The Hatterasman* back into print was a perfect first selection.

Nearly half a century after its original hardcover publication by the then newcomer John F. Blair, Publisher, of Winston-Salem, the book had become something of a rarity on Southern bookshelves. The first edition, which went through multiple impressions, was long out of print; its author was seldom remembered.

But the combination of the author's unique voice, the book's value as historical and artistic record, and the illustrator's connection with UNCW (Claude Howell was the fledgling university's first professor of art and the first chair of its newly established art department; *The Hatterasman* was the first commercially published book he illustrated), persuaded us that here was a work worth preserving in a way that would introduce it to a fresh generation of readers. Our publication board enlisted the talents of BFA student John Loonam, an intern in The Publishing Laboratory and a longtime resident of the North Carolina coast, to undertake research on the title and the preparation of a new edition, under my supervision. John was the ideal editor for the project: not only was he skilled in the methods of digital scanning and proofreading that would yield a clean and accurate new setting of type, he also brought to the task an intimate familiarity with the folkways and natural history of the Outer Banks.

storms of Cape Hatteras and reflected humanity itself in the great spaces there will not die until long after those who knew him have gone too."

The text of the present edition was scanned from the first printing and incorporates corrections made in the second by author and editor. Except for a handful of obvious typographical and factual errors (the name of the keeper of the Hatteras Light has been corrected to Byrum at his daughter's request, for instance, and the ship in chapter 26 that came to the aid of the Titanic's survivors was the Carpathia, not Carinthia, as it was erroneously given), it remains faithful to MacNeill's spellings and stylings—including a preference for the nonstandard spelling yoepon (yaupon), the rendering of General Billy Mitchel's name as "Billie," and a penchant for capitalizing professional titles and such locations as "the Island." This choice will not seem inappropriate to the reader who begins to absorb MacNeill's perspective on the land and sea that he so aptly personifies.

The type is set in a classic Jenson font similar in flavor to the Granjon which Bill Loftin of Heritage Printers used for the 1958 edition, with pains taken to maintain the generous page dimensions and minimal line-end breaks that made the original edition such a handsome specimen. Howell's line drawings have also been reproduced with care, placed within the type setting as they were in the original edition.

In one important regard this edition, to my mind, greatly improves on its predecessor. Howell's drawing for the dust jacket has been incorporated into a new cover design that more fully showcases its sparse beauty. Thanks go to John Loonam, again, for his meticulous scanning and attention to layout detail. It has been my pleasure to work with him, as well as Philip Gerard and Emily Smith and other faculty colleagues at UNCW, in bringing this volume back to life.

One further bibliographical note, in closing. When it came time to acquire a copy of the original book to be used in the creation of the new edition, I searched used-book Web sites to find one that we could disbind for the purpose. The usual practice is to slice off the spine with a guillotine cutter so that the separate pages can be easily fed into the scanner for optical character recognition.

But I'm a book collector, and my eye was instead drawn to the following entry: "1st ed. 8vo. Hardcover. Signed by MacNeill on the title page." I sprang for the twenty-dollar purchase price to buy this one for my own bookshelf.

When the volume arrived, it appeared as described, "top edge lightly sunned, in a chipped and slightly stained DJ." (Dust jacket, for non-collectors.) There was MacNeill's signature, looking quite authoritative, beneath his name on the title page. But on the front free endpaper—the blank sheet that non-collectors often refer to as the flyleaf—was a second inscription. The bookseller had missed the real drawing card: "Christmas 1958. This is about our part of the country. Sincerely, Andy Griffith."

And so it is. The students and faculty of UNCW's Publishing Laboratory hope that new readers will enjoy, as much as we have, this portrait of our part of the country.

Barbara Brannon
Wilmington
August 2007

A Foreword

This is not a history. I am not a historian, though I was once so described by a bemused Congressman groping for a word that would, to an important Committee, account for the appearance before them of what must have had the general outlines of an apparition. Most of them nodded cheerfully but not with a degree of warmth that would thaw my own dismay and convert me, by some alchemy, into a historian. But a clerk dutifully set down the Congressman's words and I suppose it is recorded somewhere that I was at least called a historian.

I am not a historian and this is not a history. There is historical matter in it, and there might well have been much more. I have undertaken to profile a race of men that have been shaped by event and circumstance in the little world of these two Islands in four and a half centuries. The idea of such a study was born on the twenty-eighth day of June in 1926, and it simmered, cooled sometimes, simmered again for twenty-nine years and eight months precisely before the first word of this text was set down on paper.

That day, in 1926, I had come down the Island at the wheel of a then very fashionable little sports roadster, driving for a man who then loomed large on the national horizon and in my own life. He had been gravely ill and was recovering. It was toward nightfall when we approached, driving the beach, the Point of Cape Hatteras. Neither of us knew our own folly. The sea reached for us and there we were. It looked utterly hopeless, for the roadster and for us. A miracle happened. Ten giants, smiling and friendly, approached through the gathering dusk. With no ado whatsoever they took hold of the roadster and toted it up out of reach of the sea. They were surfmen from Cape Hatteras Lifeboat Station.

They dried us out, fed us, and were very gentle about our folly, and the next day they rode herd on us until we were across another inlet where other surfmen, alerted by telephone, saw that no harm, born of our own ignorance and folly, befell us. My companion recovered fully. He lived in greatness for another decade. I have lived three decades with the recurrent hope that I could come back and explore a people. The result is this book.

On every page of it I have resisted the impulse to romanticize this race or to idealize it. In so far as I have been able to do so I have written the story from the inside, so to speak, especially where it gets involved with history. If an event of recorded history left any imprint on the life of these Islands, it has been explored to the last detail, both in the folklore of the Islands and in the books and the documents. All of it has been profitable, but not all of it has got set down. Some of it, sometimes requiring weeks of digging, has been omitted because there is no trace of it in the making up of the man who evolved into the Hatterasman.

There is, for mere instance, the time required to determine precisely the weather picture on the day of the wreck and the rescue of the crew of the *Ephraim Williams*. Eight days of tolerably steady digging were needed to be sure, documentarily, what the weather did that day. Out of that week's exploration three words were set down in the text . . . "Sleet was falling." . . . And the word "mustee" has not been written in a North Carolina record since 1755, and a long journey was required before I was sure of its meaning and derivation, though the context made it clear enough.

So many people have helped with the undertaking that it dismays me to so much as begin to record my acknowledgment. Thad Page at the National Archives has helped wonderfully and so also have anonymous members of the staff at the Library of Congress. But equally helpful have been some scores of just people who have sent me scraps and documents that include, even, the plans of the *Monitor* forwarded to London during the Civil War by the British intelligence agent who drew them from hearsay.

Andrew Horn, James Patton, and Miss Mary Thornton, at the library of the University of North Carolina, have vastly lightened the labor involved, and to these names should be added that of Miss Carrie Broughton, State Librarian in Raleigh, John Lockhead, librarian at the Mariners' Museum at Newport News, who found for me the needed clue to the establishment of the windmill on these Islands as early as 1723, and Missouri Rollinson Kramer, who sent me her grandfather's Journal.

In a more personal way I am beholden to the devotion of three friends who have encouraged me, and sustained me. These are Dudley and Ida Bagley, of Currituck County, whom I think of as one; Huntington Cairns, at the National Gallery of Art; and Albert Quentin Bell, the English-born doer of miracles on and about Roanoke Island, who is infinitely informed about life, especially in the Elizabethan era, and who, always, has been indulgently patient with what he calls my "natural arrogance."

. . . And there is Mr. Pegler, who is a mockingbird. He sits on his own twig outside my window and has mastered the sound of a rattled typewriter. He also has managed to take the relatively simple theme of Beethoven's Seventh Symphony and can whistle it now, which is fortunate because I have about worn out the recording of it that Dudley and Ida Bagley sent down to untangle the snarls of an Id bent too long over a typewriter.

. . . Finally there are the Coast Guard crewmen from The Station, who have poked their neighborly heads in the door and asked cheerfully "How's it goin'?" many more times than there are pages in this text. Three of them are grandsons of the surfmen who toted me out of the sea's reach thirty years ago. They still tote me, and this book is their book.

BEN DIXON MACNEILL
Cape Hatteras
April 1956

THE HATTERASMAN

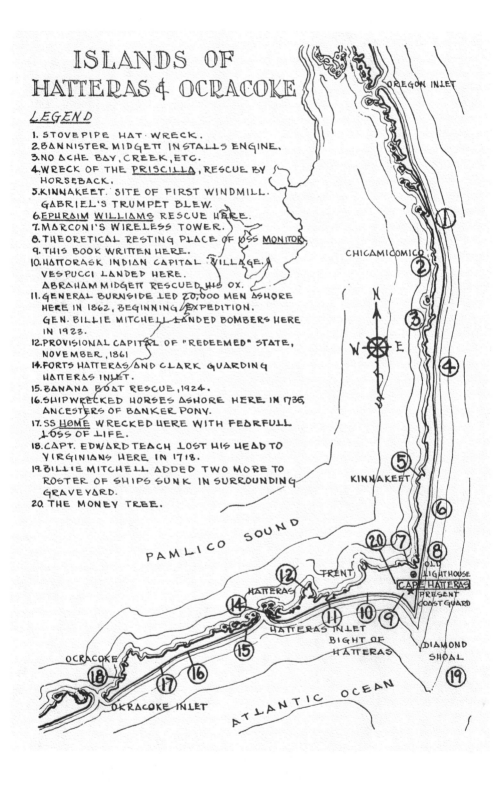

ISLANDS OF HATTERAS & OCRACOKE

LEGEND

1. STOVEPIPE HAT WRECK.
2. BANNISTER MIDGETT INSTALLS ENGINE.
3. NO ACHE BAY, CREEK, ETC.
4. WRECK OF THE PRISCILLA, RESCUE BY HORSEBACK.
5. KINNAKEET. SITE OF FIRST WINDMILL. GABRIEL'S TRUMPET BLEW.
6. EPHRAIM WILLIAMS RESCUE HERE.
7. MARCONI'S WIRELESS TOWER.
8. THEORETICAL RESTING PLACE OF USS MONITOR.
9. THIS BOOK WRITTEN HERE.
10. HATTORASK INDIAN CAPITAL VILLAGE. VESPUCCI LANDED HERE. ABRAHAM MIDGETT RESCUED HIS OX.
11. GENERAL BURNSIDE LED 20,000 MEN ASHORE HERE IN 1862, BEGINNING EXPEDITION. GEN. BILLIE MITCHELL LANDED BOMBERS HERE IN 1923.
12. PROVISIONAL CAPITAL OF "REDEEMED" STATE, NOVEMBER, 1861
14. FORTS HATTERAS AND CLARK GUARDING HATTERAS INLET.
15. BANANA BOAT RESCUE, 1924.
16. SHIPWRECKED HORSES ASHORE HERE IN 1735, ANCESTERS OF BANKER PONY.
17. SS HOME WRECKED HERE WITH FEARFULL LOSS OF LIFE.
18. CAPT. EDWARD TEACH LOST HIS HEAD TO VIRGINIANS HERE IN 1718.
19. BILLIE MITCHELL ADDED TWO MORE TO ROSTER OF SHIPS SUNK IN SURROUNDING GRAVEYARD.
20. THE MONEY TREE.

OREGON INLET

CHICAMICOMICO

KINNAKEET

PAMLICO SOUND

TRENT

OLD LIGHTHOUSE
CAPE HATTERAS
PRESENT COAST GUARD

HATTERAS

HATTERAS INLET
BIGHT OF HATTERAS

DIAMOND SHOAL

OCRACOKE

OCRACOKE INLET

ATLANTIC OCEAN

Prologue

Precisely four hundred years elapsed between the coming of Amerigo Vespucci and of Abraham Midgett to the Bight of Hatteras and there was no earthly meeting of the pair. But that defect of history has, very likely, been amended long since, and there should be no impropriety in surmising that sometimes of an evening they may sit ruminatively upon a comfortable cloud above the Outer Diamonds and contemplate the Island, whose folklore is capacious enough to accommodate them both.

By now, very likely, and if it should have appeared to matter one way or another, Abraham Midgett has amended his adjectives and no longer speaks of the Florentine as "that Spanish feller," as he did when he was subject to the limitations of folklore, of legend that was three hundred years old when Abraham Midgett's grandfather was new to the Island and to the world and beginning to absorb from his own grandfather some rudiments of an already lengthening story.

It may be that Amerigo Vespucci was a little resentful when Abraham Midgett identified him as that Spanish feller out yonder on that cloud which is almost always there, above the Diamonds, when day wanes into evening, and the sea's wind rests. It must have amazed him that his name, as a name, had never been heard on the Island as having any part of its lore, but come to think of it, some of the children had vaguely mentioned it as something encountered in one or another of the curious books they had at school.

As for Abraham Midgett, things did not exist in books and all he knew he had got from his father and from his grandfather and they had never heard of the first comer to the Bight of Hatteras except as that Spanish feller who had come there looking for fresh water in—he knew he had the date right—in 1497 when there were nothing but Indians living around here.

Abraham Midgett, as his neighbors remember him, was a bluff, lusty man, a man who never met a stranger nor made an enemy and who was, and is so remembered in the Island's folklore, the strongest man ever to breathe the breath of life on the Island. And then, very likely, he will tell Amerigo Vespucci, again, about the time his ox got stuck in the marsh yonder. Yonder back of where the old Creed's Hill Station used to be—and back of the hill upon which the Hattorask Indian village stood when the first Spanish ship let go its anchor in the Bight.

It was a Spanish ship and the Florentine navigator makes no denial of it, even though he himself was a proud gentleman of Florence. And perhaps to cover up his confusion, if he is actually confused, he consents to listen again to Abraham Midgett's improbable tale of the time his ox got stuck in the marsh yonder back of where the Coast Guard Station was, in 1897. And where the Indian village was in 1497 when Amerigo Vespucci, the hired navigator of a Spanish ship come to the western world to check the improbable tales of a man named Columbus, cast anchor while its crew went ashore for fresh water, to be had from the Open Pond yonder.

They tell the tale, with gusto and with probable embroideries, on Hatteras Island of the time Abraham Midgett's ox got stuck in the marsh. It is one of a hundred tales of his prowess that can be heard by anybody who has an ear for such tales and who is not so driven by urgency alien to the Island that he has no time to listen. It takes time to listen and it is not too much to wonder if, sometimes, the Florentine, himself eager to be about the telling of some tale of his own before that cloud begins to get restless under the rising surge of an offshore night wind, may get impatient with the telling.

There are in the lore of the Island a half dozen oxen of fabulous dimension and capacity, but Abraham Midgett's ox is fabulous only in an inverse fashion. He partakes merely of his master's storied strength. Actually he must have been a very ordinary beast. He was, as those who remember him report, named Willie and is never to be confused, or even associated, with such notable animals as Farrow Scarborough's ox Garfield, so named because he was born on the day that tidings came to the Island of the assassination of a President by that name, and whose massive horns are preserved on the Island to this day.

Willie was not much of an ox. He weighed a mere seven hundred pounds and is remembered only because he was toted derisively out of the marsh and up the hill upon which a forgotten Coast Guard Station and a forgotten Indian village used to stand, toted on his master's shoulders and ignominiously tumbled off into a pile of oyster shells left there some centuries ago by aboriginal housewives. It is remembered that the ox, Willie, gathered himself up from the garbage and slunk off down the hill to graze and that he was accompanied by his master's truculent derision.

But it is remembered, too, that none else who observed these things was so bold as to be openly derisive of poor Willie. They watched him in perhaps sympathetic silence as he departed for the grazing down the hill a ways and it is remembered also that after a while, when Abraham Midgett had eaten his supper at the Station, Willie came obediently and with proper meekness stood while his master harnessed him to the cart, and presently he set out homeward pulling the cart in which his master rested, sitting cross-legged on the floor and dozing contentedly. Willie knew the way home.

Abraham Midgett, his cart and his ox, had gone down to Pamlico Sound during the afternoon to get some oysters for the Station crew's supper. The oysters, about ten bushels of them, were dumped into two enormous coffee sacks and thence into the cart, and the total weight of the catch was above six hundred pounds. It was winter and the afternoons brief and, with night approaching, Abraham Midgett decided to take a short route to the Station, a route that was directly across the marsh. Halfway across the marsh Willie's strength left him and he, the cart, and the oysters were hopelessly embedded in the mire.

Without ado Abraham Midgett took a bag of oysters on each shoulder and, after floundering only momentarily, laid course for the Station, commanding Willie to get himself unstuck and follow him. Willie floundered some, succeeded only in getting deeper into the mire. His master came back down from the Station and unhooked the cart from the floundering ox and took the cart, holding it above his head, and carried it up the hill. Willie continued his floundering and was even deeper embogged when his master descended a second time from Creed's Hill.

Now Abraham Midgett did what was natural—for him. He rooted the dazed and exhausted ox out of the muck and picked him up. Willie's forelegs were across his right shoulder and his hind legs across his left shoulder, all six or seven hundred pounds of him, and without staggering or faltering his master ascended the hill. Willie was dumped among the oyster shells and Abraham Midgett went into the Station's kitchen where, they say, he ate two pecks of oysters raw.

"That fool ox," Abraham Midgett may be saying for the twentieth time to Amerigo Vespucci out yonder on top of that now pinkly glowing cloud, "he was not much of an ox, maybe, but he would come when I called him and he would try—he'd do the best he could, even if it wasn't much, and maybe I expected too much of him. Sometimes, anyhow, when I was feelin' good myself. And them fellers there at that Station, they did eat a lot of oysters."

And then, very likely, because he was an Islander and a polite man, considerate of an audience as of an ox, Abraham Midgett would likely suggest that the Florentine gentleman tell him how it looked around that hill, back in 1497, when he first laid eyes on it, and the Florentine's narrative would, most likely, burgeon until it achieved a comparable unlikeliness. The redness of the inhabitants, and their savageness, their ignorance of so many things would be enlarged upon with disdain born of ignorance.

Abraham Midgett's answer, if there was one, is no part of history, since history would be revolted at the idea of these two talking together on top of a cloud. But, being an Islander and so a partaker of its patience and its charity with strangers, he might say that, well, they knew how to live here even if they might not have got along so well if they had cast anchor in the harbor of, where was it now you said you were from, mister?

1

This hill was here when Amerigo Vespucci let down his anchor in the Bight yonder four hundred and sixty years ago, and there are some who give harbor to the notion that it ought to have been named, or to be renamed, for him. There are others, to be sure, numbering exactly half the resident population of the Island, who dissent, saying that with the whole continent named for one who, very likely, never set foot on it, he ought to be content.

Whether the Florentine actually did stretch his legs on this island must remain debatable and on the academic level, at least until Abraham Midgett finds some way to get word back to his neighbors in life, who are not much concerned about it anyway. It would be another fifty years before there were any other recorded arrivals from beyond, or in the Island idiom, from across the water, and it would be another two centuries before anybody got around to providing this hill with a name of its own.

Even then, in 1745, this hill had to share its name with the whole of the ridge of which it is a part, lumped together as Kendricker Mountain on the first detailed chart of the region. Diligent burrowing into the folklore of the Island discloses no faintest remembering of this Kendricker, except as a name on a chart, and it is not unlikely that the cartographer remained aboard ship anchored in the Bight during the time required for his mapmaking.

But the chart is astonishingly accurate. There is little change in the contour of the land, except the location of one of the three Indian villages that were on the Island when it was first sighted in 1497, were still here in 1547, in 1584, and whose inhabitants were, in 1710, beginning to amalgamate with immigrants from Europe and were grudgingly admitted into the sacraments of the established Church by the Reverend John Irmstone, rector of the parish in Bath.

This unhappy missionary wrote to his superiors in London a quarter of a millennium ago that these persons, half Indian and half English, were an offense to his own, and he had no doubt to his Maker's, nose and he doubted gravely that the Kingdom of Heaven was designed to accommodate such. They stunk and their condition was not improved by the amounts of sacramental wine they lapped up nor by sprinkling with baptismal waters. There are collateral reports that the rector himself had recourse to the goblet as a means toward grace in the acceptance of these heathen into communion.

But this hill was here, in 1497, when its lifting ridges beckoned the first European navigator to traverse the western ocean. Without being aware of it, Amerigo Vespucci and his ship were, and had been for many days, riding the Great River that would not, for another quarter millennium, be identified and charted by Benjamin Franklin as the Gulf Stream, sweeping northeastward at a nominal speed of four knots per hour and carrying a volume of water greater than the combined flow of all the rivers in the world.

This hill is, and was in 1497, clearly visible from the Great River. It is not a very high hill, twenty-seven feet at its eastern end near the ocean and sixty-six feet at the High Point of the Hills five miles or so to the west. When the air is clean of mist it is possible to see for thirty miles in any direction from the crest of the ridge, to Ocracoke Inlet on the west, well out above the Great River to the south and east, and across the Sounds to the mainland on the north.

Many days must have passed since Amerigo Vespucci had seen dry land in the West Indies and the sight of this hill must have gladdened his eyes when he beheld it. Back home in Europe people were being burned for just thinking to themselves that the earth might possibly be round and there were, very likely, those of Vespucci's crew who expected momentarily to come to the edge of a flat universe and topple over it into unmitigated damnation.

And besides, they were very likely beginning to be thirsty. In these hills yonder, luminous in the sunlight, glistening with the glint of trees growing, suffused—could it be?—with smoke rising above women at their cooking, there would be springs of water, wells, lakes. A gentle southwesterly wind brought them land smells, the scent of flowering things and—could it be?—the thinning smoke lifted also the odor of roasting meat. The sight, and the smell, of this ridge must indeed have gladdened the souls of these venturing Europeans.

After these weeks of blind going on an uncharted sea the sight of land must have, for the while they were feasting their eyes upon this hill, diverted them from more immediate surroundings. If the recorded experience of uncounted mariners since was also their own, the sea with not much warning became a problem. Up to here the sea had been smooth and of a deep indigo blue, the wind fair, and the air around them balmy.

But not now. While they looked landward the sea had changed. Ahead the water had turned gray and its surface writhed in a frothy agony. The ship faltered, trembling under the impact of an erratic swell that foamed above her forepeak. It could not be the wind and no cloud flecked the sky. Some force not known, nor yet imagined, in the world of the sea lay there ahead, and for all anybody knew, hidden in the mists to the north, might be the fabled edge of the world.

Off to the starboard the surface was unruffled, and beyond this smooth field of water rose the line of these hills, this ridge that gave back the sun's light, that sent up the comforting incense of land-smell and—now they were sure of it—of roasting meat. And then Amerigo Vespucci must have noticed that the ship, of its own volition, or of the sea's, was veering landward in its course.

It would be three centuries and more before his successors in navigation in the western ocean would begin fully to comprehend what was happening to Amerigo Vespucci when his ship veered landward off the Point of Cape Hatteras. The Florentine came to the Cape in the last year but three of the fifteenth century and there encountered a force that, when the twentieth century was well past its halfway mark, men were only beginning to evaluate and to measure by the simple device of taking the water's temperature four times daily at about the point where Vespucci's fragile ship began its frightened dance and its veering to landward.

Generations of navigators would come to fear it and Alexander Hamilton, when he was eighteen years old, would name it the Graveyard of the Atlantic without comprehending the simple natural phenomena that make this hundred square miles of water the most treacherous and unpredictable in all the seven seas. There is not, perhaps, much of anything that man can do about it, even when he has come to understand it wholly, but it will be just as well for him to know. It is not wholly an evil thing that happens in the water off the Cape.

For Amerigo Vespucci and for many another since, it was a by no means unhappy thing that happened to him when his ship, of its own or the sea's volition, began to veer landward. Within a little while he was able to let down his anchor in calm water, within hailing distance of the smooth sand of the beach, and with an excellent view of the village that sprawled along the near, or south, slope of an elevation that has, in times since, borne various names. Presently it is called Creed's Hill, for a man who is not remembered in the Island's lore. And just beyond it is the High Point of the Hills, around which Abraham Midgett detoured with his cartload of oysters and got bogged down in the marsh cupped between the ridges.

It is not that the sea is unkind. That is a thing that the Islanders know, an unvoiced verity. She is the mother of all life, by turns stern, austere, and implacable and she is gentle and generous and kind. But she is, immemorially, a woman, a creature of moods, sometimes unaccountably savage, inexplicably gentle, at once jealous and secretive and broodingly soft and lavishly good. She is the mother of all life—and the keeper of death. She has no patience with weaklings nor any mercy upon those who are afraid of her. She is a woman.

Something of this must have been felt by the Florentine when he let down his anchor in what would come to be called the Bight of Hatteras, and the same thing, unspoken still but felt, must come upward in the consciousness of the masters of Gloucester trawlers now when they come in at evening to lie comfortably in the Bight until morning, when they go again to the richest fishing grounds in the western ocean. Here is serenity in the lee of this ridge, and yonder the sea writhes.

Yonder, to the eastward and above Diamond Shoals, is where the northern ocean and the southern ocean meet, and never amicably. It was this age-long contending that shunted Vespucci landward when he came to the yet unnamed Graveyard of the Atlantic near half a thousand years ago. He had been blithely riding the Great River for a thousand miles since turning northward from the islands his forerunner, by five years, had named the West Indies.

When the Great River hits the Outer Diamonds a splinter of it, about the size of the Mississippi River, peels off and curls westward. This splinter swirls westward in a great eddy that becomes a series of eddies, sixty miles or so across, depending on the initial velocity of the splinter. The rest of the Great River, slowed a little by the impact of another force, is deflected northeastward toward Europe and need not be of further concern here.

It is this splinter, a surging river of warm water, that makes the Bight of Hatteras, and except when it is vexed by tropical hurricanes, the Bight is, at least relatively, calm. And it is warm. Normally there is a differential of 22 to 25 degrees within so short a distance as 100 feet of the line that divides the waters south and west of the Cape from the water north and immediately east.

And here enters the gray villain of the piece, an unlovely character whose existence was not dreamed of even by Mr. Franklin, was not definitely established for a century after America's first man of science, and who would wait yet awhile before he got a name. That is to say, he had no standing in science but navigators generally must have suspected him and the inhabitants of Hatteras Island knew him without a name. It is significant that the Islanders designate him as a masculine force. The Labrador Current is universally, on the Island, "he."

Nobody, not even the oceanographers, knows a great deal about the Labrador Current except that he originates somewhere in the polar regions beyond Labrador and slinks southward. He hugs the shore of New England, moves a little offshore under the impact of the Hudson and Delaware Rivers, is believed to duck landward between the Delaware and Virginia capes. Past the protruding waters of these sea-gates he gathers himself together again and moves in, a movement very likely somewhat forced by the expanding might of the Great River north of Cape Hatteras.

Southward of the Virginia capes and along North Carolina's sea frontier there is little to hinder him and he picks up speed amazingly, but with little rise in his cold-blooded temperature. (During the winter of this writing he has been especially virulent, his temperature dropping as low as 34 degrees.)

Navigators on a southerly heading below New York's harbor take advantage of this wicked invader at a considerable saving of fuel when he is in strength, and below the Virginia capes observers on land can see, almost any time they look oceanward, ships moving smartly southward, close inshore. But they never see a north-bound ship. These ride the Great River as far north as her strength is discernible and then, if their ports are in the northern United States, veer westward.

Twenty-five miles north of Cape Hatteras the Labrador hits Wimble Shoals, a relatively negligible protuberance of sandy reefs that project into the ocean for never more than three miles and much less than that when the current is in vigor. Then it sweeps up the sand and swirls it along southward until it comes, suddenly, upon the Diamond Shoals and Cape Hatteras. Here also is the tremendous power of the Great River, a power that has lately been calculated by a vacationing mathematician, taking into account the volume and velocity of the current, as mightier than all the steam or hydroelectric generating plants on the earth. It has been mentioned but so colossal a figure need not apologize for repetition: the Great River's volume is equal to that of 1,000 Mississippi Rivers.

Nobody has yet calculated the volume of Labrador. It seems very probable that it is only fractional, compared to that of the Great River, but as it approaches Cape Hatteras its bed is narrowed and its force greatly accentuated. At its greatest depth it is not more than 180 feet, as against a nominal depth of 600 feet for the Great River. It begins to veer southeastward, on a course of about 110 degrees above Cape Point, the distance here varying according to conditions but normally about four miles.

Fifteen miles offshore—twelve miles from the Point of the Cape, the cold Labrador water rams head on into the flanks of the surging Gulf Stream; cold water mixed with, or at least impinging upon, warm water. What happens then is a matter of conjecture among scientists, but the Hatteras Islander . . . well, to put it in the words of Martin Tolson, whose acquaintance with "her" and "him" goes back eighty years, and of Captain Walter Barnett, who is eighty-five and, commanding the Lightship in 1918, achieved the uncomfortable distinction of being the first commander in American waters to have his ship shot out from under him by a German submarine,

"They tussle around awhile and then he gives up and ducks under her and wanders off out yonder somewhere."

It sounds not unreasonable and, until the oceanographers come up with a better answer, should suffice. Island navigators who, in times past, traversed the 475 miles southeast to Bermuda, report that there is cold water on the other side of the Great River, which, off Cape Hatteras, is normally forty miles wide. Sometimes, as in the winter of 1955, the Labrador appears to get the upper hand altogether and the Great River will be shoved offshore, with the Bight-making splinter being sheared off further east and south while cold water spills over the twelve-mile-long Diamond Shoals and chills the Bight.

Many who have contemplated the relative stability of Cape Hatteras, the point and the lands north and west of it that make up the two Islands between Oregon and Ocracoke Inlets, a total distance of seventy miles, with the Cape being the anchor-point, have surmised that there must be, underlying this vast and unending tumult, a base of nothing less than granite.

It is two miles, straight down, to the nearest granite. Halfway down there is a somewhat negligible layer of limestone and above that is 4,000 feet of pure sand, omitting here and there a layer of shell, occasional coral formations. But for many hundred feet there is nothing but the sort of sand to be seen on the surface. Minute study of the geologic formations was possible when one of the major oil companies, in 1945-46, bored an exploratory well within a mile of the Point and just down the ridge that ranges westward from the ocean.

Cape Hatteras, and the Diamond Shoals that extend seaward from the Point for a distance of twelve miles, and the lands north and west from it, represent an impasse in nature. Were either of the two mighty forces neutralized the Cape and the islands that are spread out from it like half-folded wings would begin to move—somewhere. If "he" took over—but the speculation is not profitable. . . . The Great River is the sun's daughter and a right lusty wench she can be, on occasion, and maybe it is just as well that she have "him," cold, mean, and untrustworthy as he usually is, to keep her somewhat manageable.

2

This hill, this ridge, widened and elongated into the Kendricker Mountain of an ancient chart, and the extension of it westward and northward into the lean islands that make a barrier reef, or the Outer Banks—all of it is pure sand. Or mere sand, with never a redeeming rock to give it character and substance, except now and then some scattered items of granite, flint, slate gathered together in 1796 and brought here by Henry Dearborn who had a contract with Alexander Hamilton to build a lighthouse.

Add, of course, to these alien stones, smooth, rounded rocks that came to this Island in the holds of sailing ships, ballast to give them stability until they could be loaded with more seemly cargo. There are these and they are to be found even in the weathered debris at the site of Indian villages, and it is not unreasonable to think that, long ago, these people, finding a pile of stones where some ship had cast them aside, carried them, in wonder not unmixed with a sense of triumph, to their villages.

General Dearborn, with a vast and never very profitable labor —Mr. Hamilton drove a hard bargain—brought stones from his native valley in New England, lightered them ashore from the Bight below the site of the, by now, vanished Indian town, and with oxen got them to a sandy hillock a mile or so north of the Cape. Here he lifted a strong tower, near a hundred feet high, and established a beacon in the top of it, a warning to those who fared this way in ships to beware of the dreadful turmoil of strange waters.

Little of the tower remains now, but the hillock is there, its elevations and contours differing little now from the description set down by Tenche Coxe, at the direction of Mr. Hamilton and George Washington.

Sand, as an element of nature, is not very highly thought of, especially as a major component of building sites, and there are mountains of unhappy experience to support Biblical parable. Piled here within comfortable reach are six books, currently highly esteemed by reading, or at least book-buying, people and a seventh that is a fat bibliography of all the books that have been written about the making and the functioning of this planet.

None of them speaks, more than casually, of sand. None will relate how it was made nor where or why and how much, and all of them speak of it as an unstable stuff and the Four Gospels unite in declaration against it, especially for people who propose to erect a house or, inferentially, a civilization. Rocks are recommended, and for reassurance against the probability that the next big rain, or big wind, will dissolve this hill from under my house, I look out the window that discloses what the Islanders, for two hundred years, have called The Money Tree.

That the late and unfortunate Edward Teach, pirate, lover, and benefactor of his neighbors, actually buried any loot under that tree no amount of subsequent digging has verified. He might well have, because this grizzled holly was a formidable tree, well-grown and lusty long before Teach became a bloody legend, with his head impaled upon the victor's bowsprit, in 1718. But of that, more in its proper place and time.

There are those whose learning enables or entitles them to speak with authority in such matters and they assert with confidence that this gnarled holly is more than five hundred years old, and so it must have been a good-sized tree in 1447 when the Florentine established precedent for Teach and for countless other navigators who have let down anchor in the Bight of Hatteras, in the comfortable lee of this hill, this ridge unstably contrived of mere sand.

The Money Tree has outlasted a formidable tower made of alien stone. Around the base of the tree there are indications of much digging in times past and in these depressions of the ground there are now well-grown dogwoods and lusty seedlings that are children of the Money Tree—along that north slope of this ridge a bewildering complexity of growths. Within a stone's throw of the old holly are, among other things, what must be the three largest dogwoods, each of them having a trunk-girth of forty-five inches a foot above the ground.

There are liveoaks, some of them a thousand years old, these schooled fellows say. And there are scrub palm, beech, cedar and, clinging to the ground, acres of deerberry. For how many generations none can say but there is a worn place in the bark of the old tree where deer have scratched themselves in tick season, and elsewhere the bark shows plainly the claw marks of raccoons who have climbed its trunk in search of berries. It is three years now since the old tree has had the virility to produce a berry but those who have known it a long time say that the tree is resting and that it will again know the ecstasy of fruitfulness.

Scratch through the mold that lies beneath these trees, not anywhere more than two or three inches except in the wet low places, and there is mere sand. Explore further, deeper, and there is a mat-work of spreading roots. It is so of any growing thing that is anchored on this ridge, a mass of fine roots. Especially the cedars, but those whose roots are deep down in the life of these Islands will say, with an understanding smile, "These are their eating roots."

And their drinking roots?

Well, now, since you mention it, everything that grows around here has two sets of roots, one to eat with and the other to drink with. Any tree can go without eating maybe as long as a whole season but it has to drink, if it aims to stay alive. Pull up anything you are of a mind to and, well, they say any tree's drinking root, call it its taproot, has to be as high as . . . well a tree can't get any higher in the air than it reaches down in the ground. . . . But don't try to dig down and prove it—you'll have a deeper hole than you can fill up.

As it turned out there was not any need for digging so deep a hole. There came an afternoon when there were vast machines on the ridge—implements charged with the grading of a road across these ridges for the accommodation of such as would move in vehicular comfort across them. With steel cables the bulldozers laid hold upon the trunks of tall pines that blocked their way. When they came groaning out of the ground, trunk and root intact, the taproot, measured, was in every case almost precisely the length of the above-ground part of the tree.

More closely examined, the sand that was embedded in the bark of the taproot was the same, in color and in texture and cleanness, as the sand on the surface: There is nothing in the ridge but sand, which corroborated the tale told by the core taken from the exploratory oil well when it went down into the earth in 1945 to a depth of 10,052 feet before it encountered anything akin to the granite boulders General Dearborn lugged down from New England more than a century and a half before.

This hill, this ridge, this Island is sand—and what a prodigious pile of sand it is. With the foot-by-foot chart of the well-core and the erudition of the young mathematical scholars who lay out the course of the bulldozers, and a little conjecturing, it is possible to visualize what this ridge and this Island would look like if it were stripped of the sea that hides it. Here would be, in truth, a veritable mountain. It would be above 5,000 feet high, a hundred miles long, at a minimum, with foothills sloping, not too gradually, to the east and south.

Beyond the crest of the mountain, where the Sounds intervene between the Cape and the mainland, would be the high valley, almost a plateau, drained of its water. The rivers that empty into the Sounds might leave them marshy but, emerging through this ridge into the descending slope of the mountain of sand there would be, for a time anyhow, some tolerably spectacular cascades. . . . One of the young engineers, after an evening of browknitting, calculated the approximate cubic content of this improbable heap of sand.

When he read off, not quite believingly, his finding, which occupied a very large sheet of paper, he mopped the furrows of his brow and said, "All that just sand—what do you reckon holds it together? Why doesn't the ocean just wash it to—well, where would it wash it to?" The young man, with all his learning, was then mute in the presence of an imponderable thing. The notion of a mile-high mountain of sand, with him sitting in the approximate middle of it, seemed to measurably disconcert him.

Contemplation of this imponderable matter expanded the young mathematician's astonishment into dismay and to ejaculation. He said: "You mean we're sitting here on top of a sand mountain a mile high—what's to keep it—why, the ocean will wash it away, or—look at my car—the wind will blow it to hell and gone before—" He dwindled into mute amazement. A day or so before the young fellow's shiny new car, driven too rapidly against a jubilant 45-mile wind had been, on the windward side, stripped clean of its paint, which was no great disaster, seeing his post-adolescent taste ran to rose pink and pale cream. After sandblasting, the combined velocity of the car and the head wind being roughly 115 miles an hour, the body was just raw, unadorned metal on that side.

This distressing state of affairs, coupled with speculative wonder about whether the insurance company would look with compassion upon his situation, served at least to deflect his thoughts from the hazards of life atop a heap of sand that, most likely, would dissolve in water, such of it as was not carried off, no matter to where, by what he described as the damnedest wind anybody ever saw. It was a very mild wind, comparatively, and if he stays around long enough, and does not learn to come in out of it, he will experience winds that will roll his shining rose-and-cream before them like an empty shuck.

But this hill abides, changed but little in the centuries there is record of, supported, shored up by the imponderable power that made it, the two great rivers-in-the-sea that converge yonder, the Labrador Current and the Gulf Stream. There are differences between these two forces besides that of the amount of heat they maintain, that is, the temperature of their waters. There is, for one thing, a difference in color, noted already. The one is gray, the other an indigo.

And here is another difference—it is the Labrador who is primarily the sand-mover. Lacking any sort of sound scientific data, or any data at all, I have had recourse to devices of my own making. The procedure is necessarily simple, as simple as dipping up a jugful of water from each of these rivers and letting it settle. That is, letting whatever is being carried along by the stream's motion settle to the bottom of the gallon-sized jug which, for convenience, needs to be glass.

Set it away and look at it again tomorrow. At the bottom of the Labrador jug there will be a deposit of sand, sometimes as much as three inches deep in a jug ten inches in depth. This, to be sure, is extreme. The normal will run about two inches and, on occasion, when the current is quiescent, it will be an inch or less. It depends, but how much I cannot know, upon the urgency of the wind that drives the current and upon perhaps other factors.

On the other hand the water of the Gulf Stream, before it reaches the troubled area off the Diamonds, is wholly clear of earthy matter. Where the splinter veers off there is likely to be more or less sand, but rarely enough to tinge the water with its color. The Labrador is likely to look dirty. The Islanders, when they go down to the sea to discover whether it is a good day to put out their nets, determine their issue by the sea's color. If it is dirty, they abide ashore.

Of course there is a lot of sand stirred up offshore when the two currents converge, and some of it, of course, must get mixed in with the Gulf Stream water as it continues its sweep northeastward. But here again there is, so say those who venture into that area with their boats, another eddy developed and it is likely that some of the sand so stirred up makes its way northward, and westward, and again into the path of the south-flowing current.

After he is gone away with his concerns about the stripping of his new car I wonder a little if it would disturb him too much, or tax him too greatly, to lay before him another, necessarily hypothetical because none has yet computed the volume of the Labrador as it approaches the Shoals, problem. But take a hypothetical amount of water flowing past, say, the Lighthouse in a given time—easy because a small boat will drift one mile in twenty minutes—and every gallon of it containing a fixed cubic content of sand—how much sand would it move in a day and how many bulldozers would be needed to duplicate the feat? But there is no point to be settled that would change anything, one way or another. It must be clear enough to anybody that the yardage would be not inconsiderable.

But this hill abides. Rains fall upon it in volume that would devastate any conventional hill, flood the valleys below it, and bury them under avalanches of mud. I have seen fourteen inches of rain fall in the space of ten hours and, except in a little footpath of my own, there will be no sign of erosion. The sand accepts the water, holds it moderatingly until the wind and the sun and the thirst of the Money Tree and the rest of things growing, equalize it. Sometimes there may be a gathered seepage in the low places below the hill, but not for long. The ocean is yonder to take off what is not needed, or what can not be harbored conveniently.

And the wind?

3

This hill was built by the wind.

This hill, this ridge, and the four tidily-spaced ridges beyond it to the north, these Islands are the handiwork of the wind through nobody knows how many generations of days and nights, of changing seasons that require it to come to its work from different directions—south-southwesterly through eight months of the year, north-northeasterly for the rest of the time.

It is a curious thing, to me, that the Islanders have no fixed designative pronoun for the wind. For the most part they use "it" when they speak of the wind. They will say, "It's blowing a gale of wind out there," but there is no feeling of oneness with it, as there is, innately, with the sea. Their phrase, "gale of wind," has perplexed me mildly. . . .

From time to time I get down the dictionary and the encyclopedia and re-examine what they have to say about winds and about gales. It is a special kind of dictionary, somehow. It is old, and innocent of any knowledge of a lot of words that are generally current in these times. The title page of it is gone and it is not possible to determine the name of the publisher. I salvaged it, some years back, from the ruins of an abandoned Lifesaving Station. It was issued to the station on the sixth of June, 1878, by the Government of the United States.

This lexicon is generous, and a little confusing in its generosity, with definitions of wind. There is a choice of eight meanings, or shadings of meaning, including visceral gases. Back in their proper alphabetical page, gales of merriment, of laughter, are allowed, but there is no mention of a gale of wind. So I am reasonably sure that the Islander phrase is homemade, contrived to meet a special need. Island winds are likely to be rather special, and, it might be well to add, there is little evidence of wear on the dictionary. . . .

Winds hereabouts have to be versatile, seeing that they are architects, landscapers, builders and have, besides, to transport their building material, which is pure, washed sand. They have also to fetch clouds to rain upon the structures they have built and, with only spasmodic help from birds, to bring seeds and plant them. . . . It pleases me, sometimes in moments of vagrant idleness, when the wind is laughing in the night, that its glee comes from the finding of some exotic seed, brought here from Cuba, drying over on the beach where the tide has left it.

Maybe the seed of a bougainvillea, or a mere sprig of the resurrection fern which, so learned botanists assure me, is a native of Mexico. There is bougainvillea here, though it has undergone mutations that enable it to cope with occasional periods of killing cold, and there is a widening colony of the resurrection on the slope of the ridge where the Money Tree stands. It prefers mostly to live on the bounty of the older dogwoods, and it is an amazing thing to see it in one hour when a match would destroy it in a puff of smoke and in the next hour it is lushly green.

When it is engaged in these placid works of the domestic gardener the wind laughs, or so it seems to me. But there are other times when it howls and screams in utter rage, as it did three nights ago when in her anger—the gender of the pronoun is not wholly intentional—she took a middle-aged liveoak by the scruff of his neck, ripped the clinging moss away, and broke his back. He lay there yesterday, not yet dead but mortally hurt, when I walked along the ridge to see how long I must wait for the jessamine and when the deerberries would lift their shy white faces to the sun.

Not to be too fanciful about it, I think I know why the wind is in a rage, and it has nothing to do with the reasons that professional meteorologists who practice their polysyllabic science hereabouts would give for her behavior. They would speak darkly of cold masses and warm masses of air, of abysses of low pressure into whose void the wind was rushing to restore what they call isobaric equilibrium. All these things may be very true and buttressed in scientific fact, but it suits me well enough to think that the wind is irked about something.

Something like the wanton killing of a blade of grass on this ridge. Or perhaps it is a tender young cedar crushed under the uncaring wheels of a truck that weighs, without a load, five tons and which, when it is loaded, can carry six cubic yards of sand from here to yonder where they are engaged in the making of a boulevard over which people may ride comfortably to the place where the two rivers deliver building materials to the wind. It is a very puny burden, comparatively, that this massive truck carries.

In the while it is moving its tiny six cubic yards from here to yonder the Labrador has swept past, loaded with more sand than all the trucks yet built could possibly carry. Some of the sand he will loosely spill when he gets down to the eddying water above the Point, especially if the tide is flowing. A lot of his load will settle to the bottom, the tide will take over and leave—my post-adolescent engineer has calculated that one such tide will leave, if conditions are right, 50,000 cubic yards of sand to the mile of beach.

When the tide has slid back into the deep the sand will begin to dry and, tomorrow, the wind will begin the slow moving of it to wherever it finds there is need of it. Some to be picked up bodily and sifted down among the dry stalks of last season's sea oats which, presently re-enlivened by sun and watered by clouds, windborne, will send up new stalks to anchor the newly brought sand. . . . I have seen that wall-against-the-sea grow seventeen feet in eight years. . . .

Within two or three generations there might be a sixth ridge, a new one added to the five that are here. The wind is unwearying and timeless, and with unfettered resourcefulness, limitless patience. But she is also a creature of hate. She hates a bulldozer or any other instrument that man has devised to compete with her. And she hates the wanton killing of anything that she has, with illimitable patience, planted and watered and brooded over, day after night, year after year, until they have become eons.

In a sense the wind guards these hills of her own making from destruction of her own devising. The only thing that is stronger than the wind, that can say to her this is far enough, is some growing thing, no matter how small, how fragile, whether a blade of grass, whether an easily-hurt sprig of wild coffee, a fragile fern, or a hoary giant like the Money Tree. There are here, even, such tender things as a native mutation of the wild rose, and sprawling over wide acres there is a tender-blossomed variant of the clematis that has apple-green flowers.

But let one of them show weakness, let one of them be carelessly, or wantonly destroyed, and the wind strikes out in a fury that seems senseless. When this plant or that, for whatever reason, leaves its space of sand unused, the wind falls upon it with a relentless savagery that is not matched even by the sea in anger. The wind is utterly pitiless in its vengeance and it begins to tear apart what it has built, what it has brooded over, and presently the earth is bare. It is not any longer earth but mere sand.

It pleases me to think, and there can be no harm in so thinking, beyond, perhaps, the grieving of the sober-minded and the outraging of the professors and possibly theologians whose souls have been dry-kilned, that the wind is pleased when anybody plants a blade of grass. In all the earth there is nothing that the wind so highly regards as a blade of grass, and to buttress this belief I have only to look through the window at my other elbow—the south window—to where the wind's wall against the sea grows yonder at the rate of two feet a year.

This sea wall began with a blade of grass, a single, forlorn thing clinging by its roots in final desperation, on an August afternoon back in the mid-year of the 1930's. There were evil times on this Island and had been since the August Storm of 1933 and a wicked northeaster that had come that spring. The grass was gone from the whole area of the Cape, eaten down to nothingness by generations of sheep, of wild cattle. These also were gone, and those who had owned the land had given up, deeded it to the State rather than pay taxes.

Even the south slope of this ridge was naked, as barren as the plain that lies between it and the Point of the Cape, and the ridge itself was being rolled back over its north slope, and such things as grew there, the Money Tree, and gnarled massive dogwood, would within a year, or at most two years, be engulfed. In all the three thousand acres from which the wind has brought the sand to pile on this ridge, scarcely a blade of grass remained and, at storm tide, the sea rolled against the foot of the hill.

It was a bad time, and worse impended. There was the Lighthouse, the very celebrated lighthouse, the tallest brick structure in the world, the tallest lighthouse in the world—with all its superlatives it was about to topple into the ocean. When it was built the tower stood back from the sea more than a half mile, but now, the tide washed against the base of it and the beach was of a monotonous flatness.

Dismayed by the inroads of the wind and the tide, engineers came with their pile drivers and set sheet piling athwart the beach, driving it down to a depth of sixty-five feet. That, they were sure, would secure the tower against further encroachment from the sea.

They were very sure of it, but scarcely had they gone from their labors when the sea and the wind arose in remembered fury. The piles were ripped out of their depths, twisted into grotesque knots, and scattered for a mile along the beach. And the sea mounted the steps of the tower, climbing ten feet or so above the base.

It was, everybody agreed, time to move. The U.S. Lighthouse Service got ready to abandon the tower and began the erection of an unsightly steel replacement structure two miles inland on the Second Ridge. The U.S. Coast Guard, with the ground floor of its Lifeboat Station awash, began the erection of another a mile inland. And the Phipps estate deeded its ravaged holdings to the State of North Carolina, which accepted it as a tentative State park, or recreational area.

It was in the era of Civilian Conservation Corps activity, when the nation's youth were collected into camps whose main purpose was to feed them, to keep them out of mischief's way and, if practicable, find useful employment for them until times were improved. Here was a potential park, here was, man power and, well, there was no harm in trying. What would be tried was more than anybody had the time or the energy to think about. The first thought, very likely, was that the region was removed and its personnel would be, by so much, separated from the temptations presumably inherent in more thickly peopled quarters.

As director of the undertaking the authorities selected a man in his middle years, a moderately successful farmer and sawmill man, a man of sound character who would deal sensibly with his people— and who needed a job. Edward Jefferson Byrum had, in so far as he could recall, not seen the Atlantic Ocean until he arrived at Cape Hatteras with a dozen or so youths, to set up the beginnings of the project. Their average age was under twenty and their inexperience matched that of their leader.

Summer was waning toward September. The sea was calm and sunny as it can be only in this place of improbable tumult in that interlude before the season of the hurricane. There was no plan of procedure, no over-all scheme for doing anything. They were to set up a camp and do whatever, if anything, seemed possible and proper. The first consideration was, of course, to house the personnel as comfortably as might be, to feed them, and to keep them out of mischief. After that . . . .

On the second afternoon Mr. Byrum wandered over to look at the Lighthouse and at the ocean, which was new to him. It was a somnolent kind of an afternoon, and after he had climbed to the top and looked across the sand-white expanse of not much of anything, he wandered down toward the surf. He sat down in the sand and for a while he idly watched the sea, deceptively calm, illimitably blue. The wind came in almost mincing movements, but freshening as the afternoon waned toward evening.

It was a strange country to Mr. Byrum. He was used to grass, to growing things, and he looked uncomfortably about him, homesick it must have been, for the sight of just one blade of grass. He found it, not a yard away, and he reached out to touch it with his hand. It was clinging to the sand with not more than two or three dried-out roots and it had turned a rusty gray. Mr. Byrum lay back in the comfortable warmness of the sand. He remembered afterward that he must have slept.

Awakened, it must have been by the freshening wind, he glanced around him. There was a sort of chop to the sea now, and the tide had come halfway from where it had been to where he was. And then his glance went searching for that pitiful little bit of grass, something that was familiar, that was akin, though remotely, to the grass in the pasture back home, grass soundly rooted in good soil with clay under it.

Something had happened to the blade of grass. It was now half-hidden in a little mound of sand. It had reached up and caught the sand as it moved with the wind, across it, and now there was a little ridge of sand, an inch high and the length of the blade. Mr. Byrum watched with utter fascination while the fragile thing gathered, it must be, a thousand times its own weight of sand. So entranced was he with this minute spectacle that he was wholly unmindful of the sea and he was still sitting flat on the sand when the thrusting tide caught him.

Mr. Byrum went back home to his tent and changed into dry pants. After supper, in his tent and as was his custom before going to bed, he got down his Bible. He was not a bothersomely religious man but it had been his custom, since childhood, to read a chapter in his Bible every night before going to bed. He had skipped last night, but tonight, he had better get back to it, and, as he considered, it might be good for him to begin at the beginning, since he was at the beginning of something utterly strange to him down here.

And so he read down the verses of the First Chapter of the First Book until he came to the eleventh verse. There he stopped dead still in his reading and began again—"And God said let the earth put forth grass."

For a long time, as he remembered when he was old and his paralyzed hands could no longer hold a leaf of grass, Mr. Byrum sat there in his camp chair with that verse of Genesis before him. He went to bed but he did not sleep for a long time. . . . Maybe this was the answer.

Next morning, some with only the knives in their pockets, one or two with the only axes they had brought here with them, Mr. Byrum and his handful of youths went along this ridge and when they came to a dead brush they cut it. Lacking a vehicle that would negotiate the sand, they dragged it to the Lighthouse and before nightfall they had built a hedgerow thirty inches high for a distance of sixty feet, set well back out of reach of the tide. Mr. Byrum had observed that the rising tide had carried away the twig of nameless grass he watched the afternoon before—and the little ridge of sand it held.

Daylight next morning found Mr. Byrum and his boys out to see what had happened in the night. Nothing except the tops of their hedgerow of dead brush was visible. . . . Four years afterward I stood with the late Hall Roosevelt on the crest of that small ridge, by then grassed thickly and with the beginnings of cedar and yoepon and liveoak growing from it. Beyond there were two newer and higher ridges, spaced well apart, each set with grass, sea oats which the sea loves and respects.

Mr. Roosevelt, favorite nephew of one president, brother-in-law of another, and himself an able engineer, looked about him and he said, "They can move the light back here to its lighthouse where it belongs, now." (It was eleven years before the prodigal light came home on January 23, 1950.) And one of the youths who was nearby said, "Heck, Mr. Roosevelt, we can build it right on out to Bermuda if the brush holds out—and the wind keeps blowin.'"

4

For convenience and my own very private amusement I call him Lord Ocracoke. It is not a very good joke. It isn't altogether a joke, because, when occasion requires, and sometimes when it doesn't, he can be very lordly, and not unreasonably so. The blood of the Howards is in his veins, and also the blood of an Arab slave who might very well have had his own claim to noble blood. There is also, legendarily, rather more than just a tincture of native Indian blood mixed in with these other strains.

But he is, instinctively, a very lordly man. He went away from his Island when he was very young and accumulated a good deal of money and some habits of mind that are not native to the Island

and seem, somehow, a little out of place, in a superficial sort of way. Like the other day when he came up for a morning's visit. When he was leaving we stood in the doorway of this house for a moment. The house faces west; it looks down the range of this ridge and to the High Point of the Hills. . . .

"Yes, I own that," he said and he mentioned the name of the man from whom he had bought it. It is a very lordly piece of land and from time to time I have urged the National Park Service to move its boundaries north of it, so that it might, from now on, become a part of the public domain. So far they have refrained from so doing, but what plan its owner may have for its use is not clear. It will be some time, I think, before he does anything with it except just look at it and say that he owns it.

Actually he does not own it. The wind owns it. The wind built it, through nobody can know how many generations, how many centuries of patient carrying of sand, grain by grain, from the beach yonder in the Bight of Hatteras, bringing also seeds of whatever things appeared and planting them and afterward bringing clouds containing rain for watering the High Point of the Hills. By now there are great trees there, three or four of them being at least a thousand years old.

It is possible to tell the age of a tree, but the age of this hill, of that highest part of the hills yonder, is something that baffles the geologist. One layer of sand is like the next under it, certainly until they get down a mile or so into the earth where there is limestone or sandstone of a low quality, made by the weight of the earth above it. But none of them can say when the wind began its labor or how many eons of geologic time it is since the first thin layer of sand was spread over hard granite two miles straight down.

It is the wind who owns this Island and that projecting point of this ridge yonder toward the west. It is the wind, also, who owns Lord Ocracoke because the wind brought his forbears to this Island, bruising and battering and half-drowning them in the process, chastening them but not quite killing them in the bringing. There has been little of the ceremonious in the bringing, and a decade of searching has disclosed no suggestion that anybody, until quite recently, ever came to these Islands by reason of his own deliberation and purpose. The wind brought him.

Take the Odens. It is possible to document their arrival, since it happened just one hundred years ago this month (March, 1956). There are a great many Odens on the Island now, and good stout people they are, too. A great-grandson, and namesake, is general superintendent of the REA power plant which links together the Seven Villages of the upper Island and by some miracle or other he has kept his wires alive even through the most determined hurricanes. Of course the plant sometimes takes a day off in the very best weather and for no reason that Herbert Oden can foresee or explain.

But take Herbert Oden's great-grandfather, and how the wind fetched him to this island. It had been a hard winter, that winter of 1856, with the Sounds frozen over and the Island's ships grimly held to their harbors. There were then, as there are now, about 3,000 people on the two Islands and, by March, 1856, they were beginning to feel the pinch of hunger. Especially were they hungry for the taste of something besides dried fish. They were pork-hungry.

It must have been in that winter that the preacher prayed a prayer, still mentioned as an item of folklore, that if Providence had in mind the wrecking of a ship, which the preacher hoped that Providence did not, the ship would be wrecked in the Bight of Hatteras, convenient to most of the hungry inhabitants, and might have aboard it a little pork. In conclusion the preacher mentioned, with emphasis, that the Islanders were becoming pretty hungry.

Within the week word spread up and down the Island, to the remotest of the Seven Villages, that Providence had hearkened to the preacher's praying, that a good-sized barkentine had hit the Outer Diamonds, and that she was beginning to break up. The ship's name, it is remembered, was the *Mary Varney*, but that is all that is remembered of her. Where she hailed from and where her port of destination, perhaps nobody ever knew, or at any rate it has been forgotten.

By the time pieces of the disintegrating ship began to come ashore a good part of the population of the nearer villages was on hand, expectantly. More and more pieces of the wreck came in sight, and among them a body or two. Toward evening there was a great shout and then an expectant silence. Yonder, bobbing up and down with the swell, was a pork barrel. A very large pork barrel, promiseful of good eating for everybody.

There are some who maintain that among the crowd on the beach below the High Point of the Hills was the preacher who had prayed for a shipwreck yielding pork and that he alone of the crowd was not silent. He was unable to resist mentioning, as he went up and down the beach among the people of his parish, the efficacy of good praying. Not four days ago, he pointed out, he had prayed for a shipwreck and yonder, moving ever closer to them, was the answer to prayer.

Nobody paid him much mind. They were too intent upon the approaching cask, now bobbing at the break of the surf. . . . Another sea would bring it right onto the beach, and the villagers gathered themselves into tense groups at the expected point of contact. Seamen among them, which was everybody, knew out of their instincts that this wave would give the cask its final thrust toward them and they moved back a little to avoid the wetting that would ensue at the moment of impact.

Now the wave behaved according to calculation, and with a not inconsiderable thud the cask hit the beach. There was a moment's wait while the sea drained back, but it was a catastrophic moment. The cask disintegrated, its staves falling loosely to the sand. Out of the ruins rose a fine figure of a man, disheveled and here and there a little bloody. He was not edible pork. He was the first Herbert Oden to set foot upon this Island and he never left it again so long as he lived. He was done with the sea.

It could be wished that the folklore of the Island might have preserved some account of what happened to the preacher. He is not again mentioned in the extant lore of the Island. As for Oden, he went home with somebody, traditionally one of the Stowes, and in due season married a daughter of the household and afterward firmly established the name on this and neighboring Islands. It is a good name.

With variations, a similar accounting would apply to every generally prevalent family name of the Island. Every established family with any length of residence on the Island goes back to like beginnings. The family founder was a castaway. The Midgetts, the O'Neals, the Megkinses, the Farrows (Pharaohs), the Millers and the Burruses, the Daileys—the first Dailey was an English schoolmaster en route to Virginia to disseminate his learning, but he too became a permanent resident forty years before Herbert Oden—and, of course, the Howards.

The wind brought them.

With, to be sure, the possible exception of the Howard family and one or two others of the same era. Howard was quartermaster aboard Captain Edward Teach's *Queene Anne's Revenge* when she had her misfortuned duel with Lieutenant Maynard in what has become Teach's Hole at the western end of the second Island, just beyond Ocracoke village. Howard went over the side when his captain fell, traditionally with a silver goblet containing grog. He swam ashore and lost himself among the native population.

Henry Howard lost himself but not his silver cup, which is preserved, after 238 years, by his descendant who owns also the High Point of the Hills, and there is nowhere a more satisfying vessel than this when its outside is fretted with cold sweat and inside it is a compounding of ice, fresh leaves of mint, and some ancestral rum that has lived its long and respected life in a wooden keg. Especially esteemed guests in his sprawling house, hidden away among wind-vexed cedars, are favored with this attention.

More directly descended is Colonel Henry Howard, a retired veteran of the U.S. Army Engineers Corps, who nowadays takes up a good deal of his time with the duties of master of what is probably the only mounted troop of Boy Scouts in the world. To belong the candidate for membership must capture and subdue his own wild pony and ride him, unsaddled, into the meeting. The pony also is a descendant of animals brought to the Islands by the wind.

***

There is instruction to be had in a comparative reading of the roster of the census, the one of 1790 and the current rendering of Island names. With the exception of three currently numerous families, among them the Odens, the first census reads very like the last, even to first names, and the number of inhabitants does not greatly vary from decade to decade. There are Austins now and Grays, as well as Odens, who were not in the first accounting of the inhabitants of the Island.

And the same is almost equally true of other coastal communities, west of Ocracoke Inlet and north of Oregon Inlet, the geographical boundaries of what are, essentially, the North Carolina Outer Banks. In recent times the term has been borrowed, to the great indignation of the native population, to describe, for promotional convenience, the entire sandy outlying region off the coast as "outer banks." Traditionally and actually the expanse of sand north of Oregon Inlet has been called "the beach" and west of Ocracoke Inlet the banks have names of their own—Portsmouth Island and Core (Coree) Banks, and, further along, Shackleford Banks.

But the Outer Banks are these two Islands, and their people were brought here solely by the wind. Other regions have had easier access to mainlands and there have been influxes and outfluxes of people on them. When or from where people came to the Outer Banks it is generally not possible to say with any certainty, but it is always possible to say why they came: the wind brought them.

Half the people who come nowadays to this hill share a common, conditioning, compulsive experience: they have been seasick off Cape Hatteras. As crewmen on ships of war, or of merchantmen, or as passengers aboard luxury liners en route to warmer areas of the earth, they have passed here and they have been sick. Seasoned travelers who have traversed the earth's seven seas without discomfort have been sick, as they momentarily hoped unto death, in plain sight of this hill.

Some among them, they now assure me, would at that dreadful hour have cheerfully given all they possessed on this earth for the privilege of stepping from the heaving deck of their ship to the cool, the placid sand of this Island. Nobody has ever died of seasickness and nobody anywhere else has ever been quite so sick as is almost inevitable offshore here. Now that they are safe again, they perhaps magnify the depths of their suffering and the remembered longings for the feel of this Island under their feet.

Of course they promise themselves, when they are past these agitated waters, that if they ever get the chance they are coming to this Island and see what it looks like, to discover if . . . well, they just want to look at it, and from this eminence, or from the higher vantage of the Lighthouse, 196 feet up to the balcony, to see if the ocean yonder is as rough as it seemed when they were in its grip some while back. I have thought that some of them actually turn a little green from just looking seaward again.

As often as not they bring with them their wives, their children, their parents, or one who has shared and miraculously escaped the terror that stalks yonder. And, wanton that she is, the ocean is rather more than likely, on these occasions, to present a demurely dimpled face, blandly denying that she was ever in all her life other than she is at the moment. And such as have accompanied this man of endured and survived agony look skeptical and remind him that they have to get the next ferry.

But not all of them, not even half of them. When they have examined even a repentant and contrite ocean from this hill they are likely to inquire whether it is possible to buy a small portion of this Island, a site suitable for the erection of a house to which they might, from time to time, repair. There is, unfortunately, no land to be had on the Island, or not much, except an occasional microscopic lot in one of the villages, all of which are for the most part out of sight of the ocean.

These beneficiaries of a miracle of survival are about as near as it is possible to come to the state of mind with which four centuries of castaways have looked upon the Island. It is, to be sure, only an approximation. Those who had been cast ashore by the sea were not merely feeling unwell. That was behind them and they were confronted, now, by the reality of death. Their ship was broken up and they no longer had a ship's rail to sustain them in their gloomy not-caring if the ship fell apart or not. They had to achieve land, and when they touched it, felt the reality of this Island under them, they loved it.

That has to be understood in any appraisal of the feeling that the Islanders have for one of these Islands. Their forbears loved it when their hands touched it and that feeling is transmitted, down the generations. And like the current-day tripper who comes down just to see what Cape Hatteras and its surrounding hills look like, these earliest comers started right off to look for somebody who could or would sell them a piece of it.

There was then, there is now, no man on either of the Islands who wanted to sell any of his land, and so the castaways just took some land. That, too, has its continuing counterpart: when the government of the United States determined to erect the two Islands into a National Recreation Area under the National Park Service, scarcely a square foot of ground on the two Islands was surrendered to them willingly. The federal government had recourse to what is now called a "declaration of taking," which is roughly the equivalent of the procedure of the first cast-up settlers of three hundred years ago.

With the difference, of course, that the federal government, as such, is unable to enter into a marriage contract with any native-born woman and so acquire title to an item of real estate. That procedure must have been followed three hundred years ago, at least to some extent. There were, understandably enough, few women castaways. Women stayed at home as far back as A.D. 1650 when the first fragmentary records of these Islands began to be set down on paper.

Nobody need be shocked at the suggestion that male white castaways took native wives. Although little countenance is given the matter in current romanticizing of the taking of this continent, the practice has been general. Explorers, since the beginning of the tide of human migration, have been, in the first wave, all male and they have also, since the beginning, taken native wives. Reference to such practices has been deleted, out of Victorian respectability, from most of the early and unashamed narratives of the settlement of America by Europeans, and the taboo is still observed, especially by those who compound "Western" romances.

But it happened. And from time to time, among the three hundred or so Seabees who live in their tents down the hill, I sense a changed notion about having a heritage of Indian blood. It is good blood on this Island or in Arkansas, or Oklahoma, or Idaho. My neighbors are members of that battalion of the Navy's Seabees who are engaged in sundry matters hereabouts. They come, from a roster of them fetched me by their executive officer, from every state in the union.

Some of them I have come to know, of all ranks and grades, and out of this acquaintance has come the certainty that if one of them has any Indian blood in him he is going to mention it—and proudly. "I'm quarter Cherokee," one of them will tell me, and he will, without being pressed, mention his grandmother on his father's side who was a full-blooded Cherokee from Oklahoma. . . . And I remember with the very liveliest pleasure this week twenty-eight years ago (March, 1928), when Will Rogers stopped by on the way home from Mexico and we went for a week to visit his relatives among the remnants of the Cherokee Nation who live on their reservation at the other end of North Carolina. . . .

Nowhere among the almost illimitable notes that have been jotted down, as soon after I heard them as I could manage it without being observed—it is the very worst of manners to set down anything somebody has said, while he is still present: you have to learn that on this Island—is there any mention that any violence has ever been done a shipwrecked castaway on this Island. It is just not in the tradition—and it has been 101 years since anybody died by personal violence around here, so far as the records show. "King" Pharaoh Farrow beat one of his slaves, in anger, and the man died. That happened in Kinnakeet in 1855.

Perhaps the Indian villages, for a long time, were able to absorb such as were cast upon their shores, to welcome them in a fashion that did not involve killing. But in time, so busy were the winds of history in the last half of the sixteenth and the first half of the seventeenth centuries—from 1550 to 1650—that they came faster than the Indians could absorb them and, little by little, the Indian disappeared as an Indian, and was himself absorbed. Certain it is, at any rate, that a good many of the older families on these Islands, the Lord Ocracoke among them, cheerfully—they are never boastful or rarely are—lay claim to being part Indian. These are the people of the Island, but they do not own it. The Island is the wind's who built it, who broods above it possessively, and who peopled it. The people are also the wind's people, and they live, by the wind's grace, upon the wind's Island.

5

There were people here, on this ridge, when Amerigo Vespucci came in 1497. The Florentine apparently did not stay long enough to discover their name, but they must have had one. It is possible only to conjecture the impact of native upon explorer and explorer upon Islander from this first contact, and it would be three quarters of a century before anybody else came—it may have happened, however, in 1547 when a Spanish and an English ship engaged each other in battle off the High Point of the Hills and within full view of the village that lay there.

But for the record the Indians were nameless until 1584, when they were named the Hattorask Indians. Where the name came from or what its meaning, if it had one, has eluded ten years of not always patient inquiry, but by the time Raleigh's ships were here and John White began to draw rude charts of how he thought the country must look and Thomas Hariot began to set down the first account of aboriginal life on the not-yet-named continent, there were Hattorask Indians.

Later charts locate three villages, two of them on this ridge and a third on the first ridge, the north ridge, that looks down upon the expanse of Pamlico Sound and from which, on a very good day, it is possible to make out the low-lying mainland thirty-six miles away. But more often it is a mirage that you can see, in this region where it often requires a fine eye to draw a line between reality and the visionary. Nowhere on the earth, able photographers tell me, is it possible to so definitely photograph the nonexistent as it is with an Outer Banks mirage in sight. My own camera has achieved it often.

How many of these Indians there were in the three villages when the sea began her redistribution of the earth's population there is no way of knowing. In no accounting of these early voyagers that I have seen, or heard of, is there any estimate of their number. It is unlikely that any chance visitor, come ashore for whatever purpose—the need of fresh water, of fresh provision, must have been urgent for most of them—saw more than a few of them at any time. It would be entirely natural for all except the able-bodied men to get out of sight at the approach of a stranger.

Nobody appears to have bothered to count them and report their number. All that is indicated anywhere is that there were three villages, and from the examination of such data as is available for other Indian towns, and from a reading of modern estimates of them, in the three villages it is not unreasonable to assume that there were not altogether more than three or four hundred. This is not an agrarian Island. Left to its own devices, as it must have been four centuries ago, it is unlikely that more than that number could have found a living here.

There were fish in the sea and in the Sounds, and there was wild game in the woods, rabbit, squirrel, raccoon, deer. Remnants of this animal population are still extant on Hatteras Island, in that area where the ridges widen to their widest, between three and four miles. The only grain that grew here then, or now, is the Indian corn, and there were very likely patches of it sufficient to sustain the resident population. This, however, is no longer so. In these times, and for a century past, the Island could not feed itself a week if all communication were interrupted.

But there can now be no doubt about the three villages, though the middle one must have moved at some time after the first coming of the European. Either that or the first chart-makers missed one of the villages altogether. The first one, without much doubt, must have been the principal one, the one shadowed by the High Point of the Hills. Its ruins lie three miles or so down the ridge, square out the front door of this house. Its debris is there and has been recently rooted up by a not very earnest hired archeologist, unfortunately a man with whose concept of his trade it has been necessary to take issue.

It is a tolerably simple matter to root among the ruins and turn up the fragments of a pot, or of a weapon. To the professional archeologist there is not much to be excited about. These fragments are not unlike the fragments of pots that can be found in hundreds of like sites from one end of the continent to the other, but there should be better things to do with them than to test the throwing strength of an archeological arm. As archeology they are not especially important, but as Island history they might be supremely important. It is a lay opinion only.

And it is significant to me at any rate that somewhere or other these aborigines at some time or other got hold of some English dishes which were not very durable. Or maybe some harassed Indian housewife, not unlike currently neighboring wives, got peevish with her husband and heaved a plate at him. It is a documented happening of this decade on the Island and it is not inconceivable that the practice originated a very long time ago, and I'd like to know, anyhow, when these fragments in the mound yonder were English, or possibly Spanish, dishes and how they came there.

Even more would I like to know about the uncharted village that must have occupied the site of what has, within a year, become a new and presently terribly hush-hush Navy Facility a mile to the east of this house and a little north. There must have been an Indian town of some sort there, a town of sufficient importance to have some unnamed ship at some not known time take a shot at it with a chain shot.

It must be near four hundred years since the chain shot was fashionable in the expanding science of the gunpowder era, and since this missile was visited upon the Indians of a forgotten village. The Navy Department brought down a battalion of Seabees to build this secret facility, a great company equipped with monstrous machines that move an entire hill in a few minutes. Some of the people who tended these machines, hearing about my concern for such artifacts, from time to time brought me things their machines turned up.

These sheets of paper, as they become pages of manuscript, are weighted against the freshening winds of spring by half a chain shot that they brought me. Beside it is, I think, the finest piece of stone-polishing I have ever seen, a tomahawk-head of green marble polished until it glistens like alabaster. It was found in the same spot, along with some nominally good arrowheads, fragments of clay pottery—and there is not a teaspoonful of clay on these Islands—and the inevitable fragments of broken dishes.

And on another day another of them brought, and just to show me, not present, a thin gold coin. It was encrusted badly and he had polished it until about all that was left was a paper-thin piece of gold the size of a fingernail. Until these youths—and they were from every state in this union—began turning over the hills above the Lighthouse there was no mention, on the charts or in the folklore of the Island, of the possibility that here was once an Indian village. Nor is there any guessing how much stuff is there that they didn't find. A forty-ton bulldozer is not a machine adapted to archeological excavation. But this may have been a mere suburb of another village, a mile to the north, shown on the earliest charts and corroborated by recent rooting, inconclusive except as to its existence.

Two of the three villages lay on the southward slope of the fifth ridge, and it has continued something of a mystery to me why the third was on a point of land that juts northward into Pamlico Sound halfway along the length of the ridge. That is the cold side of the Island, and the winter's winds, usually north-northwest, are but little warmed by the 35-mile expanse of Sound water. Indeed, the water itself has been frozen solid at least eight times that have been documented within the past two hundred years.

Some of the Islanders advance the conjecture that maybe the natives used the King's Point town as a kind of resort, but there seems little to support such a theory. In winter the south slope of the ridge is likely to be about ten degrees warmer than the north slope and there would be no point in spending the winter on the north side. In summer the south slope, washed on two sides by the sea, is normally ten degrees cooler than the north side which, in its turn, in summer, becomes the lee side of the heavily wooded ridges of Buxton Wood.

There were three villages, about equal in size and, very likely, in population. None of them was large. It is, of course, possible that the King's Point village was used as a sort of port-of-entry for the Outer Banks, with outrigger canoes plying the waters of the Sound, in good weather, and so maintaining communication with neighboring tribes, or villages, on Roanoke Island, the scene of Raleigh's ill-starred first venture into colonization, or with the mainland, where there were other Indian villages.

When the Europeans came to the Bight of Hatteras there was no retreat open for the inhabitants. It was, and it continues to be, a long and exhausting journey across the Sounds to the mainland. When a ship let down her anchor in the Bight of Hatteras there was not time to begin an evacuation of the Island, and it seems out of character for the Island that anybody would evacuate it. There have been, since, much larger and more hostile invasions, and nobody has ever run away from them. Always, I think, the Islanders have remained and they have absorbed or have been absorbed by the newcomers.... In the brief time of their stay here five of the Navy's Seabees have succumbed to the charm of Island girls and have become husbands to them.

Whether these Island residents resented and resisted the approach of European people there can not now be any certainty, but my conjecture is that the Islanders, then as now, were ready to welcome contacts with the outside. From across the Sounds, from the mainland, it is reasonably certain that the Indians there had contact with the natives. It is a good 700 miles from Cape Hatteras to the nearest green marble mountain from where perfect tomahawk-heads might have been brought. The arrowheads here and the pots are very like those found in more definitely explored village sites far inland.

Traditionally, and without documentation of any compelling sort, the history books as far back as my own youth at the beginning of the century have the Cherokee Indians coming down here from their mountains on an annual pilgrimage in the interest of their digestive tracts. Down from the mountains they would come, in spring, to steep themselves in medicinal yoepon tea. It is, even yet, respected as a draught wonderfully potent in purging the body of winter poisons, and the Cherokees, as legend persists, would come in droves to take the cure, even as inhabitants of these western counties now come, in distressingly increasing numbers, to breathe some sea air. There were tourists here half a millenium ago.

And it is not unreasonable to suppose, but it is supposition only, that they brought something to the Island in the way of payment for their keep. They may, and probably did, swap a handful of arrowheads, or a polished piece of green marble, for medication and sustenance. Possibly the one-time owner of this piece beside me here brought also with him a more than ordinarily formidable stomach-ache and his cure entailed large payment.

But this half of a chain shot is more difficult to account for. It must have been thrown in anger, or at least in an excess of swaggering. How many centuries it lay there under that dune I cannot know, but it has come now to peaceable uses, with no more militant duty than to lay a restraining weight upon the spring's wind when it reaches in the window and would carry off this page when I am through with it. . . . There were people on this Island a long time ago, but I think they must have been a peaceable people, a lot who welcomed strangers and gave them fresh water for their ships, and fresh yoepon tea for their agues and, perhaps, their daughters for wives when they had need, or desire, of them.

Life in these villages, on the southward slope of this ridge or upon the northward slope of the first ridge, five miles or so north-west of the two that faced the sea, must have been very pleasant in its day. Yonder was the sea, and here was the wind; yonder the sun, and here this comfortable shade lying redolently thick under these great liveoaks. The sea was plentiful of food, and the Sound, too. The woods around provided deer and squirrel, and everywhere there were all manner of birds. . . . Audubon Society technicians have identified, as resident, a total of 183 species of birds, about half of them being shore birds and the others from among those who nest in trees.

Martin Tolson, who is a very lively eighty, tells me that if it were not for the gulls the Islanders would have, even in his day, gone hungry and he expects that it is a taste handed down from the day of the Indian. He insists that a gull egg, either fried or boiled, is good eating, even if you are not very hungry. But, he adds gener-ously, gull eggs are something you have to get a taste for before you like them very much and then he will add, in finality, that any kind of an egg beats being hungry. . . .

But above and beyond all this there is the Bight of Hatteras, a curving, mostly tranquil lot of blue water, warm to the touch almost always and a comfortable anchorage for such as find the going too rough yonder at the Point of the Diamonds. There is never any knowing what the Bight will produce in the way of wonders in the course of a day. . . . I have seen, in my small years here above it, two massive palm trees, their fronds still green, washed ashore. They were ripped from their moorings on some tropical island far off yonder to the south and brought here, where they were dried by the sun and, afterward, carried off in bits by some of these people who come to look at the ocean that made them so sick.

Sometimes she brings her dead and lays them there in the sun. Across the plain down the hill, a quarter mile yonder among a clump of pines that Mr. Byrum planted there, and which miraculously escaped an untended fire, there are graves. These are they who didn't quite make it when they sought to escape the sea's fury and they were brought and laid on the beach. Crewmen from the Coast Guard Station, if the sea had stripped her dead of all possibility of recognition—she likes it so, this keeping anonymous those whose death has pleased her—have brought what there was and laid it, always with the Ritual, awkwardly perhaps, but firmly, read above them.

Here were the villages to which the castaways came when they had survived the sea. The villages have vanished, except for little hills that contain such things of theirs as were not easily soluble, or which defied the rot that very soon merges man's mortal flesh with the flesh of his mother the earth. The villagers, too, have been merged with the race of mankind, and you see their ghosts, sometimes, in the dark remote gleaming of an eye that is not light, in the way that most Islanders' eyes are bright with the Nordic blondness that is also the heritage of this people.

These three villages are vanished, but new villages came to be in their stead, villages more suited to the implements and modes of a new race that arose from the old. When the one era and its villages ended and another, with its new villages, began, there is no precise knowing. Perhaps the one era merged imperceptibly into another, but it is tolerably certain that two of the villages, at any rate, are older than the storied towns of Virginia and of Massachusetts where, historically, the saga of America began. These towns began when the sea's castaways took to wife the daughters of the first villagers.

6

There is no way to determine, now, which is the oldest of the villages on these offshore Islands, often loosely defined, that stretch themselves athwart the seaward approach to North Carolina. There are no documents, no charts, and I am disposed to doubt that it matters very much anyway which of them came first into being. They were here, indifferent to documentation, when happenings in this region became important enough to be mentioned officially.

Portsmouth, on the northeast tip of the Island of the same name, both very likely deriving from a port town in England, was in 1675 one of the oldest towns between the Virginia capes and Cape Fear, and for a century it was the largest. Across the Inlet from it, a sort of seventeeth-century version of the other side of the railroad tracks, was the village of Ocracoke, occupying a pleasant situation on the southwest tip of that Island.

But traditionally, and not unreasonably, another village across the next Inlet was older. It derived its name and its initial population from the original town that lay eastward about seven miles, the Indian capital, Hattorask of the earliest charts. It was not, for another two centuries, a very lusty village and there was yet another, across the ridge from the first town, facing the Sound. It was, for reasons that remain stubbornly obscure, called Trent. For reasons that are equally obscure, the U.S. Post Office Department named it Frisco back in the 1870's when a post office was established there.

Nor did the Department's density end at Frisco. Further eastward, where a small settlement continued under the name of Cape, they ordained another post office and called it Buxton. Nobody on the Island ever knew, or can remember, why. Seven miles further along, two villages, Big Kinnakeet and Little Kinnakeet, were lumped together at a post office called Avon, for no reason that I have been able to find, though there is preserved, here, the envelope of a letter registered in that post office in 1878. The final rape of native place names occurred at the northernmost village, and Chicamicomico, definitely derived from the Indian, became Rodanthe.

But this is two centuries ahead of the story, or such story as it is possible to put together out of fairly abundant folklore and very meager mention in the records of the time, which were probably no more nor less authentic than the folklore. It is not possible even to guess who founded the town of Portsmouth and caused it to flourish until it was become the largest seaport between Norfolk and Charleston, with an annual tonnage surpassing them both for a while.

Since there is so little that is remembered, is mentioned in the folklore, it is not unreasonable to assume that the town's founders were, in the continuing term, foreigners. That is to say, they were not native to the Island. They had no Indian blood in them, so to speak. They were merchants, and these Islands had little business with merchants, not having anything much to sell and less with which to buy. No interest in them, or contact with them, except in such times as a gracious Providence wrecked one of their ships and scattered its goods along the shore for everybody to take. After, of course, decent disposition had been made of such bodies as washed up along with the merchandise.

Life on these Islands had come to feel the impact of a sort of flanking movement from the interior, with which there had been little direct contact since the Cherokee and other Indian peoples had become so preoccupied with internal confusions that they no longer came east in spring to purge themselves of winter agues by drinking the native yoepon tea. Virginia's overflowed population began seeping down into the province about the middle of the century and by 1675 were well enough established to require and institute direct contact with their home bases in England, and with customers in the expanding life of the West Indies.

For one reason or another, some geographical and some having to do with the governing authorities, these established settlers had no disposition to make contact through the ports of the Hampton Roads area, especially since the use of these places of entry necessitated dealing with the weather off Cape Hatteras. More and more of the expanding trade of the mainland began to be routed down the Five Sounds and out to sea through the Inlets at Hatteras and at Ocracoke.

And although it would be some while before Dr. Benjamin Franklin would define and name the Gulf Stream, navigators were beginning to know its mystery. Ships en route from rich ports on the far side of the Gulf of Mexico and in the West Indies began to make use of its force. They would ride this far north and, from time to time, ships from this thickening fleet would put in. Here was their last chance for fresh water before continuing northeastward toward Europe. North Carolina's first international incident of any consequence occurred when one of these ships, laden with two million dollars in stolen gold, came to grief at Ocracoke, and the ship's owners, who survived, were less than tolerant of the informal way the Islanders had in dealing with such matters. The Spaniards got their money back. And from that incident, it is more than possible, derives the instinctive mistrust in the Islands of all people of Spanish blood, and there is nowhere that I have been able to discover any indication that any Spaniard, shipwrecked and cast away on these Islands, survives in the lore of the Islands.

Portsmouth grew lustily and in 1704 numbered as many as 500 people in its population. There were other ports, to be sure, but none so convenient to the expanding population of the northeastern counties. The back country of such ports as Beaufort and Wilmington, which were not yet dreamed of, was not known to settlers nor commerce, and it would be another generation before the first of the Highlanders came up the Cape Fear River and settled in its valley. There was, of course, the settlement of the Palatines at New Berne, but they entered through Portsmouth and, a dozen or so years later, were almost exterminated by the enraged and outraged Tuscaroras.

There were few inland towns but many sizable plantations whose owners acted as their own factors. Portsmouth had warehouses whereat a planter might sell his tobacco or his turpentine or his juniper timber and shingles. There was an increasing demand for timber in the West Indies, where rich planters were building great houses and where native timber was exceedingly scarce. There was also an increasing demand, especially in the West Indies, for corn, which grew lushly in the lowlands of the mainland plantations, and there were warehouses where corn might be exchanged for salt, or molasses. Or for rum.

Small, shallow sailing vessels brought these products down from the plantations, and the docks at the warehouses were thick with them. Larger, sea-able vessels awaited them at Portsmouth and emptied the warehouses of their goods. The harbor was not notably good, and there were times when the wind and the tide played such tricks with sand that boats were not able to enter or to leave port, but in the tide's good time these situations clarified themselves. Ships departed and came back, and Portsmouth grew.

Sometimes an Island youth would ship out, or would be shanghaied, as a seaman on one of these ships, but he always managed to get back home somehow, sometime. Not all of them, perhaps, but enough of them made it to survive in tales handed down to their generations and which persist until now. Sometimes, for certain, he continued to follow the sea. He made a career of it, became the master of a ship. But always these Islands were home. His blood was here and it continues here.

It should not be supposed that the Islander villages were wholly isolated, set apart from this expanding life right in their midst. There began, and there grew, a demand for the Islanders' salt fish, cured as they had learned to cure them from the Indians. They made ready rations for the crew of a ship on the voyage home and there was always a market for these fish in their home ports. It was the only Island product suited to merchandising, except for an occasional bale of yoepon tea leaves, dried and ready for tea-making. It was known that the tea of these leaves was an antidote for scurvy.

Out of the welter of names of merchants who operated at Ocracoke Inlet two and a half centuries ago but few persist with any local significance. Chief among them were the Blounts, probably the earliest family of merchants that continue with undiminished vigor in the town of Washington and along a creek that bears the name. They lived along the Pamlico River but erected big log warehouses on a huge shell mound in the middle of the Inlet. It continues, now, as Shell Castle Island and is the abode of the largest colony of pelicans in the United States. About eight thousand of them do their nesting there in summer.

Portsmouth does not now exist as a town. It managed to survive the era of the American Revolution and continued, in diminuendo, through still another century as an identifiable place on the charts. A good many factors contributed to its disintegration, but chiefly the town died because it paid no heed to the wind and her bitter resentment of those who deal inequitably with the things she has made. She made Portsmouth Island, which is but a continuation of these Islands, an extension of them. And she also planted the grass, set the tree to guard what she had made. Trees disappeared from that Island, cut down for the timbers of ships, cut down to provide fuel. Cattle came and devoured the grass and, with her usual savagery, the wind began retaliation. Sand which had made the hills of the Island began to drift aimlessly about and to disappear into the waters round about. Never a very dependable harbor, this one was filled with moving shoals that had been dry land. To reach the site where the town was, and where nothing now is save an abandoned Lifeboat Station and a few desultory buildings, the traveler has to descend from a small boat some distance out and slog his way through about a half mile of shallow water, and this where seagoing barkentines used to anchor. The Island is a waste, washed by high tide.

There were other factors in the decline of the port, to be sure. Towns were built inland, along the Sounds and the rivers, and for a century or so the seagoing vessels, when they could get through the Inlet, went directly to their quays. Bath was the first of them, laid out and incorporated as the capital in 1704. Others followed, and afterward there were ports established at Beaufort, Wilmington, and New Berne. It is possible, too, that Portsmouth became, in her prosperity, more than a little arrogant. She did not welcome small-fry merchants, or those whose occupations were more dubious than her own.

No welcome was extended so formidable a man as Captain Edward Teach. He was compelled to anchor, when he did not proceed across the Sound and up the river to the new capital, in the town across the Inlet—across the tracks, so to speak. To be sure Captain Teach did not come to buy, and he had little business with the merchant princes who did business in the warehouses on Shell Castle Island. He had, sometimes, merchandise that he would sell, at a suitable price, but the merchants were not disposed to do much business with him. Not at Portsmouth, at any rate. He had to lay to across the Inlet and do his trading, if any, there.

Portsmouth died but it served its day admirably and more. It re-established the people of these two Islands, of these named and

re-named villages, in their contact with the sea and the world of the
seven seas. Castaways they came and, for a while, they and their generations forgot the sea in its far-ranging. But when the world's ships
began to congregate in Portsmouth harbor about 1675, at the end
of the first hundred years of amalgamation and re-emergence, these
Islanders must no longer have been, primarily, seafaring people.

It was in their blood, to be sure. Or at any rate, in half their blood.
Portsmouth, with its example and its challenge, won them back to
the sea, but with a new canniness that was part Indian and part
burnt-child castaway; that, in the generations since Portsmouth
began to die, has continued and developed. Nowhere on the earth
are there men who know the sea so profoundly, who know it and
fear it—and love it. And the sea needs to be loved, as well as Islands,
or anything else.

7

Portsmouth had no friends. It had no manners. Mariners despised it because of its navigational hazards. The native Islander despised it because it was rowdy and rapacious, populated by a breed of traders whose one thought was the making of money, not by honest industry but by sharp trading. It was a boom town, and as towns went in this new world, a big town. There were half a thousand people noisily living there in the middle of the century that saw America expand from a few scattered settlements into an independent nation.

Nobody gave the town a good name. The Reverend John Irmstone took one horrified look at the place when he arrived by way of the West Indies in 1706 and proceeded with pious distaste across the Sound and up the river to the newly incorporated capital at Bath. So also did the newly appointed governor and his chief-of-staff, Tobias Knight, who was also the chief justicer of the province. If there was any government in the town no record of it remains, though it was chartered in 1757.

But it was also a lusty town, and when a company of Spaniard ships came up from the West Indies in 1745, intent upon its destruction, they turned away, probably in dismay. The town was too big for them and they contented themselves with capturing the smaller port of Beaufort, fifty-odd miles down the coast. They held it for a day or two, pillaged it of such of its wares as were portable, burned some of it, and went away.

Long before that the government of the Commonwealth of Virginia, seated at Williamsburg, had heard with dismay that Portsmouth was an evil influence in the widening world of the west. Evil or not, it was making a deep dent in the colony's commerce, especially with the West Indies. It was 150 miles, plus the hazard of Cape Hatteras, nearer the booming market in the Caribbean and it lay, also, within easy sailing of the then mysterious force in the sea that was making it the homeward route of ships bound to northern Europe.

North Carolina, in that day, had become a sort of no-man's-land, the moribund government grandly visualized and set down on paper by John Locke at the behest of the Lords Proprietors having no longer any vitality. It would be, in 1718, another decade before the crown would take over, the king buying back the land of the Carolinas from the proprietary lords and establishing the two provinces, North Carolina and South Carolina. Virginia claimed, if it did not implement, a proprietary concern for such of the inhabitants as had trickled southward.

Quite without anybody's planning or permission, and almost before anybody knew about it, this brawling brat of a port grew up and became a bigger town than Virginia could boast of. There was a lot of resentment in high places and along the docks of the towns of the lower Chesapeake. This Portsmouth was getting business that rightfully belonged to Virginia and, moreover, it was, a lot of it, dubious business too. The Virginians laid their ailments to the prevalence of piracy rampant between them and their lawful markets in the West Indies.

Nor was there anybody to stop them when the Virginians, after scaring the daylights out of themselves by screaming "piracy," began to meditate upon an expedition to eliminate piracy and restore trade to their own ports. There was no government worth the name in North Carolina. Governor Eden had established himself at the town that has for more than two hundred years borne his name. He went there because it was the most comfortable town-in-being for him to live in. His chief justicer lived, most of the time, in Bath, which was officially the capital of the scattered province.

Something more than mere civic righteousness must have impelled the Virginia government in its fervor against piracy and, afterward, when their crusade began to backfire, they set about investigating the relations between their most noted victim, Captain Edward Teach, and the governing authorities in Edenton and Bath. When they had beheaded Captain Teach, without authority and with no special provocation, they were under the necessity of erecting him into a fabulous menace and, for safety's sake, of smearing Eden and Knight.

There survives on these Islands, and continues, a very lively belief that Captain Teach was a right considerable fellow. No better than he needed to be, perhaps, and certainly no worse than a lot of others who were too formidable to be bothered. Captain Teach was not, in the rapacious fashion of the inhabitants of the trading town on the other side of the Inlet, much of a figure. And even if he resorted, on occasion, to what is nowadays considered as piracy, at least his victims had a fair chance, or some chance. And what chance did a poor Islander have when he took his dried fish to the Portsmouth market?

And what if he did take time out now and then to travel across the Sound and up the river to Bath? It was no more than proper for him, a ship's captain, to go and make his manners to the authorities there. And did he not maintain a respectable household there, with a wife? Did he not also make gifts to the church, and to the first library ever to be established in what would become North Carolina? He was a handsome, personable fellow, when he combed his hair and his whiskers and went up river to see his family and to dine with the governor or his principal justicer. Where he got the books, what was in them, and what became of them are questions that need not be asked, now, because there is no answer to them.

There are so few actual answers to anything related to the man, but it is remembered still along these Islands that he preferred the hospitality of the simple folk across the Inlet from Portsmouth to the brawling thieves who built their warehouses and defrauded all comers on the other side the five miles or so of water. And, anyhow, what if he was a pirate? He was a respectable pirate and a good neighbor when he was around the community. To be sure he may have had an eye for any comely wench who happened to appear, but then, why not?

Captain Teach was aboard his vessel and bothering nobody when Captain Ellis L. B. Maynard and his Virginians arrived. It is remembered that Maynard took one look at the formidableness of Portsmouth and desisted from further approach. Too many people, too many ships, and they were, ships and men alike, too much for him. He drew off and looked around for easier prey. And what was easier than this lone ship, lying yonder in the smooth water of a small bay? It was armed, to be sure, but it was also at anchor.

Advantage lies always with the attacker, and Maynard attacked the unready and unwarned ship. Aroused by the attack, the crew gave a good account of itself, but there must have been little in the battle that resembled any of the subsequent moving pictures which are sometimes shown on these Islands, accompanied by hoots of derision. The Teach of two centuries of fiction must have little resemblance to the reality that was hacked to bits shortly after daylight of that November morning in 1718. Little or no heed was paid the battle by the busy merchants across the Inlet, but there are those now on these Islands who have, handed down from generation to generation, an eyewitness account of it, and it was a pretty sordid show. Captain Teach met his attackers without recoiling and so did the members of his crew, but they had little chance against a maneuvering ship, well manned and well armed, and come with the intent to destroy.

It was just Captain Teach's hard luck that he was lying well away from the cluttered harbor of Portsmouth when the Virginians came, and that he little expected them. It is remembered, and it is set down in the records, that after the Virginians hacked the man to bits they removed his head and stuck it on the bowsprit of the attacking vessel. There were no resounding shouts of approbation from the villagers who had come down to the shore at the sound of gunfire, and it must have occurred to the Virginians that they might as well get out of town before reprisals were instituted.

The wind being fair they set sail for the open Sound and the mouth of the river. It is recorded that the ship arrived in the little capital at Bath long after nightfall and that a gloomy terror pervaded the community when the head of their fellow-townsman, the Governor's friend, was impaled on the bowsprit of the ship. Maynard found no welcome in Bath and was not received by the authorities. But there were at hand no means of reprisal against him. It was not a strong government, and the following day the Virginians went back down river and put to sea without further bothering the ships at anchor in Portsmouth.

Whether there is any significance to be read into the circumstance I could not venture to say, but it is a fact that if Maynard made any sort of report to the authorities in Williamsburg no evidence of it has been found after wide searching and inquiry. Some protest was made by the Carolina government, weak though it was, against this unwarranted invasion of its territory and the killing of a man who, though not a citizen, was held in esteem. Then followed the somewhat silly "inquiry" into the relations between him and the authorities, an eighteenth-century manifestation of the twentieth century's smear technique.

"He slunk out of here," an Islander will say, near two and a half centuries afterward, and he says it as if it happened no longer ago than last week. It is Maynard they are thinking about, and from their tone one would in some fashion sense a feeling that the sea let them down when she let him get past the turn of the Outer Diamonds without some sort of retribution for his wanton arrogance. Maynard is no remembered hero on these Islands, but he is remembered.

Nor was Captain Teach any especial sort of hero. He might have been at least half as bad as the figure the romancers have made of him, but not bad enough to be "shot sittin'" like he was when he lay anchored in a tranquil place that, in later times, came to be named for him—Teach's Hole. It is not a hole, really, but a pleasant little bay, and in these days, when the thoughts of so many have turned back toward former times, there is random talk of finding his ship and raising it. It must be fire-scarred, but these sands are very tender with such.

But nobody, actually, proposes to dredge for it. They have a feeling that the sea, in her own good time, or the wind, will bring the old ship to harbor again. And in her own way. It may be a pretty rough way, when she gets around to the task, with vast winds and rolling tides. But it can happen. The like of it has happened often along the length of these Islands, and always the Islanders, when a storm is gone, go down to the beach to look.

And around a Coast Guard Station, or a wharf where men unload their fish and idle afterward in the sun, you will hear, "Wonder what that fellow done with his head?" What did Maynard do with the head of the Pirate? The last ever heard of it was when it was sighted, by moonlight, as the man's vessel approached its mooring in Bath Creek, late in the night of that November 18, 1718. There has never been any answer to that one: nobody knows. It is not in the Maynard papers.

Captain Teach, headless; sometimes, they say, walks along the shore of the little bay that is named for him, and he stares out across moonlit water toward where a big town used to be. Towns have ghosts, too, and it may be that the headless Teach and the brawling town that died of its own rapacity talk together about things that never were. And if it is proper to reflect that Vespucci and Abraham Midgett sometimes settle on some comfortable cloud to discuss changes that have come about, Captain Maynard and Captain Teach may also tenant a neighboring cloud conversationally.

And it was a considerable battle, quite the bloodiest ever had on these Islands. Forty-eight men were engaged, all told, and of these, twelve were killed outright and twenty-two wounded. In the next major hostility hereabouts, 143 years later, a total of three thousand men were engaged for three whole days. Nobody was killed, nobody mentionably wounded, though the powder burned assumed astronomical proportions. And very likely Captain Teach will say that the cutlass beats a cannon any day. He should know.

8

On these Islands they remember the *Prince of India*, and they speak of the September hurricane that littered the shore with wreckage in 1737. There is no documented record that the *Prince of India* ever existed, but the good monks in their monastery on the Island of St. Kitts recorded the hurricane, which did considerable devastation thereabouts and headed then in the direction of Cape Hatteras, which was, and is, a somewhat routine entry.

Ships and storms are remembered on these Islands, not for what they may have done to them—through the centuries the damage to these Islands has been negligible—but for what they brought with them and left. A storm may move a few million cubic yards of sand from one place to another, but tomorrow, or in its own good time, the ebbing wind will put it back where it belonged. Or it may herd all the boats onto dry land, but it is not much trouble to put them back.

These Islanders remember the *Prince of India* for its cargo, and the consequences of the wrecking have been, for more than two centuries, momentous. The ship was loaded with horses brought from somewhere in Asia Minor, probably Arabia, and they were ministered to during their long and tedious voyage by two Arabian youths. Or at any rate these Islands remember them as youths, and they must have been, as will appear, of a not inconsiderable lustiness. They continue now, in the twelfth generation, and very lustily.

None in this twelfth generation remembers with any fixity of mind how many horses there were aboard the *Prince of India* and how many of them made it to the beach when the ship broke up about three miles southwest of Hatteras Inlet and twelve miles northeast of the village of Ocracoke. About all that can be said with any certainty is that there were at least two, one male, one female. The probability is that there were about two dozen.

These were not the first horses in America, but they were the first on these Islands that are the Outer Banks. There is some question, even now, about where the animals were going when the September Storm of 1737 piled the lot on the beach here. One school of thinking adheres to the belief that they were consigned to planters around Edenton and another is of the belief that they were headed for the Virginia capes and the plantations that lay along the rivers of that province.

Wealth had increased in both regions and the ways of the English gentry had come to America. Gentlemen wanted horses proper for the hunt, and where, on the earth, were there better horses to be had than in Arabia? It is certain that they were not destined for the bawdy port town of Portsmouth. There were no gentlemen there, as these Islanders are not slow to tell anybody, and no place for riding if there had been. Or time, either: everybody was too busy defrauding honest shipmasters and even more honest planters from across the Sounds and up the rivers.

But there were horses, now, on Ocracoke Island, and very bewildered horses, too. There was no feed for them except of their own getting on the grasses that grew in the low places. Or from the leaves of shrubs. Once ashore they were on their own and they appear to have scattered in every direction. They were very likely pretty wild anyhow, and they became wilder. Nobody on the Island had any use for a horse. There was no plowing to be done, and if anybody had anywhere to go it was simpler and easier to hoist sail and let the wind do the work.

One of the castaway hostlers must have been an Egyptian and it is possible that he was named by some roving clergyman. He became, as the Islanders remember it, Pharaoh, and unaccustomed to dealings with such names, the Islanders pronounced it as if it began, in its spelling, with the letter "F," and so Pharaoh became Farrow. There are scores of Farrows on both Islands even now, and in the middle of the next century, around the 1850's, Pharoah Farrow was spoken of as King Pharoah, and his name, without regal rank, however, appears now on scores of land-deeds of that period, to the very anxious confusion of land-title agents of the government of the United States. He also owned, and mentioned in his will, numerous slaves, all of whom had been brought here by storms.

As for the other one, it may have been the intent of the church-man to name him Ahab, but somehow the native populace got the word confused with the name of the country which provided the horses and he became "That Arab." It was a word of two distinct syllables, beginning with a long "A" and both syllables evenly accented. He was A-rab. Both appear, like the horses, to have adapted themselves with little difficulty to their new situation. They, like most castaways, were in no mood to again entrust themselves to the sea.

And both—the roster of present-day inhabitants is evidence enough—presently further adapted themselves to local procedures and became the heads of families. Pharoah became Farrow and, in the course of time, Arab became Wahab, a name that endures, potent and respected on both Islands and elsewhere in eastern America. I have mentioned already the Lord of Ocracoke, who is descended from Captain Teach's quartermaster. His name is Wahab. . . . One of the liveliest intellects on that Island belongs to the same clan—perhaps tribe is the better word—and he promises to become a man of letters. He is presently editor of his school paper and a very lively link in the generation-to-generation transmission of family and Island lore.

Whether any effort was ever made anywhere to round up the scattered cargo of horses and restore it to the prospective owners does not appear. Perhaps there might have been such an undertaking, and some of them may have been retrieved. But certainly not all of them. After a few generations of multiplication, the wild horse of the Outer Banks became a notable beast and widely famed, not only for the implications of romance in his background but also because of his stamina and endurance.

There is not now much resemblance between the sleek Arabian horse and these somewhat burry creatures. It is hard living on these bleak, pastureless Islands, and it takes a lot of cajolery to induce one of them to submit to the currycomb. But when they do, and when a little grain is mixed with their marsh grass, they are a right handsome animal. And long ago the native population made common cause with the horse, came to know and use him, and for a long time the annual roundup of the year's new foaling was an occasion of wide social importance.

It happened on the Fourth of July which, for some curious and unexplored reason, has since 1790 been celebrated on these Islands with an uncommon fervor. Previously subdued horses are used to drive the entire equine population into a corral, and the Islanders, in former times, drew lots to see which had first choice of the year's new crop. Usually they were branded and turned loose to be caught and tamed afterward.

Two hundred years after he came ashore on these Islands the horse began to wane in importance. There were various reasons for it. There was the automobile, which did not appear on these Islands until after the invention of what they still call the balloon tire. This type of tire is able to negotiate the rutted sand of the beach. There was, before that, the decline of the sailing vessel after the coming of the internal combustion engine for installation in boats.

But there was a profounder reason. The horse, and herds of cattle which came or were brought to the Island—there is little in the Island's remembering to suggest when or how or why the cow or the sheep came—is fearfully destructive of vegetation, and by the beginning of this century the Islands were stripped pretty bare of grass. The sand began to move in retaliation and all sign of vegetation to disappear.

There intervened, too, the U.S. Department of Agriculture in 1919. Somebody somewhere determined that the cattle tick was a creature of extremely disruptive influence. Let a tick—and these Islands produce billions of them—bite a cow and she quits giving milk, or such as she gives is not safe for human consumption. It was not, or should not have been, any hazard on the Outer Banks, since the native human population had, like the cattle and the horses, set up a sort of immunity against the ravages of ticks as well as mosquitoes.

But the Department people were adamant. They just had to rid the whole world of ticks, and there ensued the Cattle Tick War. The Islanders fought a bitter rear-guard action, and when this failed them they embarked upon a years-long campaign of passive resistance. Along the length of the Islands, from Oregon Inlet to Ocracoke, the federal government built dipping vats and commanded the inhabitants to round up their cattle and fetch them to the vats to be purged of vermin.

It would have been quite as reasonable to have commanded them to round up the rabbits, of which there were, and are, vast numbers. The Islanders retaliated by dynamiting the dipping vats at night, but this served only to fetch a platoon of secret service people who, very sensibly, after inquiring into the matter, said that they would go away for thirty days and when they returned, if the dipping vats were found replaced or repaired, no more would be said about it.

When the federal agents, both detectives and cattledippers, returned, the vats had been replaced but nobody brought his cattle to be rid of ticks. On Hatteras Island the natives just gave up and said in effect, "The cattle are not mine, nor the horses. They are out yonder and go take them if you want them and dip them if you want to." Through the co-operation of the county authorities the federal government paid a bounty of five dollars per head for all cattle, and all horses, sheep, and hogs. The Island does not now have a specimen of either animal on it. The late Hall Roosevelt, already mentioned herein, shot the last of the cows in 1938, at a range of eight hundred yards, using an old-model Springfield rifle. The county authorities solemnly paid him five dollars, which he casually handed to the CCC youth who had accompanied him on the hunt.

But on Ocracoke the populace were of a somewhat more stubborn mind. For one thing they are in another county, which had little interest in harassing them and less inclination to bow before the rising tide of federal meddling. They just ignored the government's agents and continue so to do. When I last counted them, from a helicopter, there were 135 horses loose on Ocracoke Island and about 200 cattle.

But the Hatterasman has not abated anything of his devotion to the horse. I recall with abiding wonder a Sabbath afternoon a year or so ago when a crowd that appeared to contain every inhabitant of this Island started streaming past here, some afoot, the others riding in whatever vehicle was at their command. They were headed down toward the Point. So congested did the road become that I went down to see what had happened. The Coast Guard had brought me no report of any disaster of any sort, which is their neighborly custom.

When my inquiry finally got the attention of a passing youth he answered me over his shoulder and without looking back, "Couple of horses swum the Inlet and they're eatin' grass down yonder on the Point." He continued Point-ward, and for days the wanderings of the two horses were followed and reported minutely.

I am persuaded that if a herd of hippopotamuses had come ashore on the Island they would have occasioned no profounder wonder. They were finally caught, tethered, and sold to some tourist from Norfolk, and so, after more than two hundred years, at least two of the original shipment got to Virginia, if, indeed, that was where they were consigned in the first place.

But there was a yet greater spectacle in store. Over on Ocracoke Colonel Howard has organized what, in so far as I know, is the only mounted troop of Boy Scouts in the country. One spring day Colonel Howard brought his troop across the Inlet and encamped in the lee of this hill. They spent two days visiting me—and so did the entire population of this Island, who came just to look at a horse. And to see some of the most hell-for-leather horsemanship ever witnessed east of the rodeo belt. . . . The floor of this house must have been ankle-deep in bacon grease when they left. There were eighteen of them—and not a skillet in the crowd. And, properly enough, there was a Wahab and a Farrow among them, and one of the horses had the resounding name of *Prince of India*. Both lads are blond and freckled and blue of eye—but the name remains. Names do.

9

There has been, here, a kind of interlude, though, when the word has been set down and examined, it is not quite the right word. It is an interval, a period of time lasting 120 hours and 15 minutes, in which life on these two Islands has stood still. That is not the right word, either. There seem not to be any right words, and in a way that is as it should be. Very few words have been spoken about what has been happening.

One of the Island's own has been lost and they have been searching for him. On the third day they found his skiff sixty miles away, northeast of where something happened to him while he was planting some oysters in a bed that the State government had allocated him and which, by careful husbandry, had become a comfortable living for him. March is planting time, in these waters, and Andrew Styron was replacing the spent, empty oyster shells that had been taken from his bed during the harvesting season.

Something happened as he planted his oyster bed on a shoal halfway across Ocracoke Inlet, which lies in the lee of Shell Castle Island, where, two hundred and fifty years ago, they were erecting the first of a clump of warehouses to serve a burgeoning commerce. The oyster bed lies between there and Beacon Island upon which Alexander Hamilton directed the raising of a fifty-foot light in 1790. The beacon and the warehouses have long been gone, and the islands, such of them as remain above water, are the abode of nesting shore birds—pelicans, gulls and, where there is any cover, snowy egrets.

There have always been Styrons on these Islands. When, or from where, the first of them came there is no way of knowing. He may have been a castaway, or he might have come to forget and to begin anew: these are matters that are not dwelt upon. But there have been Styrons here a long time, as early as there is any record in the meager books that list the holders of land, of property. They were here as early as 1740 and they were disturbed about the lines of their lands.

And they were here fifty years later when the government of the new republic counted and named its inhabitants in the First Census. There have always been Styrons and when you have lived among them long enough you can begin to distinguish family markings, or, as the Islanders say, "family favor." It is so with all the families that have been here a long time, and the Styrons are a robust race, rather more than likely to put on weight after they come to their middle years. Andrew Styron was toward sixty, and he was beginning to be heavy, and his heart was bad.

On Tuesday morning he loaded his boat, and a fourteen-foot skiff, with oyster shells and set out for his oyster bed. He would, he said, be home, he thought, in time for dinner. On these Islands dinner is the midday meal. His family waited dinner for a while, but with no anxiety. Two hours after the midday they began to be a little worried, and when he did not appear—the wind was picking up—by four o'clock in the afternoon they knew that something must have happened. Word went down to the U.S. Coast Guard Station and was transmitted to Group Headquarters at Cape Hatteras.

Things began then to happen, but I was not aware of them until after supper when Gerald Williams, who had the driver duty that night, stopped by with my paper. They always pick up my newspaper after the bus gets in and fetch it up the hill. Williams is a youth of twenty-two, a yeoman-striker, and he is the fourth generation of his race in the Coast Guard. The Station is less than a half mile from here, between here and the Point.

Especially in a matter of this sort, nobody ever blurts anything. The youth did not say that they were in the midst of an alert. He just omitted to sit down, which was a deviation from what is customary. He said that Dudley would be wondering what was keeping him. This, I knew, was the crux of something. It is not required that the Group Commander—the Group is all the stations on the two Islands—stay aboard at night. He goes home but can be reached in a moment by telephone if he is needed.

And now here it all was. Dudley—Chief Luther Dudley Burrus— was at the Station. Something was afoot. Williams did not multiply words. He said simply that Mr. Styron had not come back from planting oysters and they were looking for him, or his boats. He added that Mr. Styron had heart trouble. He went away, then, and I was glad I had omitted to ask any single question. Questions are not asked on these Islands. One question will close any door and two will lock it. That much I have learned, anyhow.

Put aside also was the impulse to go over to the Station and see what was going on. Partly, perhaps, because of my long years of newspapering, and partly—well, this was Dudley Burrus' first emergency and I was concerned about how it might work out for him. He had been made Group Commander, upped in the long slow climb toward recognition, somewhat out of turn. There were those in the Group who were senior to him, in experience and in rating.

Burrus is the youngest man ever to have the command, and it had not come easy. There had, inevitably, been mutterings. He was commanding his own people. Three-fourths of the hundred or so men in the Group are Island-born, and there are immemorial rivalries. Burrus had had more experience off the Island than most. He was not quite twenty-one when he put a landing craft ashore on Guadalcanal in 1942. The landing craft contained the first wave of Marines.

Afterward Burrus had been pinned down behind a coconut log for eighty-four hours by Japanese mortar fire, with no relief except to poke a carbine over the log from time to time and take a crack at anything that looked like a Japanese. He was without water for the last two days. Later on in that campaign he took the Marines off and put ashore the first elements of the relief divisions of the Army. Then they put him in a hospital for a long period of recuperation. When the war was over he made it back to duty on his own Island. But I stayed away from the Station.

Dawn the next morning brought the sound of aircraft and, throughout the day, I caught occasional glimpses of them as they made their pattern, but they were more audible than visible. They were flying low, and the search was over the waters of the Sound. Now and then, against the blue water of the Bight, I could see one or another of their vehicles as they searched the beach. From the sounds that came with the shifting wind I knew that there was one B-17, three Sikorsky helicopters and, most of the time, two Martin Mariners. The reverberation of their engines dwindled at dark, and I heard the exhaust of the rescue boat's engine as she returned, after dark, to her mooring.

It was late when they brought the paper. I had almost concluded that they would not come at all, when the door opened, as it always does, without any knock. Jasper Williams, a man of the very fewest words, was there. He was sorry they were late. He had been out on the boat. Had not found a thing, no sign anywhere. And he had to get going because he had told Dudley that he didn't mind taking the night run along the beach. No, he was not very tired. He liked being out in the boat.

Well, here it all was, and again I managed not to ask any questions. The search was continuing, it had so far been fruitless, and the crew had fallen in behind Dudley Burrus and they were all doing a job. Thursday was a repetition of Wednesday, in so far as sounds in the air went. But the wind shifted west, then northwest, and by midafternoon I knew that the machinery at the Weather Bureau was recording gusts up to fifty knots. This house, atop this hill and in the path of all winds, trembled a little, and I knew that anybody out in the Sound in a boat, or any crew in the air above it, would be taking a beating. But the engines droned on toward dusk.

That evening it was Gerald Williams with the paper, which was indication enough that the emergency was still on. He has duty only two nights a week, and this was not his night. He couldn't sit down, no. Collins Gray had found a skiff and they were bringing a man up from Ocracoke to identify it and he had to get along. He would meet the Hatteras Inlet surfboat at the Inlet and bring the man along in the power wagon. The skiff had been found in the marsh twenty-seven miles north of here, which is about sixty miles from where it had been last seen.

Friday afternoon, with the week's work behind me, there was time to idle over to the Lighthouse and meet an official of the State government whose duty is in part concerned with these Islands. It had nothing to do with the tense search and, in so far as I knew, he had heard nothing of it until one of the patrol vehicles, with a youth I had not seen since the beginning of the search, slowed down abreast of where we stood and he took the time to say, casually, "It was the boat." My official visitor appeared not to have heard him and I think he took no notice of the incident at all. But it had in it all that I needed to know. They were keeping me wholly informed.

Andrew Styron's towed skiff, not the 18-foot boat with an engine in it, had been found, intact, sixty miles northeast of where he had disappeared. There had been a stiff southwester developing through the afternoon of Tuesday, and the skiff had been driven out into the Sound and north and east. The vengeful westerly wind of Thursday afternoon had driven it into the marsh on the Sound side of the Island. Where the other boat had gone, and what had become of the man it had contained—these were the unanswered questions.

Since the time of my coming to this hill it has become the custom, at eleven o'clock Sunday morning, for one or another of the Station's vehicles to appear at the foot of the hill. A member of the crew will come up and say, "Time to go get dinner." I have let nothing break this pleasant routine. Arrived at the Station, when the dinner gong sounds, the crew troops into the mess hall. The senior duty petty officer, by inflexible custom, invites me to sit at the head of the table.

This I have never done. It is the unwritten law of the service—I have observed it elsewhere also—to invite a guest to sit at the head of the table. I have also seen a three-star admiral decline to sit there. But it is the guest's right to be asked. I have wondered what would happen if, sometime, I did sit down at the head of the table. The consequence, very possibly, would be that on the following Sunday the vehicle would not appear at the foot of the hill.

In accordance with custom, at 11 a.m. on Sunday the vehicle appeared, in the custody of the second class engineman who had slowed down his truck on Friday to mention that the boat had been identified. No mention, now, of the search, or of anything except that it was time to go and get dinner. Burrus being on duty, and he being the senior member of the crew present, it was his turn to indicate the head of the table, which he did. I took my proper place at his right hand and dinner began.

There was no mention, directly or indirectly, of the search and I did not know until the Boatswain's Mate standing by at the teletype, the telephone, and the radio, laid a yellow slip of paper beside the Group Commander's place that it was continuing. He glanced at it, nodded to the man who had brought it, and continued with his dinner. Burrus laid the yellow paper beside my plate and I glanced at it. The search would continue. When they got up from the table he said very casually to the Chief Engineman to take the afternoon patrol. Pick anybody he wanted to make it with him. The message was from the pilot of a helicopter who had landed forty miles north, at Oregon Inlet, to refuel.

Down the long table the crew talked about whatever was at the top of their thoughts, but there was no syllable about what lay underneath. They all looked fearfully weary, as men do when they have slept only patchily for five days and five nights. They ate with abstracted hungriness, not with appetite. Those who had duty with the Loran Station, most of them specialists and not native to the Island, were curiously wholly silent. They were in the presence of something grim, something they were not a part of, something they did not understand. There must have been a lot of questions in their minds, but they did not ask them.

It was not that anybody was secretive, or withholding. It was, I think, that here was something that was bred into the crew, the native part of it. Here was duty and here was something to be done and not talked. The sea had taken a man, an Island man, and they did not know, not yet, what she had done with him.

After dinner I did not stay. The driver who brought me home did not cut off his engine but waited until I had got down, and then he went straight back to the Station. . . . It was his grandfather who was skipper of the Lightship that August afternoon in 1918 when a German submarine shot the boat out from under him.

It was toward five o'clock when Dudley Burrus came up the hill. He looked immensely tired as he climbed up through the pelting mist from his own car parked just off the road. He said that the search was ended, except for routine patrol of the beach, and would not be resumed. Andrew Styron's family had said, a little while ago, that they were content and the helicopter in which his son had flown as passenger-observer had put him down at home and returned to its base. He had called in all the search boats, and radioed the aircraft to break off. The search was at an end.

And he thought he would go home and take a nap. Come to think of it he had not been to bed since Tuesday morning, nor left the Station. . . . No, he didn't feel very tired, but he expected he would when he got to resting. "It's been five days since I've seen my boy and I expect he is so grown up now I'll not know him," he said with a not very successful laugh. Junior is now seven. And then the tension departed and he relaxed in his chair. He talked for a long time, till the mists had shut away the sun for the evening.

Everybody had done a fine job. Nobody had hung back, or loafed, or questioned. Come to think of it, it was the biggest search he could remember, with more elements involved. "The Marines even sent us two helicopters yesterday," he suddenly said, seeming just then to remember it. He said that he didn't know they were coming, that they just came in on the radio and said they were in the searched area and could they lend a hand. "I picked them a channel and they got into it and didn't go home until they reported every foot of it covered. Right nice of them."

And he went on. "We have covered every square yard of land on these two Islands, and every bit of the water in the Sound and for twenty miles offshore. I figure there is about two thousand square miles of it. We've had every kind of aircraft I know of. There was even a Navy jet reporting for a while Saturday. He just picked up stuff and joined in while he was flying in this area. They've walked the beach, and the Boy Scouts down at Ocracoke even got their horses and covered that Island, plumb out into the marshes.

"Only time I got worried was the other afternoon when the wind shifted around to the west and I had five boats out there in the Sound. Four of them I got word to and they made it to safe anchorage, but there was still Edison Midgett and his 83-footer. I asked him for his position and gave him the weather and put him on his own. I have known boatmen who would have put in at the nearest anchorage, but in about three minutes Ed radioed in that he was taking her back to Ocracoke.

"That boy is a born seaman. He took that boat right down the middle of the Sound with the wind blowing fifty miles on his quarter and didn't loosen a peg in her. He took on some water, but half an hour after he got to his dock he called in to say that he had topped his tanks and got the water out of his chain locker and was standing by for orders. That boy is not but twenty-six years old but he could take a boat anywhere. Everybody did a good job. I think these boys flying the helicopters did—well, they were calling in Saturday morning after the wind calmed down that the water was so clear they could make out crabs on the bottom. . . . But for my book I believe the hardest job anybody had, and they all volunteered for it, was the fellows that walked on their feet from Oregon Inlet to Ocracoke Inlet and looked behind every bush they come to."

And then I asked the only question that had not been answered. He looked a little startled and said, yes, the Admiral called a while ago and said from all the reports they brought to him it looked like we had done a good job down here. . . . And then he yawned mightily and said that he believed he was getting sleepy. . . . Which was not surprising; it had been 132 hours since he had been to sleep. . . .

It was an old story he had been living and had, at last, been telling me—but new to his experience. He inherited the makings and the tradition. Now he knows, and his men know, that he and they have, in these five days and five nights, been proving their heritage. When he was gone I remembered that not once had he mentioned the probably lost Andrew Styron. It was the search, the duty, the inherited obligation, that had mattered. And the Admiral had called, on a Sunday afternoon, to say that they had done a good job. . . .

10

Grubbing archeologists, both the amateur and the professional who makes a living by teaching his science, have climbed this hill lugging their wonder after them. They wonder why Indians built themselves a village about two miles north of the Lighthouse, which was not there at the time, of course. Why would they build right there on the open beach, where the Island is not more than three hundred yards across from ocean to Sound, and sometimes Sound and sea actually merge?

It seems never quite worth while to tell them. It would upset their beliefs, and it would work havoc with their plan to get back across Oregon Inlet before nightfall. Normally they look upon the necessity for abiding the night on this Island with misgivings matched only by the misgivings of the Islanders to have them stay. Not that there is anything sinister about either the grubbers or the grubbed-among. It just seems to happen that they always plan a day's outing from a base north of the Inlet, and the Islander is wary of a man in a hurry.

It would take more time than they have at their disposal for an Islander to begin to get ready to tell them that the Indians didn't build a village on a narrow beach, protected from neither Sound nor ocean. It may be that the Islanders would be hesitant for the reason that the time-driven grubber in the earth might not be tolerant of the truth as it is remembered on this Island and indicated on the earlier charts. There was a kind of a mountain that extended northward from this ridge, facing the ocean, and it was in the lee of this lost eminence that the Indians built their village.

Within the lifetime of many of my neighbors and still vivid in their recollection, there was a ridge and it was fifty feet high. It was an utterly naked ridge, as they recall it, like the dunes that wander, disconsolate and treeless, along the beaches beyond the Inlet. . . . Not even an accredited geologist can quite believe that a dune containing two million cubic yards of sand can move a hundred yards in the course of a single night—in a dry wind.

Not longer ago than 1900 this ridge lay there, where nothing now is but a flat beach three hundred yards across and sparsely grown with beach grass. It was, as many remember, fifty feet high and it extended "pretty well up the beach," Martin Tolson assures me with what, for him, is sufficient definiteness. In his mind the statement is wholly precise. That is to say, it was not a round hill, or dune. It was a sort of broken ridge and, in times past, it extended northward toward Kinnakeet. There is now no sign of it.

Nor was the Island so narrow at that point when the Indians had their town there. It must have been all of a mile wide and, like their neighbors five miles or so to the west, they had their town on the Sound shore. There are remnants of it remaining and fragments of their utensils are sometimes brought to me. Presumably also other fragments have been carried away in the knapsacks of the grubbers who desist always from their excavation in time to get across the Inlet by nightfall.

But the Island was, back in that early time, about a mile wide at this point, which is now next to the narrowest place on the 70-mile length of the Outer Banks. There is here, under my hand, the earliest Coast & Geodetic Survey Chart of this area (1856), and it shows plainly the tide line a thousand yards east of where it is now. It indicates also a considerable elevation of land along there. The current detailed chart indicates a maximum elevation of only eight feet in a few scattered hummocks presently mapped in that area.

And now I look at this flat blankness and wish that it might somehow have been spared the leveling and the attrition that have happened to it. This hill is the site of the first completely documented happening on these Islands. Somehow there has been preserved, through the two centuries that have passed, this narration of blood-spilling on the eastward rise of the hill that isn't there any more. And historians who are unable to extend credence to anything unless it is documented, and unless the ground conforms also to the narrative, are disposed not to believe any word of it. The hill is not there.

But it was there, in 1746, and in its existence and in its non-existence there is wrapped up a whole era of life on these Islands. If the five British seamen who came ashore to plunder the Island of its cattle had survived and if they had made off with the cattle, the hill might still be there. But this is spilled historical milk and the seamen died, the cattle remained, and now both cattle and hill are gone. They are all linked together in the chain of events, and the two Islands, in one or another degree, have suffered. Not altogether figuratively, the cattle ate down the hills.

For some while I had been wondering about this northerly ridge, since it turned up on the first surveyed chart of 1856, but I had at least learned that the way not to find out anything on these Islands is to ask a direct question. And then, on an afternoon when the wind was riding the Labrador Current hard—that is to say, a cold northeaster was blowing and threateningly, one of my neighbors, a contemporary in years, stopped by, possibly in notion that it was about that time of the day. That time of the day is the hour when, in this house, it is proper, in the vernacular, to have a transfusion. That is, to drink moderately of bourbon.

Driftwood crackled in the fireplace and my neighbor settled in his chair, his weathered fingers caressing his glass. He glanced again out the window to the eastward and said, "She's goin' to get rough." The whole earth and the sky were gray with portent of bad weather and the ocean rumbled beyond the Lighthouse. Now and then my chimney seemed to hold its breath but, after a moment, the smoke surged upward again. My neighbor savored his bourbon and said that a little grog did taste good on a day like this.

Halfway down his drink his memory kindled. He looked for a while at the fire and then he said that this day reminded him of a day, maybe fifty years ago, that was just like this. Along about the middle of the evening—the afternoon, that is—the wind started to blow, just like it had this day. He was a young fellow then and he was coming down toward the Cape. "I was goin' gallin', I guess," he put in. In the vernacular of my own youth you went courtin', but along these Islands the term is "gallin'," though I've never been too sure how it should be spelled.

Anyhow, my neighbor was young and he was headed to this vicinity to see a girl. He rode his horse and the wind blew. It began to spit sleet at him and he knew it was going to be a rough night. He remembered that he saw an old sow—there were wild hogs in those days—and she was going about in a sort of panic. She had a mess of pigs and she was trying to make them get up on top of that hill. He looked up that way and she had made a kind of bed of seaweed on the lee side of the top of it, and he wondered what she was going to all that trouble for.

A hill? Oh, yes, there was a good-sized hill there then. But there was not much of it left when he went along that way the next morning. He abode the night with his girl's family, bedding down with about three of her brothers. It had not rained but it did blow.

It was a dry blow and most of that unanchored hill had moved over to the Sound.

"Beach was mighty near flat when I got along there the next day," he remembered. And he added, "I just never did hear what become of that old sow and her pigs. But that hill never did get back like it was. It just kept moving over, inching along until it was all over there in the Sound." He looked again toward the rumbling beyond the Lighthouse and said that this was going to be another sand-mover if it didn't turn into rain and wet the sand down. He said that he guessed he had better get moving. He descended the hill and by some kind of necromancy infused his prehistoric automobile with life and motion.

Above the noise of it and of the wind he called back, with a kind of ageless amusement, to say that he reckoned the wind must have "blowed that old sow away, and just as well on account of she would have drowned if she hadn't got on top of the hill. It was just her time," he added, and his vehicle lurched Lighthouse-ward.

And so—the hill. It was there when he was a boy and that was not too long ago. Time and man and his cattle, his horses, his sheep, and finally his old sow and her pigs had stripped the hill naked and it was inevitable that it would go, in a night, as this one had gone. It must have been, in its day, a right noble hill. I have inquired of one of the youthful engineers who are currently busy hereabouts to estimate for me the cubic content of a hill about so high, about so wide, and about so long, stretching a "good ways up the beach yonder," and after some knitting of his eyebrows and borrowing a pencil, he handed me a piece of paper with figures on it. He said he expected there were about two million cubic yards of it.

Once it had sheltered a community of Indians. Not a very large one, probably, but a town. But now the hill, passing cleanly over the residue of the town, has disappeared into the Sound, has become a vast complex of shoals and reefs, shallowing the water until boats no longer come there. Some while back, when a major oil company was intent upon drilling a hole in the earth to see if it contained oil, their dredges came and scooped out a channel along which massive machines were brought to land. But by now, after a decade, their fifty-thousand-dollar channel is smoothed over and the dock they built is rotting away. The ghost-hill wanders around still, not much troubled by the wind perhaps, but knowing no peace. The water still moves.

And there is blood mixed with it, with this sand that was swept in a single night from its immemorial place. Two centuries ago it must have looked very like the plain below this hill looks. Here the wooded dune and below, stretching to the ocean, a more-or-less level plain, grassed over with tough beach grass, and set here and there with a stout cedar, or a clump of hoary liveoaks. It was more than a thousand yards, possibly much more, in distance from the hill to the sea, and in the plain cattle grazed. And horses and sheep and perhaps the ancestor of the mentioned sow also rooted in the sand for the roots of the Indian potato, whose blossoms enliven the landscape here, in season.

Offshore a ship went its way and then its sails drooped and the vessel lay to, close inshore. From her stern a small boat dropped down to the water. Men were in it, five of them, and they turned shoreward. These maneuvers had been observed from the top of the hill, and there must have been a messenger dispatched in considerable haste to the villages to the north and west. The landing party was in no great hurry to get ashore and there was time to assemble and organize resistance.

When they came in and beached their boat out of reach of the tide it was perfectly clear what they had in mind. They wanted some fresh meat, and the simplest way to get it was to come ashore and shoot a few head of beef, butcher them, and carry them aboard. They deployed inland toward the hill. The cattle grazing very likely took fright and moved away from the beach toward the hill. The landing party pursued them, thinking very likely that the cattle would stay their flight when they got to the cover of the woods that covered the hill. It was an English ship and its master complained with great bitterness to his government. Not one of the five members of the landing party returned to the ship, from which it was possible to see what happened. They were killed, the last man of them, when they set about skinning two steers that they had shot. They were themselves shot from ambush by people lurking in the woods above them, on the hill, and after waiting until the next day in hope that some of them might have escaped and would return to the ship, the master hoisted sail and departed.

This protest was relayed to the not very stable government of the province of North Carolina, delayed very likely by the fact that the governor then had no permanent seat and the capital was wherever the royal governor happened to be at the moment, which was likely to be anywhere, in his search for a suitable place for establishing his government. Indeed, it must have been near twenty years before the document found a resting place, after Lord William Tryon set up a permanent seat at New Berne.

If there was any official action contemplated it must have been confused by the inability of the Governor's staff to determine where the outrage happened. There was nothing to show whether it was in one county, or another county, or indeed, in any county at all. As a matter of fact the geographers on the governor's staff had neglected to include the Islands in any county, and it would be another fifty years, and in a new republic, before the question of including them in any county was acted upon.

The incident is remembered on the Islands, but only as one of many that occurred in the course of the century or so after the Outer Banks became cattle-raisers. Nowhere, perhaps, was there a locality less suited to the production of cattle, but they were here and, like the inhabitants, castaways for the most part and they did the best they could with what they had. The Islands had also the misfortune, as cattle country, to be very near to the lanes of an expanding fleet of commerce.

It was a very simple matter, as many shipmasters thought, to put in and rustle a few cattle, but the affair on the hill above the Lighthouse must have been something of a discouragement, though looking back along the centuries, one could wish that the Islanders had not been so quick on the trigger. It would, in a very definite sense, have been better for them if the last cow had been carried aboard ship the afternoon of the bloody reprisal. The cattle remained to almost destroy the Island. They ate away the grass, and the wind came and on a final night of vengeance swept away altogether the hill from which the defensive resistance to the rustlers was mounted.

There is now neither cattle, nor hill, and some night, if she really put her mind on her work, the sea could very handily cut through the Island altogether where once a forgotten race found shelter, and from which the Islanders resisted hostile invasion. It was not a great distance from where the hill was that another hostile landing party, seven in number this time and riding in a rubber boat, came ashore in the night. They were not after cattle. There were no cattle in 1942, and there was no hill from which to resist them. But the story is not essentially different from the earlier story: none of the seven lived to leave the Island. But of that, something more in its proper place.

11

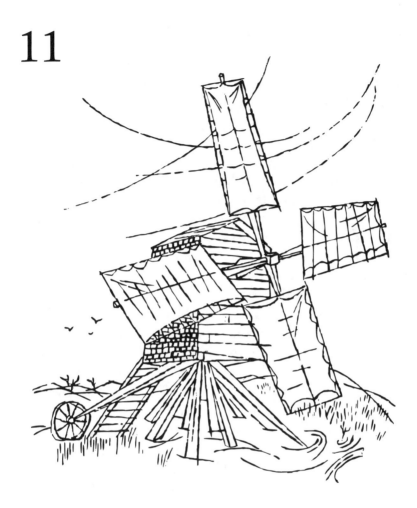

Alexander Hamilton passed Cape Hatteras on a summer's night in 1773, and thereafter, remembering the night's terror, he spoke of that portion of the sea as the Graveyard of the Atlantic. He was seventeen years old. When he was thirty-three years old and second ranking member in the cabinet of George Washington he set his First Assistant Secretary of the Treasury at the task of buying four acres of land upon which to build a lighthouse overlooking the Graveyard.

Not until some while afterward, when his agents were negotiating for lands that nobody wanted to sell, did the Islanders begin to be aware of a man named Hamilton and to associate him with what had started as a smudge of smoke on the horizon and, when dark was come, became a stubby pillar of fire. After a while the flame died out, but those who watched from this ridge could not tell whether the sea had swallowed it. Morning brought no telltale wreckage. It had been a rough night.

Hamilton's ship was named the *Thunderbolt* and he had sailed from St. Kitts, in the West Indies, as supercargo. New York was the port of destination, but because of what happened off the Cape the ship limped into Boston ten days later, not much more than able to keep steerageway after she left the propelling current of the Gulf Stream. Most of her mainsails were charred rags and there were other evidences of the sea's wrath. The *Thunderbolt* had taken a beating, and so had its crew.

Whether the ship's master, whose name is not preserved in the Island's remembering, took too long a chance and in his eagerness to get to New York cut in too close to the Outer Diamonds is a matter that the record leaves to conjecture, but it is the belief of generations of Islanders that it must have happened so. There was a moderate southwest wind, as there often is at that season of the year, and when the ship cut a corner, intent upon leaving the Gulf Stream and riding a favorable wind directly to its port, it cut across the point where the Labrador Current makes a confusion.

Whether or no, when the ship got to that place, which good navigators avoid, it rolled drunkenly, and the ship's furnishings began to slither around. Among the things that got toppled over was the brazier in the cook's galley. The ship caught fire and flames climbed the rigging, and for a while it looked as if the ship would be burned unless she sank first. In either case the prospect of escape and survival seemed meager, especially when the flames worked down into the cargo holds where raw sugar was stored. Sugar, as every Islander knows, can make a lot of smoke when it gets to burning.

It is not unreasonable to assume that those aboard must have looked landward, calculating their chances of making it to dry land if they had to abandon ship, or if the ship went down. There was, of course, no lighthouse there but there did show on the horizon evidences of habitation. There were at least three massive windmills in sight, their wings turning smartly in the brisk southwest wind. And there were, of course, these hills—plus the one that lay to the north, toward a village with the largest of the windmills.

The sight was certainly not unfamiliar. There were windmills on every island in the West Indies, useful in turning the machinery that crushed out the juice of sugar cane, and for turning the stones of mills that ground corn brought from somewhere on this mainland. Where there were windmills there must be settlements—but miles of frothing water lay between them and the smoldering, rolling ship.

Young though he was, Hamilton must have known about these windmills here long before he embarked from St. Kitts for whatever destiny had in store for him on the continent. Since he was twelve years old he had virtually run the vast warehouses of Nicholas Cruger, first merchant prince of the West Indies, and often enough he must have checked the incoming and outgoing cargoes of ships that plied between Portsmouth on Ocracoke Inlet and the Cruger docks.

There were shiploads of corn from the Carolina plantations, and shingles from its juniper swamps, timber from its uplands. Outward bound there were, on occasion, millstones, destined for the towns in North Carolina. (There is no actual record of this that I have been able to find, but learned geologists, after months of study of specimens, have come up with the definite answer that millstones still to be found on these Islands are basalt, and that they undoubtedly came from the deposits of such rock in the volcanic regions of the West Indies.)

Kinnakeet—the Avon of the Postal Guide but still Kinnakeet in Island vernacular—seven miles north of the Cape, was very likely the site of the first windmill for grinding corn on these Islands. It was, and continues to be, spoken of as Big Kinnakeet and it was, from other records, the center of community commercial life, apart and distinct from the foreign commerce centered at the now dead port of Portsmouth. It had a harbor sufficient to its needs, and there was a considerable activity there. The first of the "King" Pharaoh Farrows settled there about the time of Hamilton's passage.

There were windmills. The first record of them, in so far as it has been possible to document it, was set down in 1715 when the Provincial Assembly, meeting that day at the Williams plantation on the west bank of Pasquotank River, a distance of about ninety miles north and west from Cape Hatteras, made provision for the establishment of windmills, or water mills where the flow of a creek made it feasible. Any man undertaking to set up such a mill was to be given public lands to put it on.

The first of these windmills was erected at Avon in 1723. There were toward the middle of the nineteenth century at least fifty-three of them in the tidewater areas of the State, and eleven of them stood on these two Islands. The application of the steam engine to domestic uses and, later, the invention of the internal combustion engine, put an end to the windmill—and to the sail.

How deeply embedded in the living of the Islanders did the windmill become can very simply be stated by my own experience in finally laying hand on the root of the story. George Oliver O'Neal is a Kinnakeeter, now well past seventy. For a long time he sailed the Five Sounds and the seven seas in ships and then he came home and started a small store in his village. Customers were and are no great bother to him and his real avocation. He set out as soon as he got set up in his store to whittle out a model of every ship he had ever seen service on.

There are now, scattered around his little store and shoving his merchandise into any odd corner, more than thirty ship's models, each of them in perfect scale and each in detail, even to a ship's cat asleep in the lee of the wheelhouse. It is always a Hatteras Cat, which is a peculiar intermingling of every breed of cat that ever sailed the sea. They say that no ship's cat was ever drowned: they get ashore and, like any good castaway, go native.

Since I first saw them I have wished that I owned one of the O'Neal models but I have, by acquired wisdom, omitted to suggest that he sell me one of them. They are not for sale. He likes for people to come and look at them, and he lent Joseph Baylor Roberts every sort of helpfulness when he came to photograph them for the *National Geographic*, through the whole of five hours that it took to set up the picture and make it. He was patience embodied. But when the picture was done he himself, declining anybody's help, put each item back in its own place, back to where it belonged.

One day when I had stopped by the store to look again at the collection and to listen, gratefully, to one or another happening that occurred when he was mate on this or that ship, modeled here, I mentioned that I had heard of a photograph of a windmill and I wondered if, when I got the picture, he would undertake to make me a model of it. He agreed readily to do the best he could with it, and I saw that there was a kindling glow in his eyes.... But I was not prepared, when I went back, jubilantly bearing the picture which had come that day in the mail, to find, sitting there on the counter in the store, a perfect scale model that, when photographed, could scarcely be told from the original photograph done more than a half century before. Captain O'Neal, when he was a boy, took corn to that mill, now long since gone.

The Islands, and the Islanders, remember.

They remember, of their own recollection, how the Island looked and what happened on it in 1880 and, out of their inherited recollection, how it must have looked to Alexander Hamilton when he glanced shoreward in the waning light of a summer evening in 1773. It is not remembering altogether: it is a continuing of awareness on an Island "where yesterday is tomorrow and tomorrow is yesterday and today is compounded of them both," which is a sentence I contrived long before I knew wholly the meaning of it.

This model of the Bateman Miller windmill at Kinnakeet, long since carried away by an importunate curator to be preserved in the Smithsonian Museum, unlocked a lot of doors to a lot of remembering. There is, and has always been, a lot of rivalry among the Seven Villages of Hatteras Island and they combine and make common cause only when they are pitted in some matter against the single village on the next Island—and in turn they all combine, both Islands as one, when there is some conflict, usually against the upper end of the county, or, that part of it lying to the north of Oregon Inlet.

When the O'Neal model was established on this ridge and the story of it put together, I began to have visitors. They wanted to see the model of the windmill and they examined it very critically indeed, and then they would add that they could show me a place where there was a better windmill than that. Show me the exact spot where it stood. I went to all the proffered sites, ending up two hundred yards offshore in the Sound, down at Trent—Frisco, if you want to mail a letter to anybody there—where there are two perfect specimens of basalt millrock that used to be turned by the Rollinson windmill—"and it made the best meal on this Island."

My guide and informer on this expedition was a boy aged fifteen. He remembered, too, although it was about the year when his great-grandfather was fifteen, that the mill went down in a hurricane that blew in from the northwest. That blow also began to eat away the Sound shore, which is why the rocks are now two hundred yards out in the water. On the two Islands I so discovered a total of eleven grist mills that were turned by the wind.

They were all what the meager literature on windmills describes as the German type, which is a sort of mystery that I have found no solution for. The German type differs from the Dutch type fundamentally. In Germany the millhouse, with its huge sailed wheel, sits about twenty feet from millhouse floor to the ground on a huge pillar. There is a massive outrigger beam with a wheel fixed against the ground, and with every shift of the wind the miller gets down and rolls the beamed wheel around until the house heads into the wind. In the Dutch type the works are fixed on a tower and only the roof of it is turned to head the sail into the wind.

There is very likely sound sense in it, as there is in most things that have been tried by long centuries on these Islands. With the Dutch type there is some lack of fixed contact between roof and house, and that just wouldn't do in the winds that prevail around Cape Hatteras. The whole thing has to be a single unit, firmly fixed together. Else, come an able-bodied wind, the roof would take off and likely not stop this side the Sound. But about that I have been able to elicit no fixed opinion—they were just always built that way.

Mr. Hamilton—it is so that they speak of him on these Islands—would have understood something else about life along this sandy narrow strip of earth. He had seen much corn and other grain imported from Carolina plantations to the West Indies because the islands there were not suited to the growing of such crops. Neither Hatteras nor Ocracoke could feed itself with bread of its own growing. But they did and do have the advantage of being almost within sight of the lushest corn-producing area of the United States, in the rich, black lands of the mainland across the Sound.

With a favorable wind a bugeye could make it across the Sound and back in a day, if there were urgent need. On the inbound trip the smart, sturdy little sailboat would carry four or five tons of dried fish and find a ready market. There were increasing numbers of slaves over there, and dried fish was a good ration for them. And it was cheap, besides. They got for their fish pound-for-pound in corn, and other merchandise for Island-made brooms. There was a great demand, even as late as 1875, for Island-made brooms, fashioned from the scrub palm that flourished and continues to flourish. It also made good palm-leaf fans, a work that women were good at and in exchange for which coveted cloth could be had.

In time there came, for a century or so, to be produced on the Islands enough sheep's wool to suffice the needs of cloth-making, and weaving was generally done at home. Sometimes the boats would bring home raw cotton from the mainland, and this would be carded and spun and woven by Island women. But mostly the commerce was in corn, sometimes when it was plentiful and cheap, salt pork. In time each village had at least one windmill and, where there was need because of the inevitable factionalism that exists perhaps everywhere, two mills were required in at least three of the villages. People of one family, or faction, would sooner go hungry than eat bread made of meal or flour ground in a mill owned by one with whom one did not speak.

Mr. Hamilton's ship rode the Great River yonder and when he looked wonderingly toward the land it may be that he was reassured by the sight of the three windmills turning briskly in the wind. He did not come ashore and he did not again entrust himself to the sea. The record indicates that he traveled overland from Boston to New York. Five years and he was an officer on the staff of General George Washington and at the beginning of an acquaintance with Henry Dearborn, also a lieutenant colonel, who made a career of having known people.

It might well be that when Mr. Hamilton looked landward from the smouldering deck of the *Thunderbolt* he missed something that should have been there. It is reasonable to suppose that he had heard of Cape Hatteras and the dangers that were to be met there by any who committed himself to journeying by sea. The area must have loomed large in the affairs of the man for whom he had worked since he was twelve years old, in the West Indies, a man whose major concern was with shipping. A good half the company's business was with North American ports, and no man of the sea ever passed Cape Hatteras unaware of it.

There was no lighthouse there in 1773, only these hills and the windmills that have been gone a long time. It is possible that there were other ships, also caught like his, in the unpredictable turmoil of impinging rivers. Since the beginning of navigation that point has been perhaps the most sighted and logged geographical point on the charts. It sets conjecture back on its heels even to begin to wonder how many ships have passed the Cape and mentioned the fact in their logbooks since the beginning in 1497. Hamilton must have thought about it.

Last year it occurred to me that people had been wondering about how many ships pass within sight of the Cape in any given time for long enough and that it would be a very simple matter to count them. When the matter was suggested to Admiral Russell Wood, commander of the U.S. Coast Guard in these parts, he readily agreed to have a record of them kept aboard the Lightship that sits in the inner edge of the Gulf Stream. It surprised him a little that it had never been done, when he came to think about it.

In that year, 1955, the ships that passed within sight of the Lightship numbered 7,786.

Very likely this is not all of them, but it will suffice. It is forty miles across the Great River here, and a ship is visible, from the lookout of the Lightship, for a distance of twenty miles in good weather. By custom and good navigation, ships bound for Europe from the ports along the Gulf of Mexico, having no business with American ports, keep to the far side of the Great River. That brings them nearer to their ports of destination at least by the width of the stream, and they are generally not observed.

But there is a good round figure in the number of 7,786 ships sighted from the Lightship in the course of one year. Nothing like that was happening, to be sure, in Mr. Hamilton's day, but it is reasonable to assume that there were, even then, a considerable number plying that route. It is very probable that the number was even larger in the final days of the sailing ship, beginning with the time of the Gold Rush in California in 1849 and continuing down into the era which ended on August 16, 1933, when the G. A. *Kohler* wrecked twenty miles above the Cape. She was the last four-master.

Tucked away in eight feet of records and notes that completely fill the shelf above my fireplace there is the record of 2,268 ships that have been lost within sight of this hill in four hundred years. Perhaps two hundred of them were victims of man's savagery, lost in time of war, but the others were taken by the sea. It is a story that was beginning to be old even when Mr. Hamilton sailed in this sea on the only voyage that he ever permitted himself. It is possible, too, that it had already been named and that it remained only for him to give the name currency.

At any rate it is not surprising that he included Cape Hatteras in the first recommendations that he made, as a member of the Cabinet, to the First Congress and that, on August 4, 1790, Congress heeded him. The day has come down, as a public holiday on these Islands, as the Birthday of the U.S. Coast Guard. Included in the request was provision for a lighthouse on Cape Hatteras.

Nine years would elapse before the beacon's light reached across the turbulence of the Outer Diamonds. It was no fault of Hamilton's that so long a time was required. Plans were drawn, by Hamilton's friend and fellow staff-member, Major General Henry Dearborn, and submitted with a bid for construction. Hamilton approved the plan, took it to the President for his signature, and with that done, turned the project over to Tenche Coxe, the first Commissioner of Revenue.

There were, of course, difficulties. The first of them was the reluctance of the owners of the land upon which it was proposed to erect the lighthouse to part with it. The federal government, in that day, had little authority. It could not own a piece of land without the legislated permission of the state in which the land lay. With that permission, the federal government could proceed to negotiate with the landowner, in this case the four minor children of John Gaskins. Altogether eight years were so consumed.

And so it was that John Adams, as President, had the duty of signing as approved the final documents involved, including some adjustments in the price at which General Dearborn figured that he could do the work. He had planned inadequately, proposing to gather a few barge-loads of stone from his native New Hampshire, float them down the Connecticut River, and so to Cape Hatteras. The final agreed cost was to be $35,558, and to be included also and in addition was a wooden beacon tower on Beacon Island at the entrance of Portsmouth Harbor.

Some of the stones carted down here by General Dearborn and fashioned into a 96-foot tower make a kind of fence in front of this house, and on a little rise, back along the ridge and not far from the Money Tree, there is a tumbled mass of them that were, in so far as I can determine, used to secure the burial place of five members of the crew of the U.S.S. *Monitor*. These stones around the front door I lugged here, at odd times, largely out of sentiment, and in these last weeks I have known a youth, a member of the Seabees and a native of the county in New Hampshire from which the stone came.

This youth, big and blond and taciturn, which the Islanders remember was also the way of those who came in Dearborn's hire a century and a half and more since, looks upon these stones about my door with a sort of dumb understanding. Among them is a shining, untarnished piece of flint a good twelve inches thick. Before he was transferred he used sometimes to come up the hill and just pick up that white shining rock and look at it for a long time. He was, I supposed, homesick like an Islander would be if he came somehow, in a far place, upon a little heap of sand from home.

Another day he came, still taciturn, and wanted to know if I would do him a favor. Such as? Well, he reckoned it would sound silly, but would I take his picture over yonder, with him sitting on top of that nub of the old tower that still sticks above the sand? That is all that is left of Mr. Hamilton's lighthouse now, but it is sturdy and it looks as if it will stay there a long time. So the picture was taken, to be sent home to his folks, with him sitting on a pile of home-grown rocks, and with the newer, but by now old, candy-striped brick tower yonder in the background.

And when the picture was done he observed, shyly, "It ain't a very big world, after all, is it?"

12

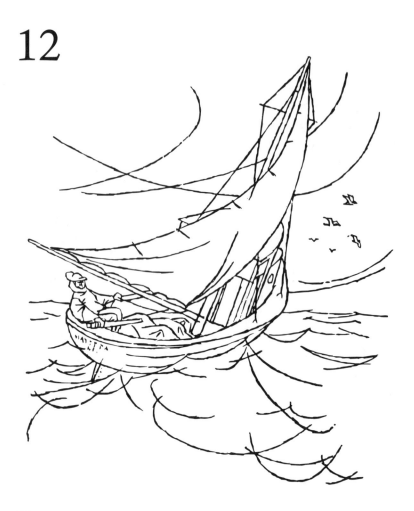

Even now, a hundred years and more since the tea industry vanished from these Islands, anybody who finds himself itching for a fight can get himself accommodated by approaching any native of the village of Kinnakeet and uttering three words. The consequences will be immediate, bloody, and conclusive, and he who got hit, if he is able to remember anything of the moment, will remember hearing the one who hit him say, "Now shut up or I'll cut your tongue right out of your head."

It has never been necessary to cut anybody's tongue out of his head, and there is no account of anybody ever approaching a Kinnakeeter a second time and saying, "Kinnakeeters!—Yoepon

Eaters." These are the three infallibly provocative words. It matters not at all where the Kinnakeeter is when he hears them. It is my belief that if he were sitting astride the North Pole and had not seen a human being since year before last and somebody approached him with these baleful words the answer would be a swinging fist.

Here is an embedded hate of astonishing intensity and the roots of it lie deep in the past. It is now 155 years since the phrase was first uttered in disdain and since the Kinnakeeter, Edward Scarborough, knocked the mocker cold in Elizabeth's pothouse up Pasquotank River in 1801. It made no difference that the man was not sober, or that he meant no harm when words were uttered in derision. Like most of those who inherit his name, Edward Scarborough was a quiet man and a man of vast physical strength.

And withal, a shy man, proud and sensitive. And that evening, when he tied up his bugeye at the rude dock before the pothouse that grew into a small city without changing its name, he was very likely as weary as it is possible for an Islander to get. The winds, as they are likely to be in winter, had been adverse, and it took a lot of seamanship to work the five-ton vessel up the Five Sounds and finally the river itself. Edward Scarborough was tired and cold and, very likely, hungry.

And it is also likely that he was worried about the security of the cargo he had brought to market. Packed in neat bales under the covering tarpaulin was the entire fall curing of yoepon leaves, and if the tea had been wet by the seas that were taken aboard, despite the man's craftsmanship as a sailor, a year's work would be gone—and with it a year's provisioning of such things as could be had only in these upcountry markets.

Edward Scarborough, when he had secured his bugeye, stood in the doorway of the pothouse, blinking against the sudden light. Behind him stood his half-grown boy. Here both were on unfamiliar ground. There was no such place as this on the length of their home Island. It was crowded and ribald, and one among the not very sober men, probably a maker of shingles further up the river in the edge of the Great Dismal, saw him there. And he said with ribald mirth—"Kinnakeeters! Yoepon Eaters," and his words were greeted with loud laughter.

Edward Scarborough did not laugh. He hit the man and the man dropped in his tracks like a pole-axed ox. Edward Scarborough waited for a little, ready. And then he turned back into the darkness, with his son. Nobody followed him, none hindered him. The next day he sold his cargo elsewhere, bought what he could with what he got for it, and set sail for home. He brought with him a rankling hate that continues unabated into this day.

It has now been fifty years and more since yoepon tea was produced commercially on these Islands, and not in my decade on this ridge have I so much as seen yoepon tea or tasted it. It is rather more than likely that the youth who will gladly knock your head off if you utter the three words has never tasted the stuff and has no remotest notion of the processes used in the curing and the brewing of the leaves of the shrub that, for two centuries, provided his forebears with their principal commerce.

As medicine and as beverage, yoepon tea was in use on the Island when the Indians lived here in tranquil isolation, and it was the basis also of such commerce as they had with their neighbors on the mainland. Its use continued through the centuries when castaway and aborigine were fused into a single race, but it was not until the latter half of the eighteenth century that it began to attain a place in the commercial structure, about five years after Alexander Hamilton passed this way.

Not in any direct sense did Hamilton's passage have anything to do with it. The time was a century after tea was brought to the western world from the Orient, and the expanding British Empire had made it a government monopoly, heavily taxed. Tea had become the first fixed international habit, and the people who were settling the continent had to have their tea. Events that led to or precipitated rebellion were deeply entangled with tea. And then there was no tea to be had.

Whether yoepon tea is a satisfactory substitute is a matter of opinion and of taste, but in 1775 and for a long time thereafter there was no choice. Denied their tea from normal sources Americans began to look around for a substitute. They made themselves tea with the roots of sassafras, the leaves of sage and of catnip, and the leaves of yoepon, which is a much nearer approximation of the tea of India or of China. The chemical content of the leaf is not greatly different.

Yoepon, so the books say, is a variant of the ilex or holly, indigenous to the coastal lands of southeastern America, and is seen from Mexico to the Virginia capes, but nowhere does it grow with such luxuriance and abandon as on these two Islands.

It is of relatively slow growth and nowhere does it attain anything of tree-like proportions. It is not unlike the boxwood of the higher latitudes, but crowd it and it will shoot upward. Along the ridge where the Money Tree is there are many specimens as tall as twenty-five feet, and five inches through the trunk just above ground.

There is a very likely specimen just out the window that looks toward the Point. It was set there when I came to this hill, with a companion at the northwest corner. They have thrived abundantly and are now a good ten feet high. But both have been fertilized and, when necessary, watered. Both have rewarded me with prodigal crops of round red berries that remain in place until they are pushed away in May by a new crop—or are eaten by Mr. Pegler or are shaken off by the wind.

From time to time I have considered the notion of experimentation with some leaves of the two yoepon bushes, the plucking of them, the drying of them in a very slow oven, and the making of tea from whatever might result. The process has been suggested, but not recommended, by some of my Island neighbors. This is one thing they continue in reticence about and, remembering what happened to the man who derided Edward Scarborough in 1801, and subsequently, with variations, to any who made bold to mention yoepon tea, I have put off the experiment as not well timed. And anyway, it would be a sin of sorts to mommick up my yoepon bush.

Not that the bush would seriously mind, I think. Very soon it would repair such damage as might be done it. Of that there can be a certainty. For as long as 125 years yoepon tea was, it is certain, the principal output of these Islands, after fish, and in that time a tremendous slaughter of yoepon must have occurred. But even so, the yoepon is now, and I suppose has always been, the most prevalent item of Island flora. Even in Kinnakeet, where the industry centered, this is so.

Historians have never made much ado about it, but in addition to losing most of a continent the British lost also the market for their world-monopoly in tea. Americans quit drinking tea for the duration of the Revolution and never got around, very wholeheartedly, to resuming the practice. They had their yoepon tea, and there are yellowed bits of record, stowed away in a cheese box under this table, that indicate that yoepon tea, as late as 1840, was produced here and sold in Philadelphia.

In that same cheese box, which contains the records of the Hoopers and the Farrows of Kinnakeet for about 150 years of merchandising along the Five Sounds and in Norfolk and Philadelphia, there is record also of shipments of coffee that came to this Island from South America by way of the West Indies as early as 1830. It was landed in Hatteras—not Portsmouth—and was distributed to the trade. That may well have been the beginning of the decline of the yoepon tea trade.

There is here among these papers also a manifest of the cargo of the last ship to make port, one jump ahead of the Federal fleet that came in late August of the first year of the Civil War. Among other things there were ten bags of coffee, which were gleefully taken over by the invaders as something supremely prized. Americans had begun to demand their coffee, and other nations, too.

. . . On April 12, 1942, a German submarine surfaced beside an Island fisherman in the Bight of Hatteras, and its commander, with the utmost civility, inquired of the fishermen if they had any coffee and sugar aboard. It happened that they did have two cans of coffee, about five pounds of sugar, some canned milk.

These things the Germans took, politely paying for them in good American money, after which they returned to their business of sinking merchantmen in nearby waters. . . . The incident was repeated at least five times that spring.

Thereafter coffee got to be rationed everywhere, and on these Islands the inhabitants again had recourse to their yoepon tea, as they did when war interrupted the flow of green coffee from the West Indies in 1861.

It has become a part of American folklore that the present vast tobacco industry, the predominance of the pipe and cigarette over the cigar, derives from a taste acquired by Federal troops when they occupied the tobacco-growing area of North Carolina and Virginia late in the Civil War. The rise of the improbable Duke fortune was from the simple circumstance that the father of the Dukes had a considerable quantity of smoking tobacco on hand when the Yankees invaded his county. All of it was promptly stolen, but so well did they like it that the thieves, when they got home after the fighting and pillaging were over, wrote back to old Washington Duke offering to pay him for any tobacco he could send them. He sent and they paid and the Duke fortune, within sixty years, became five hundred million dollars.

Nothing of such magnitude happened to the yoepon tea of these Islands, though 20,000 Federal troops quartered on the Island at one time or another drank yoepon tea because there was nothing else to drink, and it did assuage dysentery. Afterward there came letters from Indiana, from Massachusetts and New York—these I have seen—inquiring if it were possible to get some of that tea the writer had while he was stationed around here. Whether they were ever answered there is no way of knowing, but the chances are that they were ignored. People on the Islands became as bitter about occupation troops as they already were, most of them, about inquiries for yoepon tea.

Yoepon, as an item of commerce, tied these Islands, even if loosely, to life on the mainland across the Five Sounds and to a community that was being drawn away from the sea. They had moved the capital two hundred miles inland, which was not unnatural. More of the population of the State had come down the wagon trails from Pennsylvania and Virginia than, all together, had entered through its seaports. Indeed, the only direct migration of European people into North Carolina had been the Swiss Palatines, through Ocracoke Inlet to the ill-starred settlement at New Berne, and the Scottish Highlanders, who began a fifty-year migration through the Cape Fear in 1735. Secondhand immigrants moving along western trails provided the bulk of the population, in 1800, and they wanted their capital near them, conceding only the name to Sir Walter Raleigh who, despite a widely-held contrary belief, had never seen North Carolina. The East lost its dominance, first because of the ox and then because of the railroads, and its port towns, except in a very local sense, died.

Relatively, however, it was a much easier and often shorter trip from these Islands to St. Kitts, or even to London, than it was to Raleigh. Easier on a man's feelings and his emotions, at any rate. To him it was natural to travel with the wind for his ox or his stagecoach horse, and I have encountered, at least once, remnants of the sheer terror experienced by an Islander when necessity compelled him, about 1812, to journey westward by stagecoach, to the seat of a government that was utterly stranger to him. It was some matter that had to do with the federal courts.

No man ever faced the unknown of the sea with more apprehension than did this westward faring Islander confront the mystery and the abundant agony of riding in a coach day after day toward a destination that appalled him. By some miracle he regained the Island in time and thereafter harrowed his neighbors and his posterity with a narrative of hardship endured, and by God's mercy only, survived. There was little commerce between these Islands and the inland country. They had, among other lacks, little knowledge of yoepon tea.

13

"She's a woman, I tell you," Martin Tolson will remind me, "and you got to be patient with her. Give her time and let her think she's done it on account of her just wanting to do it, and she'll get around to it. Like this wife I've got now—she's my third but they've all been pretty much alike—I get sort of tired waiting for her to fix my breakfast or something sometimes, but like as not when she gets around to it she's fixed something I didn't even know I wanted but I did."

Martin Tolson is an Islander by birth, three times an Islander by marriage, and he is likely to say that it is a habit that he got into when he was young, this practice of taking a wife, when in need of one, from among the daughters of the Island. It began sixty years ago when he was an apprentice lighthouse-keeper and it continued through more than forty years of active service and into comfortable and still vigorous retirement. He says that he expects the sea to yield him a 70-pound drum—channel bass to foreigners—on his hundredth birthday.

There would be nothing strange about any of it. If anybody could reasonably expect to become a hundred years old it should be Martin Tolson. He lives in relaxed, understanding neighborliness with the sea, and he knows that if you will just be patient with her, humor her a little when she is in a cantankerous mood, go away and pay no attention to her when she is in a tantrum, she will reward you in astonishing ways. "Why," he is likely to ruminate, "when I was needing lumber to finish my house with and no way to get it, she knew what a fix I was in."

And what did this ocean do when she heard that one of her children needed some lumber? She arose in the night, looked around until she found an overloaded schooner wallowing northward with a cargo of fine heart-pine lumber. She was deck-loaded and lay deep in the water. It was a very simple matter to loosen the timbers that held the deck load in place, and for a little time the surface was thick with lumber.

It was a very fortuitous arrangement, not only for the man perplexed with an unfinished house for his second wife, but for the master and crew of the schooner as well. With the deck load gone the vessel was able to ride out the storm, which presently abated anyhow, and proceed without further event to Boston. The wind held on long enough to shepherd the lumber shoreward, and the tide, when it ebbed, left it high and reasonably dry on the beach. There was enough, not only to finish the half-built house but for other Islanders in like situation, and even those whose houses were no further along than the wishing stage.

Lumber schooners no longer ply the sea, and the problem of building, or finishing, a house now involves such complicated expedients as commerce with a lender of money and with those who buy and sell building materials and deliver them right on the site of the projected structure from the deck of vast trucks that take up the whole road and from which ascend obscene odors of combusted petroleum. But even yet the sea is mindful of her own along these Islands, and when she gets her hands on even a few boards somewhere she will fetch them, and some among the Islanders, remembering her motherly solicitousness, will be down on the beach to gather them together and put them to good use.

Indeed there are those who, when they have projected a new house and have had recourse to all the necessary expedients, will not lay hand to hammer or saw until they have found somewhere along the beach a piece of timber suitable for incorporation in the house. There is no pagan superstition no propitiating gesture, no weakly silly invocation of good luck. Rather, I think, it is a natural and altogether wholesome deference to the force in nature that built these Islands, that holds them in the palm of her hand, that brought these people here, and withal has dealt kindly with them.

There are some hundreds of notations here of the sea's largess, and together they afford a random accounting of the sea's sometimes blind-seeming concern for the well-being of her children on these Islands. . . . On August 16, 1899, when the whole country wallowed in the backwash of the Panic of 1893's poverty, the sea brought three hundred barrels of flour and placed it, little the worse for the watering it took, within convenient reach of everybody halfway along the upper Island.

These Islands have never, in so far as there is any mention of it, produced a single grain of wheat, and flour has to be brought in. Or take an item from the John Rollinson (1827–1906) Journal set down fifteen years to the day before the *Priscilla's* barreled flour came ashore to be generally distributed along the length of the two Islands, a barrel for every family. John Rollinson never learned to spell very well but, to the unending joy of such as would inquire into the ancient time, he did learn to write, and faithfully.

The Journal: "The bark Cedorus loaded with coffee stop on the Outward Shoal of Cape Hatteras in the evening. Thursday morning

I went to her in my pilot boat. Got 21 sacks of coffee and brot it to the Beach. Friday I went back and got 20 more. Sea got ruff Friday evening and she went to pieces."

In this wise did the sea provide the Islanders with coffee at a time when there was need of it. Because of John Rollinson's freewheeling way with spelling there was some trifling difficulty in checking the Reports of the U.S. Coast Guard and in finding out what happened to the crew. There were five men aboard the *Codorus*. They were taken off and cared for at the Station. She was out of Sao Paulo, bound for Baltimore, and apparently her master undertook a short cut across the Shoal.

That John Rollinson could read and write at all is due very largely to the sea's chance, and that there was paper for him to write on, wholly to the sea's intervention. When he had need of some paper, in December, 1845, the barque *Ontario* had about the same hard luck as befell the *Codorus* forty years later. John Rollinson was then a youth of eighteen, an able man with an oar and with a sail. He went to the wreck and brought off, among other things not recorded, what he most needed. He brought off some reams of good English rag paper, some of the barque's extra-heavy sailcloth, and some linen thread.

Eight years before, when John Rollinson was a lad of ten, the sea brought these Islands their first schoolteacher of record. Schools there had been before, but their existence was intermittent. There still smoulders, at any rate on Ocracoke Island, a handed-down resentment against the booming port of Portsmouth because they would lend no support to local effort to maintain a school in Ocracoke. The rich merchants sent their children away to school, either on the mainland or back to England, and there was no fruit for the native effort to establish and maintain any sort of school.

Three days before Christmas in 1837 the sea brought Hatteras Island a young schoolmaster. His name was Joshua Dailey and he was an Englishman, bound, by way of the West Indies, to a teaching job in Virginia. It was at the beginning of a rough winter, and the season's worst gale was in the third day of its malevolence when the brigantine *Ralph* got caught in its confusion. The ship went to pieces in the breakers just east of Hatteras Inlet and abreast the village. The crew and the passenger got ashore with some help from the Islanders, and the passenger disclosed the fact that he was a schoolteacher.

Thereafter and for the rest of his life Dailey taught school on Hatteras Island, and for the most of the time in the village of Trent—six miles eastward from the Inlet and about halfway between the Inlet and the Cape. Here was, in a sense, the center of population, and here, for one reason or another, at the time the economic center of the Seven Villages that dotted the length of the Island.

This schoolmaster left a mighty imprint upon the Island that continues now, down through and including the fifth and sixth generations of his posterity. But it is this generation's misfortune that he was so busy enlightening the young of the Island that he had never any time to set down his own story. There are glimpses of him in the Rollinson journal, and his death is recorded in it, but there is not much else by which to appraise him except his posterity. They are an able and formidable race and became mighty men with an oar.

It is remembered that Dailey brought nothing away from the wrecked brigantine except his virtually naked self. He had none of the implements of his trade, no books, no attestation of his professional endowments. He came to the Island, as most have, naked and destitute. But no matter. The Island understands that. And the Island needed a schoolteacher. Now that it had one, it lent little encouragement for him to continue his journey. As long as he would stay, and would teach the untaught young of the Island. . . . Dailey stayed.

Joshua Dailey stayed and made do with what lay to hand. He had no books from which to teach and there were none to be had. So he taught "out of his head," and for writing, there were geese with quills and ink was to be made from the juice of pokeberries and from small plantings of indigo maintained by women for dyeing their wool. Paper was come by with difficulty and at considerable

cost, as the Islanders reckoned cost, but the school prospered, continued, endured.

John Rollinson's father was a man of some substance and lived
comfortably. Teacher Dailey lived with him in Trent, and when
John Rollinson came back from the wreck of the *Ontario* with paper
enough for making a book, teacher and pupil set down a textbook
on arithmetic. It is written obviously with a goose-quill pen, and its
chapter headings are set down with the most fashionable flourishes.
As penmanship alone the book is a veritable wonder, and there is
no need anywhere in the hundreds of pages of it to puzzle over the
identity of a letter or a figure. It is astonishingly clear.

The whole of the book was bound, stitched with stout linen
thread, in covers of heavy sailcloth, fortified with varnish of an
enduring toughness. (The book was brought to me, utterly without
any preliminary warning, and I have committed it, for safety's sake,
to the vaults of the library of the University of North Carolina, not
as a textbook but as a running account of what happened on this
Island between the time it was put together as an arithmetic and
the day of its maker's death in 1906.)

On the last page of the first section of the book John Rollinson
set down the text of a contract he had entered upon to teach school
in the village of Hatteras. He was nineteen years old, and the
ascending fortunes of the village made it desirable that they have a
school of their own. Portsmouth was on a decline, as a port and as
a place-of-origin for students in mainland or continental schools.
John Rollinson taught, and he did more.

As there was need, other paper was acquired and incorporated
within the varnished covers of what had become the Journal, and
when this was exhausted temporarily, the schoolmaster set down,
on odd corners of pages, where there would be vacant space left
after a problem in long division that extended from the upper left-
hand to the lower right-hand corner. Nothing trivial was set down.
A man might be mentioned when he was born, when he married,
when he died, and a wrecked ship, or that "George Willis and his
wife and his son was frose up at the mouth of Rone Oak river
twenty days and then George walked to Plymouth on ice."

None of those who came down the generations from this schoolmaster, and bearing his name, became teachers. He was not physically a man of great stature, and the next generation of him was not a formidable man in size. He was a man of the sea, and his tombstone yonder among the cedar and yoepon and liveoak of the Second Ridge has graven upon the face of it the likeness of the Congressional Medal of Honor for Lifesaving. He was the first man to achieve it, and he bluntly declined it when those in high place would have accorded his crewmen a lesser honor. They, in his thinking, merited it equally with him, and there was no gainsaying him. They shared an equal honor.

That was a day when a veritable building boom in houses was begun on the Island, when the sea in an abandon of vengefulness piled the beach high with a hundred thousand feet of good lumber. But the crew, every man of them, was brought ashore, five miles through seas that continue to be remembered as about the worst the ocean, up to now, has been able to contrive. Benjamin Dailey, recording it, but not until the ninth day afterward because his hands were so blistered and swollen that he could not write, observed merely that "after a hard struggle we got to sea."

But that was around the point of the Cape to the north, and John Rollinson ignored it. The Bight of Hatteras was his. Neither of them lived quite long enough to set down the fact that a great-grandson of the schoolteacher, on the night tick of Guglielmo Marconi's wireless station above the Cape, was the only man to communicate directly with the doomed *Titanic* when she hit ice two thousand miles away. He wonderingly transmitted the intelligence to his headquarters in New York and was reprimanded for cluttering the wires with ill-considered foolishness about the sinking of an unsinkable ship.

But the sea, mindful ever of her own, and by some vagary that still puzzles men of science, had remembered her own, had brought them tidings from far places of improbable happenings. Even as, when the Island began to be fretful of its lack of schools, she brought them a schoolmaster, in time brought lumber when he was in need of lumber to build himself a house, and was mindful of her own in such a trifling matter as there being no coffee on his pantry shelf.

But . . . she is a woman, I tell you, and you have to humor her and be patient with her when she is in a bad notion. . . .

14

The sea talks to these children of hers.

It was a long time before I could begin to comprehend that simple fact and longer before I could understand a single syllable of what she would be saying. It is very likely that the first time I heard one of these Islanders say to another, "Did you hear the ocean talking a while ago?" I must have laughed in my ignorance but, happily, the laughing was inward and nobody heard me.

After that I listened and in time one sort of sound began to be distinguishable from another. Sometimes the sound she was making would be loud and clear, sometimes a soft murmur that was scarcely audible. Then, sometimes in the night, other times in the clear light of noonday, she would be brief, peremptory. And one Islander would look at another Islander understandingly. They would nod, without making any sound themselves. They had heard her and they had understood what she was saying to them.

In the presence of an Islander, of any age, it was proper to be very circumspect about this business. It would have been presumptuous for me to speak openly of having heard the sea talking. It would have made me look a good deal of a foreign idiot. It takes some hundreds of years to get a fair working knowledge of this curious speech, and although the Islanders would have been, as they have always been, tolerant of brashness, they would have, none the less, thought their own thoughts about me, and if I could have read them there would have been no flattery in them.

Time and waiting and listening brought me a kind of recompense that I have, these many months now, cherished, and circumstances provided a wholly suitable object upon which to demonstrate my learning in the language of the sea. He was a Brooklyn-born young fellow, very smart, in his books and in the ways of life that are the peculiar charm and social obstacle of people deriving from that fabulous borough. He was in command of a large detachment of Seabees who had elected to establish themselves as my neighbors. They live just down the hill from here.

It happened on an especially calm Sabbath afternoon. Rarely had I seen the sea so calm, the wind so still, the sun so benignly bright. Nowhere was there any premonitory sound. Even the radios that, even yet, send up a babel of sounds from every tent in the village at the foot of the hill were somnolent. The paper had contained no mention of any especially untoward event anywhere in the world. The word hurricane was, for that day, out of print completely. . . . And then I heard her.

It came across the mile or so of plain between here and the Point like the crack of a heavy-calibered pistol. Just once and then she lapsed into still silence and the sun continued to shine and the wind was utterly still. The surface of the sea yonder was glassy smooth, blue as it can be only when warmed by a tropical sun. The long slow movement of vast water in the great eddy of the Bight was just barely perceptible. But I had heard her.

When it grew on toward evening I bethought me to wander over to the Lighthouse and look at her close up. I had heard her, and I just wanted to look her in the eye, so to speak. Along the way I encountered this young, vastly energetic and, when he thought of it, urbanely mannered young lieutenant, whose men called him a slave-driver. He had been swimming and his young Nordic hair lay close against his lean young skull. He felt very good indeed. He stopped to chat a little.

And then I told him. Within forty-eight hours there would be a hurricane roaring up out of the ocean yonder and his tents, if he didn't secure them, would be shredded to rags. He looked politely incredulous, and then he looked at the sea from which he had a little while ago emerged. And he said, scarcely able to keep the derision out of his voice, "What do you mean, hurricane? Just look at it—not a cloud, not a ripple. And there hasn't been a thing about a hurricane on the radio."

With that he removed himself from the contaminating company of an old crock who said he had heard the ocean talking. Still not too sure of my interpretation I went over and looked at the sea. Half a mile down the beach, toward the Point, she, very suddenly, let go again with that pistol-crack. I looked to see what had happened. Nothing had happened that the eye, or at any rate my eye, could detect. There had been, I thought, a curiously-shaped wave, but I could not be sure. The ripples from its ebb made a little pattern against the waning light.

Actually it was fifty hours before the hurricane hit. That night the radio had become alert and a perceptible disquiet began to pervade the camp down the hill. One or two of the petty officers came up after supper to say that they had heard somebody say that they had heard on the radio that there was a hurricane brewing and that it would likely hit Cape Hatteras. . . . That, out of lengthening and confusing experience, is routine—all hurricanes, when they are first found, are "expected to pass off Cape Hatteras at. . . ."

Monday saw a freshening of the wind, a roughening of the sea well beyond the making of the wind as it blew in the area. But the young lieutenant couldn't be bothered with hurricanes. He had had nothing official on it, and young lieutenants have to have it in writing from someone in authority before they give any countenance to even a hurricane. Work proceeded throughout Monday and until the middle of the afternoon on Tuesday, when the freshening wind loosened a corner of a tent and ripped it from its framing.

Official word arrived about the same time that the outfit was to be placed on Condition One at six o'clock, and that was the first time that this high-sounding term was heard on the Island. There was a considerable confusion, and the young lieutenant came up to know if he might move in, with his command post. He couldn't. Four young petty officers had already asked and were even then trudging up the hill with their gear. They had secured their tent and the young lieutenant was moved, alone, into the house next door. . . . The blow lasted four days and four nights, a thing of moderate but persistent intensity that bothered no Islander. The center of it passed seventy miles to the west.

There is no mystery about this business, about any Islander who heard the sea talking knowing that a hurricane was impending, nor that it was known on the Point of Cape Hatteras certainly as early as they had word of it a thousand miles away at the tip end of Florida. It has a sound scientific basis, and a simple one. It was explained, with charts and pencil and paper here one day by Captain Donald MacDairmid, who is recognized among oceanographers as knowing more about the surface movements of ocean water than any man living. He learned by landing aircraft—and wondering why he sometimes misjudged some of the essentials. He, nor any other who has studied his reports, needs now to wonder.

Among the things that MacDairmid didn't know, needed to learn, and did learn, was the speed with which a surface impulse travels. It ranges, depending on its initial thrust, between 250 and 300 miles per hour. A tremor of water set up by a hurricane in the West Indies will travel outward from the center at that rate. It takes from eight to ten hours for an impulse, a wave, to travel from a new-born tropical hurricane to the Point of Cape Hatteras.

And the Cape thrusts out into the Atlantic Ocean as no other projection of land on the continent. If there is a wave passing, it will register on the Point, often with a crack like the shot of a pistol. Not every one of them, perhaps, but enough of them to make a sound pattern that needs no scientist to interpret it. You just have to learn to understand what she is saying when the sea starts talking. She speaks with an infinite vocabulary, and it will take a lifetime of listening, and ten generations of inheriting, to understand her fully.

There are those thus schooled. The sound of the surf pounding the shore north or west of the Cape, and sometimes both, has a significance and meaning that is bred into an Islander. For them the sea always telegraphs her punches, to borrow from the argot of the ring, and unfailingly she sends out warning well ahead of time if there is anything imminent that the Islander ought to know about, to the end that he may take such precautions as seem indicated. It is a matter of actual record that no tumult of storm has ever taken a life on the Islands.

When she feels an attack of any sort coming on it is the sea's wish that her children get away from her, that they get to some place on dry land and stay there until the time of stress is passed. And it is not without sound reason that any Islander will tell you that here is the safest place on the earth in time of storm. Nobody has ever been hurt by one—provided he took the sea's warning.

Alliteration shades into synonym . . . Hatteras and Hurricane. After some centuries of it, nowadays intensified by gargled hysterics of the radio announcer, to think of one is to think also of the other. The hurricane is by no means unknown on Cape Hatteras and along these Islands that make the Cape's angle into the ocean. About one in five of them comes within range of the Cape and, on occasion, the Cape can and has produced a hurricane on its own account. So also has Cape Cod. Not all hurricanes are spawned in the West Indies.

Since I took a sort of stance on this hill (1947) and began to observe what goes on around and above and below it, there have been twelve hurricanes. Thirteen, counting the one that was hatched within plain sight of me about twenty miles to the southeast in the middle of a June morning. Winds have attained a velocity of 135 miles per hour, in 1949, but not one shingle is missing from the roof.

There is, come to think of it, a shingle gone, but that got detached on a morning when a frolicksome Marine helicopter teetered there for a while and a casually blond Marine corporal dangled his bare feet out the back door of it while he tinkered with some fishing gear. He waved genially, and the same downblast of rotor that detached a shingle fetched down his words when he said, "Hi, Pop." He was, and it probably would not have mattered to him, not aware that the other elderly crock who stood, looking up at him, was indeed the father of the helicopter, who chanced to be extending an acquaintance of long standing that morning.

These shingles were, to be sure, nailed on by natives of the Island, and they considered the possibility of winds of one kind or another when they drove their nails. There were also hurricanes around before I became a tenant, the records indicate. There were before my time in the house twelve other hurricanes after the house was built, including the monster of 1944. Altogether, including the one that was put together here in June, 1950, that makes a total of twenty-five hurricanes.

These same records report that there have been, since the house was built in 1939, a total of 118 hurricanes, all of which, at one time or another in their lives, were reported by some radio announcer or other agency of harassment to be "headed for Cape Hatteras." Some of them did make it, twenty-five of them, and they brought with them just about everything a hurricane can tote, including winds of 142 miles per hour (1944), but the house is still here on this hill, structurally undamaged except for the shingle missing because of a Sikorsky helicopter.

Three applications of paint have been scoured away, to be sure, and the planking is probably thinner from the sand-blasting it gets when the wind really gets in some licks. In a regulation blow all the leaves are whipped off the yoepon bush, and it has been left stark naked not less than three times since it was planted under the window. But it promptly grows some more leaves, summer or winter, and is green again before the pines have regained their proper color. Driven salt spray will turn pines brown in a day and they look for a while as if fire had swept them.

The birth of a hurricane is a wonderful spectacle to behold, and it would have had a lot more wonder in it if I had, then, known what was going on. It was an unusually clear June morning, cloudless except for the low-lying bank of rolling formation that lies above the Gulf Stream at most seasons of the year. It is not a large area, there where the two currents, cold and warm, meet. Almost always the cloud bank is there at sunrise, but it normally goes away when the sun is up.

But this morning it stayed, and there were some premonitory cracks in the rhythm of the surf. After a while it was noticeable that the center of the cloud bank was rising above the flanks of it and that it had begun, lazily, desultorily at first, to rotate very slowly. The mass was white under the sun, and it began to swell, darken. Within an hour it was moving outward from the rotating center, which had climbed higher. The sun was suddenly enveloped and the cloud blackened.

And then it began to rain, in brief gusts, then steadily. Within the space of three-quarters of an hour four inches of rain fell on this hill. . . . Next day I looked for the published report of the weather observatory twelve miles west of the Cape—it is now in process of moving back to the Cape, where it was established eighty-five years ago—and to my utter amazement, not a trace of rain fell into its measuring cups. There was then no radar equipment with which to pry into the maw of a disturbance, and the radiosonde balloon that ascended during the blow here took off in the opposite direction.

This hill was caught in the outer rim of the burgeoning hurricane. The next village to the north, Kinnakeet, seven miles away, was left wholly out of its sphere and no drop of rain fell. The thing moved to the south and east and presently the sun was out, the sand drained away the sudden flood. It was twelve hours before anything more was heard from it. Ships at sea began to sputter. One after another reported that they were in the clutches of something that behaved just like a hurricane. Three were, for the time being, disabled, and the Coast Guard's rescue machinery began to turn.

It was another twelve hours before anything like the whole picture came into focus, not from the Weather Bureau but from the Coast Guard. There was no doubt, now, about it. A relatively small but very potent hurricane had been hatched right off the point of the Shoals and, perversely, it started down to the West Indies, to the consternation of ships in that part of the ocean. She continued south and east for twenty-four hours, lost a good deal of her force, and decided that she had as well turn back and look in on the Island of Bermuda, which is 442 miles south of east from the Lighthouse.

This one is not in the Weather Bureau's books. Inquiry directed to their historical section three times for an official report on the phenomenon has met only with silence. But they do have in their official records, together with chart, the report of a somewhat similar happening that formed southeast of Cape Cod on October 3, 1913, moved southwest, passing Cape Hatteras well out to sea, curved inland at Charleston, and wore itself to an innocuous end 125 miles west of Cape Hatteras on October 9.

There is not much that anybody has been able to do about hurricanes except count them. An astonishingly convincing job has been done at that, over the centuries, beginning with Columbus himself and continuing on down to now, since the first of these Western Hemisphere phenomena was observed in Santo Domingo on June 16, 1494. In the course of the next 461 years a total of 1,512 appear to be a matter of record. From such sources as I have been able to command, ranging from Island folklore and record to Andreas Poey and his successors, it is my belief that 306 of them hit in the vicinity of Cape Hatteras.

Some of them, many of them, were of an intensity that left indelible imprint in the lives of the Islanders. They are remembered, and these go back to 1702, when the sprawling port village of Portsmouth was made into a shambles and the wreckage of ships was mixed with the wreckage of houses. That one is remembered on the Islands, since, among other items of wreckage, there were two Spanish merchantmen freighted with gold stolen from the Incas. They were able to gather up their loot and load it into other ships.

There is, by now, a formidable literature on hurricanes, but these massive disturbances stubbornly avoid being analyzed by machinery. Meteorological science is pretty young for such a task, and their accounting machines, which feed upon little cards with holes punched in them, yield only meaningless gibberish after such feeding. Martin Tolson who, between his surf-casting on the Point, explores his Scriptures, has as good an answer as the calculating machines have so far produced. He cites the eighth verse of the third chapter of St. John . . . "The wind bloweth where it listeth."

At any rate it suffices an Islander, and it does not hinder them when they add, for expediency's sake, a third nail when they are anchoring a shingle on their roof. Not that they are opposed to Andreas Poey counting the hurricanes, or to the meteorologists who punch holes in little cards and feed them to a machine. The word of the Beloved Disciple contents them, that and the Voice of the Sea when she is disposed to communicate something. Nor does the Islander take it amiss that a learned young fellow can look down the throat of a hurricane and see her teeth, so to speak.

The sea has already, very likely, told the Islander what it is that the young scientist is going to see, and some among them may indulge themselves an inward sort of a snort when the young fellow is too intent upon his radarscope, or to the tinglings sent down from 80,000 feet by radio swinging under a balloon, and Captain Bernice Ballance may observe, not without sententiousness, that he can see the moon from where he is sitting and don't they ever bother to look at the moon any more? Or just look out the window. But the room where the radar machinery is situated has no windows.

Andreas Poey's name does not loom very large in the histories, and even now the modern scientist insists on a certain amount of editing and excision before accepting his remarkable work. He was born in Cuba, got to know about hurricanes from practical, and no doubt often disturbing, experience. Most of his life he devoted to the exploration of monasteries and other depositories of ancient records in the West Indies, and in 1856 he appeared in Paris with a chronological record of every hurricane that had been reported in the West Indies from the time of Columbus' second voyage.

Six years later his work was published in English in London and it has now become one of the rarest books on the earth. The Congressional Library has one of the few known copies of it in the United States. It has been edited and reissued, in the light of what purports to be newer and more complete evidence and, in one guise or another, is continued down to the present and to include hurricanes after they got to be named for girls instead of the Saints upon whose days they chanced to be born.

By whatever name they are named, they continue to be the most appalling phenomena known to mankind, and naming them for girls has not made them in any wise girlish or maidenly. Loose estimates of their inherent power compare an able-bodied hurricane to a dozen, or to three dozen, nuclear explosions of war-worthy intensity. And when they have found out all that can be known about a hurricane, even if they expand their learning until they can feed a machine little cards with some hope that it will not mock them with its vomit, there will still be little that anybody can do about them.

Hurricanes just are, and all that anybody can do about them can be handily encompassed by the third nail for a shingle. That is the ultimate wisdom. There are, to be sure, corollaries. Don't disturb a blade of grass. There is Mr. Byrum's dyke yonder, erected by the wind with the help of fragile twigs. (For some reason, though the engineers have not yet seen it, a slatted snow-fence is no good. The wind will not leave her sand for such a contrivance.) When the wind had finished her work they planted some grass, some sea oats, and these blades of grass have a powerful magic. They alone have stopped the sea and the wind.

Twenty-seven hurricanes have had at that dyke and its grass since it was raised up. Some of them I have seen, and they were very terrible hurricanes, especially the September, 1944, blow, when the wind went past the 140-mile mark and the sea arose in a great gray-green wall to engulf a village and stir the dwelling places around as one might stir with a stick leaves floating in a pail of water. Of the 112 houses in the village 99 were anywhere from one foot to one mile from their moorings. Nobody, to be sure, was hurt, or even greatly inconvenienced.

Even my neighbor Gibbie Gray can and does now laugh at what happened to him that day. He is a merchant, and in his store there was, and is, a very heavy iron safe. It contains mostly the savings of his neighbors, a bond or two in a packet, some money in another. Anything that they want to keep in a place that is reasonably safe from fire or like hazard. On that day, when the waters came, and the 140-mile wind—Gibbie Gray thought there must have been in the neighborhood of sixty thousand dollars in money or securities, the lifelong savings of his neighbors. There are no banks.

With houses floating around like worried ships Gibbie Gray got to worrying about the contents of that safe. If the store floated away, it would carry the safe, and then where would he and his neighbors be? He dumped it all into a heavy sack and lashed it to his back and started home. Before he got there he was overtaken by surging water that now, astonishingly, was coming from the Sound. The wind had shifted and the sea receded. But the Sound came up even higher. The water's surge lifted Gibbie Gray and his burden upward. He caught the lower limb of a massive liveoak that has been standing in that village for a good half millennium. He took firm hold and climbed. He attained a place of comparative security halfway up, and he settled down there and rode out the storm.

Afterward he hauled his store back to where it belonged and restored the contents of the safe to its keeping, and the savings came in very handy when his neighbors began to retrieve their houses from wherever they had happened to lodge. All but two, that is. These were carried over to the beach, and they took off for some strange destination. They have not been seen since, and their occupants were confronted with the need of building anew. Which they did. Not one inhabitant of the village was missing. They were the sea's children—and they are.

15

Thoreau's most quoted sentence is not heard on these Islands. The mass of men on these Islands do not live lives of quiet desperation, and in the middle of Thoreau's next paragraph there are some words, which few anywhere have ever bothered to quote, some words that make more sense . . . "New people put a little dry wood under a pot, and are whirled round the globe with the speed of birds. . . ." Meaning, of course, steam.

These Islands have never liked steam, have never trusted it altogether, and its introduction as motive power was ignored as something that had neither divine nor natural sanction. Had not the winds been ordained to move mankind and his goods from one place to another? The will of the wind was the will of God, and the only allowable departure from natural and spiritual law—well, it was no sin for a man to take a stout oar in his hand for short distances. But the fires that men built under pots to make steam to blow them, even against the wind—well, such fires were akin to the fires of hell itself.

Steam was a long time coming to these Islands and it never got a firm foothold. In so far as can be determined it was in the fortieth year after Mr. Fulton had ascended the Hudson River with a fire under a pot that steam came to this Island in any but the most detached sort of way. That night, with every villager, numbering about six hundred souls, within his hearing, Anderson Gray delivered what comes down in folklore as the longest, and most vigorous, sermon ever delivered on Hatteras Island. He was against steam, and he literally scalded his parishioners with invective, likening the fires under a ship's boilers to the everlasting fires of eternal torment.

They still tell the tale, and it is so with all handed-down lore, with such a sense of immediacy that it is often difficult to keep in mind the fact that this happened a hundred years ago and not just week before last. I have heard the tale told at least five times, and in its essentials it varies in no smallest detail, but nobody can pin it down to a precise year in time. Time has no very special significance on these Islands, and this event could have happened anywhere between 1847 and 1874.

From collateral records, among them such formidable works as Dr. Christopher Crittenden's scholarly and profoundly documented treatise on Transportation in North Carolina, I am inclined to fix the time, not altogether arbitrarily, as August 4, 1847. For one thing, it had to be prior to the Civil War, because in that era the Yankees came, bringing with them a total of eighty-two vessels, most of them propelled by steam, and they ranged the scale of Naval architecture from Brooklyn ferryboats to battleships.

Steam, with all its iniquitous connotations, had appeared on the horizon as early as 1825, but no vessel so propelled had ventured willingly into the harbor at Portsmouth, or had approached Hatteras Inlet. Islanders returning from foreign parts brought with them improbable tales of ships propelled, at least in part, by steam. Still, mankind had no conclusive faith in it—they still had sail to fetch them to port if the fires went out under their pots. But now and then, looking to the sea, there would be visible foul patches of smoke issuing from fires that had boiled waters for the turning of wheels. . . . It was sinful and no good could come of it.

Twice within a year, lacking one day, terrible evil had come of it. Once, first, thirty miles north of the Cape, in clear weather, a ship named the *William Gibbons* propelled by steam had, for no reason other than its own flouting of Providence, come upon disaster. And, squeaking within the year by a single day, another ship named the *Home*, wickedly depending on steam and proceeding at a reported speed above and beyond what Heaven had ever intended that mankind should travel, had hit the beach twenty-five miles southwest of the Cape.

In neither case had the sea's state of mind had anything to do with it. Not the wind nor sea, but the engines, had driven them ashore in calm, clear weather in which any ship propelled as God had intended them to be propelled would have gone unhindered, helped even by the winds that were blowing. If they had sails, that is. Neither ship was designed as the sea intended them to be designed. They were flimsy craft, built mostly to slip through the water, propelled by engines, at great speed. One of them was said to have been able to travel as fast as sixteen miles in one hour.

That was especially wicked. What possible difference could it make to anybody whether he made the trip from New York, past Cape Hatteras, and down to Charleston in three days instead of five or six? Something dreadful was bound to happen and there would be little hope for them, either as they came to disaster or when they entered the hereafter, as was rather more than likely. Nobody was lost when the *William Gibbons* hit the beach before daylight at New Inlet. (There is no longer an inlet there, but the site of this disaster is only a mile or so south of where the *Flambeau* and her cargo of no-longer-fashionable hats hit the beach thirty years later.)

This unhappy incident is not to be ascribed wholly to the circumstance of steam propulsion. The wreck was due to the incompetence and the carelessness of the crew. They had mistaken the beacon on Bodie Island—there was no Oregon Inlet until the Great Storm of 1848 cut it twelve years afterward—for the light on Cape Hatteras, and the navigator thereupon laid a southwesterly course, which brought them hard aground in a little while.

These Islands saw rather more of the passengers, about eighty of them, than was desirable. That part of the Island was then, as now, not inhabited except for fishing camps. The now-closed inlet was very shallow and used only by small fishing craft. In the confusion the passengers were set ashore and herded toward John Midgett's (he was grandfather to Captain John Allen Midgett, to be mentioned again) fishing camp. One account says that there were 119 of them, but the Islanders say there were about 80.

What the Islanders could see of the efficacy of steam, from the beach, was not impressive. The ship undertook to wallow herself off the beach, but to no avail. As might have been expected, the crew became gaudily drunk and the situation worsened. The wind, not liking anything that it saw, appeared to have made up its mind to end this foolishness. The sea rose and in a night broke the ship in pieces. Nobody was lost, and with the help of native small craft, propelled by sail, all were transported to Elizabeth City and thence to Norfolk, each with his magnified tale of terrors endured.

This occurred on October 10, 1836. A year later, lacking one day, the *Home* hit the beach six miles east northeast of Ocracoke, and the bodies of ninety people, most of them women and children, littered the sand. Forty members of the crew and male passengers survived. The record books ascribe the disaster to a hurricane that is called the "Racer's Storm" because of the savagery with which it dealt with a sloop of that name. The hurricane is not remembered on these Islands as one of unusual intensity, and Andreas Poey records that it passed to sea off Charleston on October 9, 1837, three hundred miles south of Cape Hatteras. Except for two small sloops no other ships were reported lost.

But the *Home* was not designed for the sea. She was made for steam and for speed. With an over-all length of 220 feet she had a beam of 22 feet and was registered at 550 tons. When the going was good she made the run from New York to Charleston in sixty-four hours, to the accompaniment of applauding clamor in the newspapers. She left New York on October 6 with the widely heralded intention of cutting four hours off the running time to Charleston. Seventy-two hours had elapsed when she rounded Diamond Shoals.

Racer's Storm had long since sounded its warning against the Point of the Cape, and the *Home* had felt the outer thrust of the disturbance as far north as the Virginia capes, 130 miles above Cape Hatteras. But the fires under her pots burned brightly, eating greedily into the store of fuel aboard, and when she rounded Cape Hatteras and headed into the seas she found there her steam pressure was dwindling. There was water in her woodpile, and she faced the ordeal, the outer fringe of the hurricane, without power.

There was still steam enough left in her boilers for her to creep ahead in the uncertain lee of the curving shore of the Bight, but when her engines finally faltered her master had no recourse but to turn her head toward the beach. It is not a pretty story, any of it. Islanders remember that they heard it from their grandfathers that the ship's hull writhed like a snake in agony and that as soon as her bow was against the beach she began to break amidships. She was built for speed, for steam, and not for the sea and the wind.

For three days the Islanders gathered up the terrible offal that a human body can become when life is no longer in it. They buried them wherever there was a place that would hold a grave. The survivors, moving across the Inlet to Portsmouth, found passage in sailing ships and went away. The dead remained, and there remained also the Islander's growing mistrust of steam. And the survivors, without bothering to explain why they were the survivors and not the women and children the Islanders had buried in the sand, deflected criticism from themselves by rather hellish accusations against the Islanders.

Some of these tenaciously persist.

And there persists also the inborn mistrust of the devil's element put under a pot of water to make it boil and so produce steam for turning a wheel. Of these things only disaster on earth and damnation in eternity could be reasonably expected, and the total experience of the Islanders, from the first steamer that passed along the lane of the sea onward to that August afternoon in 1847, was in support of the belief that steam was something conceived in mortal sin.

Kinnakeet had become, toward the middle of that century, the First Village of the Two Islands. Portsmouth was declining. Ocracoke had not yet taken over wholly its neighbor's fading fortunes. Hatteras Inlet had come upon evil times and its channel would need the scouring-out which it got in a later storm. Kinnakeet flourished. Here was the seat of "King" Pharaoh Farrow, perhaps the richest man ever to inhabit these Islands. He had ships. He had slaves, taken after shipwreck as castaways, or bought or traded for. He owned, or appears to have owned, 241 tracts of land on the two Islands, if one can believe the yellowed pieces of paper that currently appear when the federal government undertakes to clear title to this or that area of its proposed National Seashore.

There were two Kinnakeets—the big one and the little one about two miles north and also facing the Sound. The two became one fifty-odd years ago when the entrance to the north village's little harbor closed. The villagers loaded their houses onto barges and floated them down to Big Kinnakeet which, by then, had become, in the Postal Guide, Avon. Nor was King Pharaoh the only citizen of consequence. There were the Hoopers, for generations merchants to and for their neighbors, and whose records, finally, were stuffed into an empty cheese box about 1875 and so rest comfortably under this table at this moment.

Kinnakeet, seven miles north of the Cape, was the Island's capital in 1847, and its docks were thick with Sound traffic. Near by also were the shipyards where both the Farrows and the Hoopers built ships, when there was need of them, and their windmills provided the power for the slow turning of crude sawmills that converted liveoak into such timbers as were required for the ribs and bows of shipbuilders as far away as Maine. This was the end of the liveoak forest that once covered the whole of the Island and the beginning of its century-long denudation by wind and tide. August came, with its torpor and its flies and its mosquitoes. It was a dull time of the year and, as was customary not only along these Outer Banks but everywhere in this part of the United States, the time of the August Meeting. It was the season for the revival of religion, and there was fervid exhortation to repentance, by day and by night. The practice continues, with diminished intensity, and in August, traditionally, the Islanders repent of their sins, renew their vows of devotion to the true religion which, until the Civil War rent the Island asunder, was the faith as revealed to John Wesley.

Anderson Gray is remembered as a man of immense stature, of profound piety, especially in August, and of massive eloquence. It is remembered that he could be heard as far away as Little Kinnakeet, a distance of two miles, when he verbally held some unrepented sinner over the flames of hell and shook him. But it was rarely that an inhabitant of Little Kinnakeet abode at home in these seasons of revival. He either left the Island altogether or came down to Big Kinnakeet to hear repentance preached as well as to see sinners wrestling with their sins.

Always toward the end of the season of revival Anderson Gray bore down upon the imminence of the end of the world. There were signs and portents of an unmistakable sort. There always were, but each year he managed to bring them down to date, and for days people went about as if expecting that each moment might see the dissolution of the universe. The moment would be preceded, to be sure, by three spaced blasts of a trumpet wielded by the Angel Gabriel. Anderson Gray, it is remembered, could and did produce, out of his vast throat, a reasonable approximation of the anticipated trumpet blasts.

It was a trying time, not only because of the imminent dissolution of the universe and the descent of sinners into the pit of
hell. The weather was hot. The flies were worse than anybody could
ever remember them being, and all these were pointed up as sure
signs of the end of the world. Nobody could get his mind on anything else. All industry, the building of boats, the curing of yoepon
tea, the selling of goods, even fishing, was in a state of suspense,
and there was just nothing to do but fight off flies and mosquitoes
and wonder if this place would last through the night.

Not disturbed by the preaching but mightily discommoded by
the heat and the flies, the cattle, the horses, the swine, the sheep,
and the goats on this afternoon had waded out into the shallow
waters of the Sound in search of some surcease from the heat
and the insects. No breath of wind blew. The heat and the flies
were also an inconvenience to Anderson Gray but he did not, for
understandable reasons, follow his neighbors and their cattle into
the Sound. He took with him one of his sons and walked the three-
quarters of a mile eastward to the beach. The ocean lay like a mirror
there. Father and son rested beside the surf and wished that from
somewhere there might come a breath of wind. None came. They
may have dozed off in the somnolent heat.

Father and dozing son were wrenched back into awareness by
an appalling sound. It seemed to come down out of the sky and
to fill the whole of space between them and the zenith. The earth
trembled under its shattering weight. Father and son looked
wordlessly at each other, and then doom cracked again. "You hear
that?" Anderson Gray croaked, and his son croaked.

"Yes, papa." Without a word they got to their feet and started
back toward the village. And then it came again, this time louder
and nearer. They began to run.

Before they got to their village they met and were engulfed by a
tidal wave of people, of horses snorting wildly, of cattle bellowing,
of pigs squealing, of sheep bleating. Some of their neighbors
were screaming wildly, some in hysterical repentance of hitherto
nameless sins, but mostly just screaming in unrestrained terror.

Anderson Gray's son joined them, adding his voice to the uproar, but Anderson Gray stood dumb, with his eyes uplifted. In a moment the sky would open and the ascension would begin.

There is some small divergence, now, in estimates of how long a time this state of affairs continued, but it is remembered that one hardened sinner, a habitual absentee from the preachings and one who was often mentioned as a horrible example, cerainly the first to be snatched down to the pit on the Last Day, came casually into their midst. His name is not remembered, or at least not to me. He very likely has many descendants in the neighborhood now, and good people, too. He came from the direction of the little harbor.

At first people stared at him in unbelieving horror, fearful of seeing what must, any minute now, happen to him. So far, however, he was unhurt, and he was grinning amiably and trying to make himself heard above the uproar. He had to repeat it nobody remembers how many times before anybody could actually hear him. And then, of course, they did not believe a word of it. This was a devil's trick being played upon them by the devil's own child. But toward night, when there appeared to be some small delay in the explosive termination of the world, some of them followed him, at a distance sufficient to put them beyond the normal reach of a bolt from heaven if it struck him, to the harbor.

This nameless fellow pointed and said, "Yonder she lays, like I done told you." And there she did lie, the small steamer *Neuse*, out of New Bern, come to fetch King Pharaoh Farrow some goods he had sent for. Somebody aboard took hold of the *Neuse's* whistle cord and yanked it smartly and, for the fourth time that day and in its history, Kinnakeet heard the appalling sound of a trumpet, a steam trumpet. And they were, very likely, considerably relieved, and that night there were few who heard Anderson Gray preach. Some think that he didn't preach at all but joined his neighbors down at the dock to just look at the appalling apparition that had appeared among them.

16

With his goose quill freshly sharpened and with some new ink, John Rollinson set down fifteen words on a page of his Journal already crowded by a dissertation entitled Vulgar Fractions. As was his apparent custom, he opened the book at random and set down whatever he had on his mind in the first open space of his homemade textbook on arithmetic that he found. There was not, on this page, room for more than fifteen words, so he compressed history.

"Troops arrived at Hatteras Inlet to Guard the Inlet on Thursday, 9th of May, 1861."

It is not much, but the event is not elsewhere recorded in history. For these Islands the Civil War had begun and, curiously enough, on an adjacent page of the homemade arithmetic that became a source book there is another equally brief entry minutely related to the fact that it was to this place that the first troops armed by this State not yet formally out of the Union were dispatched. The neighboring entry states: "The first vessel went through Hatteras Inlet February 5, 1847. *Arthur C. Havens*."

Hatteras village had become the pre-eminent town on the Outer Banks, and within the year after the troops came to guard the Inlet, Abraham Lincoln, by proclamation, would designate it as the provisional capital of the retrieved State of North Carolina, and it would become the port of embarkation for the most elaborate campaign of invasion, combining land and sea forces, undertaken by Federal forces in the war that was coming, then, toward the peak of its frenzied violence.

Hatteras village had become the capital of the Outer Banks, and it was so because of the violence of a storm that was brewing in the ocean's torpor in the autumn of 1846. There is a brief note about it in the Journal, and the effect of it is indicated in the entry for February 5, 1847. The storm scoured out Hatteras Inlet, until then a waterway of negligible importance, too shallow to accommodate ocean-going vessels.

It was not an especially violent storm as it is remembered in the folklore of the Islands, but it had its peculiarities: it scoured out the Inlet, made it deep enough to take heavy traffic, and thereafter it replaced, for a long time, the entrance into the Sounds at the dying town of Portsmouth. Oregon Inlet was cut through the next year, but there was no town there with facilities for storage and for transshipment into smaller vessels more suited to the shallowing rivers on the mainland.

Something must have happened to the *Arthur C. Havens* somewhere because there is not again any mention of the vessel, except as is found fleetingly, and a little vaguely, in what people can remember was told them when they were very young. It is likely, because of her name, that she was owned in Washington up the Pamlico River. The name is that of a family then and for long afterward active in the mercantile life of the river country. There are some who say she set out on a voyage to the West Indies and did not return.

But she was replaced. There is periodical mention, in the carefully kept records of John Rollinson after he became Collector of the Port of Hatteras, of the schooner *I. W. Hughes*. She was owned by the Havens establishment in Washington and plied between there and the West Indies for many years immediately preceding the outbreak of the War and the paralyzing of the business of the port. On some days there are as many as five entries of arriving ships, and they averaged, in season, a ship a day during the decade after the village was established as a port-of-entry when its Inlet was opened.

Toward the end of that decade Portsmouth had virtually disappeared as a shipping town. Hatteras was rather better than well-situated for the shipping business. It was the nearest seagate to Elizabeth City, Edenton, Plymouth, and Washington, the river-ports that served the upper half of North Carolina's sea frontier, and each, with the exception of Elizabeth City, had a good up-river country to be served with flat-bottomed river boats that could not venture out into the Sounds.

Beaufort, to the southwest, had its limitations as a port of entry because of the tortuous approach through its back country to New Bern, where river steamers took what freight the Neuse River could carry. Wilmington's port, with the far-reaching Cape Fear River, as well as deeper water, accommodated a larger tonnage. Many vessels, outward bound from Edenton and Elizabeth City, used Oregon Inlet for shorter access to the sea, when the weather was good, but Hatteras had the advantage of being located southwest of the Cape and the Shoals, eliminating this hazard for the West Indies trade.

Since there was no port-of-entry at Oregon Inlet, all incoming cargoes bound for the northeast section had to come through the port and pay their duties. There was no outward clearance required for shipping and no record of it exists, but the outward-bound cargo usually was made up of corn, cotton, some tobacco, but predominantly timber products and turpentine. There is tucked away in the Journal an advertisement of the sale of the cargo of a Sound-wrecked schooner "consisting of 2,200,000 shingles."

Hatteras village waxed. It was a booming decade, these years that ended with the coming of the troops to guard Hatteras Inlet. New houses were built and John Rollinson built a store (cost: $73.71), which he rented out to a neighbor. The village became in a way a melting pot for the Islanders. There are not any new-to-the-Islands names in the census lists for the period, but names that were, until now, found only in one or another of the Seven Villages of the Island began to appear as Hatterasmen.

The Rollinsons moved down from Trent. The Grays came from Little Kinnakeet, and the Midgetts and the Meekins families began to be represented. The Stowes and the Styrons and the Burruses were there already. People moved into the village from other villages, but there is no indication that there was any influx of people from the outside, except as they came as castaways, like the Odens came. And there were Farrows, come from Kinnakeet and from Ocracoke, and Fulchers who came up the Islands from beyond Portsmouth and remained.

Both Trent and Kinnakeet declined measurably in the decade and Hatteras became ascendant until it was larger than Portsmouth, than Ocracoke, or any other town north of Beaufort, which was from the beginning a mainland town set apart from the peculiar life of the Outer Banks. Hatteras was not the seat of any government and, as were other sections of the Outer Banks, never quite sure for some generations whether it was a part of any county, or which county. It, as convenience suited, was a part of Currituck, of Tyrrell, and of Hyde, and not until 1870 did it become consciously a part of a county as such. Portsmouth belonged to the county of which Beaufort was the seat, when it became finally necessary for it to think, in its dying, about which county contained it. John Rollinson records that he was named a Justice of the Peace for Hyde County.

But the town became, for a deluded while, the capital of the reclaimed state of North Carolina, and for the whole of one day it was solemnly discussed by President Lincoln and his cabinet, who had sitting with them a rather brash but able young New York man who managed to have himself hailed as the conqueror of Hatteras and became almost forthwith a brigadier general, while the man who actually reduced the two forts by devising a naval technique new to war was relegated to obscurity and was not heard of again.

There is no sense of surprise in the Rollinson Journal at the circumstance that North Carolina, eleven days before it had formally left the Union, mobilized what troops it had on hand and dispatched them to Hatteras to guard the Inlet. Hatteras was the most important port on the State's coast, in 1861, with an annual tonnage that surpassed Beaufort and was about equal to that of Wilmington, certainly in the essentials of war-making. And it was the nearest one to the Northern enemy.

There are vestiges of the two forts still remaining, and, if examined from the air, still recognizable in their original contour. On the ground they are just some more grass-studded hummocks, but looked at in the whole, the hummocks take the form of the original forts that were erected on the east, or upper, side of the Inlet. It was a back-breaking labor, and withal it must have been sorely disillusioning to the thousand men who had, in a surge of enthusiasm, volunteered to go and shoot some Yankees.

There was, naturally, Fort Hatteras and, when that seemed not quite adequate for the purpose in hand, a second one a mile nearer the village was erected and named Fort Clark. They were mere sand redoubts of conventional design, but the sand could, and later did, absorb without damage all the ordnance a considerable fleet could throw against it. Such cannon as were available, numbering twenty-two guns of assorted sizes, were installed on the seaward side of the forts.

As mentioned, troops began arriving on Thursday, May 9, 1861. They came, as the older citizens heard from their fathers and grandfathers, from every which away. There were troops come from

New Bern, from Washington, Plymouth, and Edenton. Elizabeth City, apparently, made no contribution to the defense of the Inlet, fearing rather they might be set upon themselves from the north. As it turned out Elizabeth City was the first inland town to fall before the offensive afterward mounted from the captured village converted into capital.

Ships continued to arrive and to depart from the port, and among them there were some hastily-fitted-out privateers. It is not recorded nor remembered that any ship was actually owned in the village that became capital. They were, for the most part, owned about equally by the merchants in the inland towns and by New England traders who bought wherever they could and sold the same way. There were those who, in the light of some of the more vigorous representations made to President Lincoln, mostly New Englanders according to the allegations, were playing both ends against the middle for their own profit.

It does appear to be a matter of fairly clear record that one of three loaded ships taken when the fleet reduced the two forts was owned by a man from Maine, whose allegiance was to his own profit and who had, a few days before, taken as a "prize" a ship of Massachusetts registry which had no notion of trafficking through the port of Hatteras. He was hurrying home with a cargo of tropical fruit, mostly bananas, and the first Federal troops to go a-pillaging in the village set upon the by now overripe cargo. I have seen a grave said to contain what was left of several of these after dysentery from overindulgence in bananas had wreaked a havoc among them.

Hatteras was divided in its sympathies. It is recorded in Rollinson's journal that in an election held on November 6, 1860, Lincoln got forty-three votes and Douglas got forty-three votes. Why this was so can be explained only in conjecture. The slave issue was largely an ideological issue. Slaves there were on the Islands, but held mostly by one or two families. These were not bought and imported, except in one case where King Pharaoh Farrow deemed it expedient to buy a female slave as company and solace for a black he had acquired by picking him up after a shipwreck. The girl was bought on the mainland, and the transaction had its implications of eventual profit.

Slavery was an academic matter on the Islands since nobody had, or needed, or wanted any slaves, except such men as Pharaoh Farrow. There were two or three families of free Negroes on the Islands who took the name of families that had befriended them, but they were not, in so far as I have been able to discover any record or mention, absorbed into the racial picture of the Island. They existed, they fished, and for the most part, lived to themselves. They were a negligible element, mostly disappearing with the invaders, though some families continued down into this century.

The advent of a thousand North Carolina troops into the community must have had an impact that only such an Island could absorb with composure. Some few among the young men joined them, but for the most part the Islanders held aloof from the impending war. There were those, to be sure, among the resident population who welcomed them. Rollinson was among them, and he records in his Journal that he, together with his wife, went over to the fort on Sunday and had dinner with the commanding colonel.

But by nightfall there was ominous word from the Cape. The lookout in the Lighthouse reported that a fleet of ships had passed, well out to sea, and were even then rounding the Point of the Outer Diamond Shoals. And there was an entry in the Journal, hastily scrawled: ". . . the Bombardment of Fort Hatteras began on this Wednesday August 27th, 1861. . . ."

17

James Buchanan is remembered and mentioned on these Islands, not as the fifteenth President of the United States, or as one of only two bachelors to attain that exalted status, but as the uncle of Harriet Lane. She was the daughter of his sister and during his occupancy of the White House his official hostess. In her own right she must have been a young lady of great sense and charm and her name became a verb on these Islands. To be harriet laned is a discommoding experience.

Miss Lane is not remembered as herself but as the smartest and the most deadly ship to approach this coast in the nineteenth century. She was not a Navy ship until a Presidential order, in 1861, made her one. She was the first engine-driven cutter built for the U.S. Revenue Service, designed and constructed by William H. Webb. Her Allaire engine, working on two paddle wheels, could drive her ahead at speeds approaching twenty miles per hour, and the Prince of Wales, who had yet to wait forty-five years before he mounted the throne of the British Empire, said that she was the smartest ship in the world, and the fastest.

And certainly her crew thought so, and when Harriet Lane came aboard, as she did when the heir to the British crown was passenger, they thought also that the ship was worthily named. Harriet Lane and the *Harriet Lane* were of a kind and each worthy and representative of the other. The ship was known also in Japan and, in some part, must have become the prototype of that awakening empire's aspiration to have a navy which would be the equal of any on the earth. The Imperial Commission visiting the United States, with Miss Lane aboard as hostess, traveled from Washington to New York aboard her.

On the tenth day of July, 1861, the *Harriet Lane* approached within gunshot of Hatteras Inlet and let fly with three salvos directed against the forts being erected there by Confederate volunteer troops. These were the first hostile shots fired by the U.S. Navy at Southern-held territory. There was no damage, except pandemonium among the sweating soldiery engaged then in the erection of the two forts. There were no casualties of record, but the tale persists that two mainlander soldiers were drowned while trying to escape the Island by swimming Pamlico Sound.

This sleek cutter was no stranger to these waters. From the time she was commissioned, the *Harriet Lane* was busy. When she was not serving as a conveyance of visiting royalty she was at sea, patrolling the eastern coast of the United States, and her log relates that she had traveled as far south as Patagonia. It does not explain why. The immediate concern of the government was smuggling, especially slaves, and she from time to time looked in on the port of Hatteras. The Treasury Department did not leave everything to the Collector of the Port.

Compared to anything else then afloat the *Harriet Lane* romped instead of sailed. She was a proud ship. Members of the crew would, when she hove to off the Inlet, point out to anybody who came aboard—these included John W. Rollinson, though his intermittent journal is curiously silent about it—just where the youthful Prince of Wales stood while holding the hand of Miss Harriet Lane. It was there, on the top of the starboard paddle box. . . . And here rested the emissaries of the Emperor of Japan—and here, at this point on the rail, the chief of them had stood while emptying his stomach of whatever it contained.

Any young Coast Guardsman whose roots go down into the sand of these Islands can provide unrehearsed details. She was not a Navy ship. She was a Coast Guard boat. Not actually and technically, of course, but she belonged to the Cutter Service, which was combined with the Lifesaving Service in 1915, at the insistence of Josephus Daniels and William Gibbs McAdoo, and that made her, at least retroactively, a Coast Guard craft.

Nor do they hold it amiss that the *Harriet Lane* lobbed the first shell at this Island and so began the most dismaying epoch in its history. When she had delivered her premonitory salvo the ship departed to the northeast and rounded the Outer Diamonds. But seven weeks later, to the day, she was back again, jubilantly, and perhaps a little disdainfully, out-sailing and out-maneuvering every other ship in the horizon-filling armada that tagged along behind her.

Here were gunboats and battleships; troop transports and even a wallowing ferryboat taken off its harbor run in New York, leaving people who needed to get out of or into Brooklyn little to do but wait for the next ferry or get themselves a rowboat. The *Harriet Lane* came leading them, and with speed enough to scamper ahead, or to circle back and around her convoy. She was having a very splendid time, and those who watched her from the shore were sick with dismay. She had, somehow, turned traitor to them.

Some among those who watched her coming from the shore, from the parapets of the forts, sensed that she was not perhaps as frisky, as gracefully agile as she used to be when she had no graver task than peeping aboard some schooner to see if she had any black ivory from Africa. She didn't maneuver quite like she had and, as the Islanders were to discover within a day or two, there was sound reason. She carried, mounted on her open deck forward, the biggest cannon in the Western Hemisphere. It was a considerable load, the cannon itself and her ration of ammunition stored below.

After she had taken a few token cracks at the forts-abuilding seven weeks before, the *Harriet Lane* was ordered to Baltimore for refitting. The prodigious 15-incher was emplaced, and her whole armament renewed. She was stripped down for battle, but even so she was not as responsive to the wheel as she had been in the days of her blithe innocence. She was no longer, so to speak, the sea's sweetheart but a grim amazon girded for war. Still, she could knife through the water at twice the speed of anything else in the armada, and it was so that she came, of a Sunday afternoon, in late August.

All told there were seven ships mounting cannon, and behind them ranged the transports carrying troops and supplies. Their number and identity remains somewhat cloudy, and it cannot be said with any finality how many troops they fetched. One impregnable authority says there were 800 soldiers, and another, with equal authority, says there were 1,018, and about all that can be said with any certainty is to quote a lad of seventeen or so, currently a high school senior wrestling with an assigned theme. It will not be set down in his term paper, but privately he quotes his grandfather who, as a boy, witnessed the matter. Grandfather said there "was a hell of a mess of 'em."

About the cannon-carrying ships it is possible to be more definite, or at least to quote the Navy Records. The ships were the *Minnesota*, 47 guns; the *Wabash*, 46 guns; the *Cumberland*, 24 guns; the *Susquehana*, 15 guns; the *Pawnee*, 9 guns; the *Monticello*, 3 guns; and the *Harriet Lane*, 5 guns. The total is 149 guns, and it is reported officially that the aggregate of the seven ship-crews was 1,972.

And to oppose them there were two forts. Fort Clark, a square redoubt of sand stabilized with muck and grass from neighboring marshes, stood nearest the Inlet and the sea. It contained five elderly cannon of assorted calibres. Fort Hatteras, a mile eastward, halfway between the Inlet and the village, was a more pretentious structure. It was bigger and contained more cannon. There were twelve mounted 32-pounders and five not-yet-mounted guns, including a 10-inch Columbiad.

These are the totals in what would come to be called firepower. The invaders had 149 cannon and the defenders had 17 cannon mounted and five not yet mounted. The defenders had also 1,000 muskets, which meant that every man in the two forts could have had three muskets each if he had any need of them. The two forts were manned by 350 men of the Seventh North Carolina Volunteer Regiment commanded by Colonel William F. Martin. It is not clear, and has never been, what had happened to the rest of the outfit that came down in May, eleven days before North Carolina withdrew from the Union, and began building Fort Clark.

Some of them had been dispatched to Ocracoke under the command of Lieutenant Colonel G. W. Johnson. There is nowhere any intimation that any of them had been dispatched northward to man the newly erected fort commanding Oregon Inlet. But it is abundantly clear, in the recollection of the Islanders, that, militarily, it was not much of an outfit and that few or none of them knew anything about soldiering. Nor, on the other hand, was there ever any evidence that the invading troops, when they got ashore, knew much more.

It was not the Islanders' war and it never became the Islanders' war. It was at best a deplorable something that had come here to happen, and except for three or four men who somehow managed to get themselves caught in the fort when the shooting started and were so included among the prisoners of war, nobody had any hand in it except as unwilling spectators, as more-or-less innocent bystanders. The five hundred inhabitants of the village and the thousand or so inhabitants of the villages up the beach were a bewildered minority.

When it came to the somewhat academic matter of choosing between Lincoln and Douglas—afterward Tilden would overwhelm Hayes on the Island, which very likely has its significance—they could be sharply divided in their sympathies, but not to the extent of shooting anybody about it. They are just not the killer type. They had heard, of course, a lot of blood-hungry talk among the Confederate troops since they arrived in May, but few Islanders partook of this vengefulness.

What very likely concerned them more was, for instance, when would the *I. W. Hughes* be able to put to sea with her cargo of two hundred bales of cotton that had come down from Washington a good while back, headed for somewhere in the West Indies to deliver her cargo to some England-bound ship and fill her own holds with barrels of molasses. Molasses was coming to be pretty scarce around the village and in the upcountry. And that cargo of bananas that had come in, oh, it must have been two weeks ago, it was beginning to smell pleasantly of ripeness.

From Ocracoke Inlet to Oregon Inlet the Islanders waited uneasily. The smooth tranquillity of life was ruffled. Some of the Confederates were pretty overbearing, especially in their ruthless commandeering of boats and in demanding accommodations that did not exist and stores that were never heard of for the use of their forces. That stinking little boat, the *Neuse*, which had so upset Kinnakeet a dozen years before by pretending to be the Archangel Gabriel, came and went importantly, bearing messengers and colonels and other disturbing essences.

These were disturbed times. They had even taken the light out of the Lighthouse, and that was a profoundly disturbing thing to have happen. Some people, soldiers, had come down the beach with it in a cart, arriving on the heels of the messengers who had come with tidings that a strange fleet was passing southward offshore. The lantern, with its curiously-contrived reflectors, was hustled aboard a small steamer and carried off up Pamlico River to Washington. . . . It eventually got to Tarboro and there disappeared from history. Years of inquiry have disclosed no slightest clue as to what became of it thereafter.

For sixty years and more the light had been a sort of core of the Island's awareness. Whether one was on land or on sea it was there, and so long as it was there all was well with the world. Now it was gone, and there were those among the elderly devout who likened it to the Ark of the Lord, to the Pillar of Fire by Night. It was a bad thing to look up at night and not see Mr. Hamilton's Light burning. . . . Next thing the massive granite tower would be . . . no, that was unthinkable.

But it happened. No Islander can say, and no historian of either side has said definitely, what actually happened to the tower, but there came a morning when not much of it was left. Some maintain that the Confederates destroyed it, and others maintain, with equal vigor, that a Yankee gunboat came close inshore and knocked the top out of it. All that can be said with any certainty is that about thirty feet of the tower was gone. After their hold on the Island was secured the Federal forces set about repairing it, fetched brick from somewhere and restored it, adding about fifteen feet to its height. A new lantern was brought and once more the light reached out above the troubled Graveyard.

It was not Mr. Hamilton's Light, as the Islanders had spoken of it. Despite the absence of any record of these operations, it seems clearly indicated that repairs had been effected as early as the end of 1862, since on the night of December 31, 1862, the U.S.S. *Rhode Island*, with the *Monitor* in tow, logged the report at eleven o'clock that her position was eight miles east of Cape Hatteras Light.

Consternation came with the sight of the Federal fleet when the *Harriet Lane* led it across the Bight of Hatteras. Panic would be the more accurate word. Colonel Martin looked out of his fortification and dispatched messengers. Some went to Ocracoke, whither he had allowed half his command to go. He summoned help from wherever it might be found, and, to their credit, none who got the message hesitated. It is remembered that the forces deployed to Ocracoke, seventeen miles away, arrived at the height of the bombardment and landed, without casualty, under fire.

Commodore Samuel Barron emerged briefly into history. How he came to be in command of the Confederate forces in the eastern region, or his whereabouts when he got word from Colonel Martin, is obscure. But he arrived, and the first thing that Colonel Martin was aware of was that here was superior rank, here was somebody upon whose shoulders he could place responsibility that he was, apparently, unwilling to carry himself. At Martin's insistence Barron assumed command of the defense of the Islands.

It was Wednesday before the invading force was ready to launch the attack. The *Harriet Lane* led off, coming confidently inshore, well within range of the Confederate guns. She let go with her monstrous cannon, and the earth shook under the impact of its roar. Her massive shell fell against the outer face of the fort and exploded with another hellish roar. No damage was done the fort. Under Barron's direction the guns of the two forts answered this insolence, but ineffectively, though the vessel was hit at least five times on subsequent thrusts.

It was commodore against commodore now, 17 guns against 149 guns—and a new concept of naval tactics. Silas H. Stringham was in command of the Federal fleet. There is nothing in the books about where his new concept came from, and in the absence of anything of authority it may be reasonably assumed that he applied the *Harriet Lane* procedure to the entire operation. The lithe little revenue cutter had not even slowed her engines when she let go with her ponderous cannon.

Thereafter Stringham put his fleet in a column of ships and they steamed past the forts and, without stopping, as was naval usage, delivered broadsides from a moving platform against a fixed target. The little cutter, however, had only to aim her prow at the target and fire point-blank. Stringham's tactics were effective in a surprising degree. Most of his shots hit the target, and little of the return fire, when his ships were within the short range of the forts' guns, was able to hit a moving target from a fixed mount.

The bombardment continued throughout the day. A considerable tonnage of ordnance was lobbed against the forts, with only negligible damage, and toward nightfall the ships withdrew, breaking off the action until the morrow. But meanwhile the transports had worked their way inshore, and from them was launched the first wave of the landing force. This operation was undertaken three miles northeast of the forts and a mile beyond the village. A rising tide made the landing operation moderately hazardous and only partially successful.

And here was something else that was utterly new to the villagers: they heard for the first time blasphemy in the German tongue, but unmistakably blasphemy. The first to undertake the landing venture were elements of a German regiment raised hastily in New York, mostly from German immigrants, and mostly with previous military experience in the Prussian manner. They were good soldiers, but not for such undertakings as confronted them here. They were not good boatmen, and a lot of them got dunked in the ocean. None drowned. All swore in their guttural native tongue. Some were said also to have prayed.

But more was in store for such of the villagers as ventured out from the village to see what was going on. The bombardment was beginning to be tiresome. There appeared now some persons garbed in the most outlandish uniforms yet seen in combat on the American continent. They were elements of the Ninth New York Infantry, an organization patterned and named after French Zouave battalions that their commander had observed while touring Europe. Their garments were baggy-kneed as to pants and multicolored as to jackets, and the whole was topped off by a piratical cap that could have served also as a stocking. They looked no better than Webber's Germans when wet, but they swore in Irish.

Webber made another try at coming ashore and 318 of his men made it, under the baleful eye of Major General Benjamin Franklin Butler, who observed the landing from the quarterdeck of the *Minnesota*, which had withdrawn from harassing the forts to cover the landing. Night came on and Webber's men encamped wetly on almost the precise spot from which, sixty-two years and eight days later, Brigadier General Billie Mitchell would take off, in an undreamed-of ship, bent upon sinking two battleships off the point of the Outer Diamonds by dropping 1,100-pound bombs on them.

Night arrived, and quietly. There were now Webber's 318 wet troops encamped a mile northeast of the village, and within the two forts, there were, counting new arrivals—there had been no casualties—618 troops of the Confederacy. At nightfall the ships had withdrawn to deep water to anchor until morning. There arose discussion in the forts as to what to do. Some of the men wanted to take muskets and attack Webber's outfit three miles up the beach, insisting that they could be wiped out very thoroughly and simply by shooting them. It was generally assumed that their powder had also got wet and they couldn't shoot back which, as the Islanders remember, was quite literally true.

Commodore Barron had had enough shooting for one day. He had sent messengers to New Bern and to Washington and elsewhere for reinforcements. He elected to wait until he had sufficient troops for the offensive, and not one of the 1,000 muskets in the fort was loaded and fired. They were, along with all hands and equipment, surrendered the next day at noon, and so ended a battle that was to be heralded throughout the North as a stupendous victory, wholly offsetting the humiliating rout of the United States Army at Bull Run some weeks earlier.

Commodore Stringham resumed the bombardment of the two forts at seven o'clock while Colonel Webber's men dried themselves in the sun. Some elements of the Ninth New York, not very resplendent now in their wet red pants, got ashore, but no move was made to march on the two forts. Stringham then got it into his head that it would be helpful to bring some firepower to bear on the forts from inside the Inlet, since it was apparent that the defenders were huddled against the seaward walls and could not be brought into direct range of his guns.

Not surprisingly this task fell to the *Harriet Lane*. She was fast, heavily armed, and of shallow draft. Captain John Faunce viewed the undertaking with a degree of skepticism, and Stringham became peremptory. The *Harriet Lane* pointed her nose toward the forts and let go with all she had in her boiler and in her ammunition locker. She would turn to point her big gun at the fort, and while it was being reloaded, she would get back on a course that would take her through the Inlet. It looked, some of the observers reported and the inheritors remember, as if she was going to climb right out of the ocean and land right in the middle of the fort's quadrangle.

And then two things happened simultaneously: a white flag was run up on the fort's flagpole, and the *Harriet Lane*, as Captain Faunce had protested that she well might, ran aground. But for the white flag, and if there had been any man in the fort who felt like firing even a small cannon, she could have been pounded to bits as she lay helpless there with a sand bar under her keel. Her paddles were barely touching the water, and they thrashed away with great impotence. But the battle was over, and the Germans were marching boldly down the beach with some of the baggy-pants Zouaves wheezing mightily in an effort to march past them and get into the surrendered fort first. It was a dead heat.

Some remembered but nameless person among the sweating soldiery chanced to glance seaward and there observed a frantic agitation among the signalmen. Their wig-wagging, being interpreted, said for them to desist from their marching, and presently General Butler descended into his gig and was rowed ashore under the walls of the capitulated fort. In landing there was some evidence that the sea is no respector of rank, and the General's pants were somewhat bedraggled, even when he was taken on the shoulders of some of the boat's crew and toted out of reach of the tide. His whiskers were in some disarray as he trudged toward the fort to lay hold upon the palm of victory.

These matters went unobserved aboard the *Harriet Lane*. By now she was canted up on her side in the chop of the sea and her master afterward remembered this as a not unhappy circumstance. The wind freshened and the seas broke against her bottom instead of over her decks. And this also facilitated such expedients as became presently necessary. The pot-bellied cannon, the fabulous 15-incher, was loosened from its moorings, and it toppled into the Inlet where it still must remain. It was not salvaged and the sand took it for its own. All other cannon aboard were dumped overboard, together with all munitions and such stores as were not immediately needed.

There was other damage. Her boiler had become unseated, and her engine's shaft, the axle upon which were impaled the hubs of her two massive paddle wheels, was out of plumb. The *Harriet Lane* was in a considerable fix and nobody, in the excitement of victory, or of defeat, offered her any attention. The crew were compelled to do the best they could, which, within forty-eight hours, was enough. She floated, hoisted some sail, and was maneuvered out of reach of the sand bars that were thick and treacherous around the Inlet. It required three days more to get her boiler back on its bed, her engine back in plumb.

Thereafter she limped, almost unobserved, away from the war and headed for Newport News whither, as she had hoped, she would bring first tidings of great victory. It was September 6 before she made port in Hampton Roads, and news of the operation against the forts at Hatteras Inlet was blazoned already across the front pages of every paper north of Washington. There were bonfires and surging parades in New York where, as it appeared, the Ninth had, with virtually no help from anybody, subdued the rebellion against the United States. Webber's Germans were scarcely mentioned as being among those present.

It was the end of the *Harriet Lane's* glory. She limped up to Philadelphia for repair and refitting, and there ensued one of war's more stupid confusions. The Navy Department refused to pay the crew's wages, and the Treasury Department also declined to pay them on the allegation that the ship was no longer in its service but the Navy Department's. Through all the months of her refitting, the crew, including the commander, moped moneyless about Philadelphia until the red tape was untangled. The crew got their pay and discharged their debt to the Girard House, which had decently extended them credit they did not have with their own government.

But there was no longer magic in her name. She returned to service, but not with a massive cannon. For a year or two she patrolled the coast when the war was over but was soon sold to private owners and renamed the *Helene Ritchie*. Once or twice she came to Hatteras and to the Inlet when she was in the West Indian trade as a schooner. She was lost in a hurricane in the West Indies in 1877, and she is remembered in the Coast Guard and on Hatteras Island as the smartest and ablest-manned cutter of her day. The Islanders bear her no resentment but, rather, share the pride with which all Coast Guardsmen remember her.

General Butler entered the fort and was greeted with uneasy silence. Commodore Barron had quit command of it, and the surrender was negotiated by Colonel Martin. He surrendered the fort, himself, the commodore, his officers and men as prisoners of war. It is remembered on the Islands that General Butler was somewhat surly in his transaction of business and that he looked around from time to time "wondering what they had done with the bodies." There were no bodies and the General appeared to take it amiss that there were none. All that powder and shot and nobody killed.

After a hundred years there is perhaps nobody to care very much, one way or the other, but at the moment there was very bitter dissension, and some nose-bloodying, about which of the troops got to the fort first. There were street fights, between Irish and German immigrants, in New York, and the Irish appear to have won history's argument. So it would appear that Colonel Rush C. Hawkins, twenty-nine years old, beautifully mustached and wondrously caparisoned in red pants, sword, pistols, and other appurtenances, had got ashore, rallied the elements of his Ninth Regiment, and was on hand to take over the fort.

The fort and the prisoners. These, numbering 670 men, including the commodore and the colonel, were herded together, and the following day, while the *Harriet Lane* still struggled with the sand bar, they were taken to the anchored transports standing offshore. Small boats that landed detachments of soldiery from the transports carried back cargoes of prisoners, and by the Sabbath day all troops were ashore, all prisoners aboard, mostly on the chartered steamer *Adelaide*, Captain H. S. Steelwagen of Philadelphia, master.

Prisoners, after processing at Fortress Monroe, were sent first to New York, where they were observed with a joyful clamor, and thence to Boston, where they were deafened by the jeers of the populace. Most of them were afterward exchanged, and the Seventh Regiment was reconstituted and gave a good account of itself in the war's later stages. It is not clear what became of the 1,000 muskets which were surrendered unused, or the cannon, which had been used to such little effect.

So soon as they were ashore the invaders tucked themselves in. Headquarters was established at the already mentioned point where the German regiment had got themselves wet in the interest of national security. Pillage began immediately and was sternly suppressed by Colonel Hawkins. Or at least orders to that effect were promptly issued but were not observed with any notable fidelity. Perhaps the effect of eating too many too ripe bananas had more weight than orders, but five men had already succumbed to dysentery. The shipload of cotton was seized and sent to Boston.

Many of the inhabitants had fled. What proportion of them can not now be determined, but it is very likely that everybody who could get away was gone by the time the troops began to deploy from the surrendered forts. It is related in John Rollinson's Journal that he, with his family, got as far as Cape Hatteras, twelve miles away, by nightfall, and that they spent that night with the Williams family. The next day they continued northward and on Monday crossed the Sound into Hyde County. These Islands had become occupied territory and would so continue for a long time to come. Within two months Hatteras village, tenanted almost wholly by the invaders, was proclaimed the capital of the reportedly retrieved State of North Carolina. By then John Rollinson was negotiating for the rent of a farm in Hyde County, where he grew considerable crops of corn in the next four or five years. There was nothing to eat on Hatteras Island.

18

They remember, on these Islands, the day Johnny Barnes went out of life. It was September 2, 1861. It is not likely that a direct question will get you an answer, certainly not until it becomes clear why you have asked, and then the answer will depend. It will depend upon whether the Island's instincts suggest that you would understand how they feel about Johnny Barnes if they told you about him. It is not that they don't know about him. They remember him, and the memory has shaped the feelings of the Islanders for almost a century.

In life Johnny Barnes was not a figure of consequence. Five times the census enumerators passed him over, and even the official report of his killing speaks of him merely as an unidentified rebel who was shot because, instead of halting as he was commanded to do, he started running. The sentry did not know and his superiors did not bother to discover that Johnny Barnes was, and had been from birth, stone deaf and that he was running to get home and protect his aging and widowed mother from the advancing horde of people who wore baggy red pants.

It happened in Little Kinnakeet, the north village that is no longer there. The forty-odd houses that were left when its little harbor filled up were loaded on barges and moved down to Big Kinnakeet which became Avon. But the house in which the Widow Barnes lived alone with her only son, deaf Johnny Barnes, had long since passed into other hands. The name vanished from the Island and the last record I have found of it is a listing among the purchasers of some items from the estate of Isaac Hooper, deceased. That was eighty years ago.

They remember on these Islands that Johnny Barnes was a magician when it came to woodworking tools and that all of his life he worked in the yards where ships were built in the two villages of Kinnakeet. He knew only his work and his devotion to his mother who, alone among the people of the villages, could understand his look, his gesture, the rudimentary sounds that he could make with his lips. . . . There was none left, after the strange and ferocious men in baggy red pants came, to carve his name on a cedar slab, but the Islanders remember that he was fifty-three years old when he was killed in September, 1861.

Johnny Barnes was the only man to die by gunfire in the fantastic battle for Hatteras Island, or in the mounting of the offensive from the Island against the mainland of North Carolina and southern Virginia. At one stage of the campaign there were not less than 25,000 troops on the two Islands and, especially in the days immediately following the surrender of the two Confederate forts at Hatteras Inlet, there was an improbable expenditure of black powder. Perhaps never in the history of war has there been so much shooting and so little killing.

Occupation of the two Islands was effected with so little blood-letting because the Islanders, for the most part, fled. There was little else they could do. It was not, in fact, their war, and those who had come to repel this invasion of them had surrendered without much resistance. There was, in the Kinnakeet villages, only a handful of the inhabitants left. Johnny Barnes and his mother had remained, very likely, because neither could quite comprehend what was happening and could be expected to happen when the soldiers from the North came.

Actually they came from the south. Within a day after the landing was effected at the Inlet, after the forts surrendered, the Ninth New York was in full cry, and their young colonel was sending urgent word back to the command at Fortress Monroe for the other six companies of his regiment to be sent to him at once. General Butler had repaired to Fortress Monroe, leaving Hawkins in command to cultivate "friendly relations with the inhabitants" and to cajole them back into the Union.

Hawkins' scattered Ninth New York, some elements of which had been deployed about the countryside in Virginia when the Hatteras Expedition was mobilized, were reunited on Hatteras Island. Webber and his German volunteers drew the assignment to Ocracoke to suppress rebellion, and no more was heard of them. They were replaced on Hatteras Island by the Twentieth Indiana Infantry under command of Colonel W. L. Brown. But the over-all command of the expedition was in the hands of the young New Yorker who had been so taken with the smart appearance of France's Zouaves.

Colonel Hawkins was not a professional military man, though he became a good soldier after some seasoning and, or so the Islanders heard, was wounded at Antietam some while afterward. But his major task on the Island was to maintain, in the higher echelons, the fiction that a massive victory had been achieved on these Islands and that more troops were required to keep the inhabitants in a submissive state and to continue the wresting of territory from the enemies of the United States.

As the Islanders look back upon it the victory must have been vastly magnified in the North, and as fast as communication and transportation would allow there began to arrive a motley crew of persons who hoped to have a helping of glory, and of such profit as might accrue. The historians, on both sides, for the most part ignore the campaign, the Southerners because there was little in it that they could recall and record in pride, and the Northerners perhaps with a measure of shame because of the gullibility that had magnified a relatively insignificant encounter into a great battle.

Hawkins had his troubles and soon. There was not a hostile soldier on the Island after the surrender of the forts, and within a week half the native population of the Island had fled to the mainland. There was, to be sure, a half-finished fort on the north shore of Oregon Inlet, fifty miles away, and there were scattered troops on Roanoke Island, a dozen miles above. But they were scarcely a menace to anybody, and it is unlikely that there were as many as a dozen muzzle-loaders among the native population. They were not and are not yet a gun-toting people.

But it was an active time and every day there were expeditions sent out from the headquarters at Hatteras village to explore and subdue. On the seventh day of September a detachment numbering about two hundred men was sent north to repel what was reported to be a counterattack mounted from Oregon Inlet. Some of the Islanders had reported that a thousand men had landed at Chicamicomico and were marching southward to recapture the Lighthouse, which, by then, had suffered mysterious damage.

There was, again, no fighting. A scouting detail, looking eastward from about where this house stands, sighted a little group of Confederate scouts looking at the Lighthouse from a point about the same distance north. Each group must have reported to its leaders that they were about to be attacked in full force, and both detachments repaired precipitately to their bases. The Confederates retired to Chicamicomico and to their three little boats, and the Zouaves trudged twelve miles back to their camp. The Confederates had twice as far to go to reach their base. There was no gunfire, and no shedding of blood, but marching in these sands, in September, can induce a lot of sweat.

And now the first blow to Colonel Hawkins' pride befell. There arrived from Washington a fat civilian, with important connections, who wanted a helping of glory. He arrived quite drunk, and Hawkins bluntly disdained the orders he presented and refused to accept him into his regiment, much less assign him to top staff duty. There had arrived also a full brigadier general, remembered as General Williams, who did have authority. Upon Hawkins' refusal to honor the fat one's credentials, he was relieved of command of his own regiment.

Outraged and jobless Hawkins took off for Washington. He was technically under arrest, but there seemed to be nobody around ready to undertake the enforcing of confinement. Hawkins went to Washington. He saw not only the entire cabinet but President Lincoln himself, and for the better part of a day he presented a persuasive picture. There had been a great Federal victory at Hatteras and the whole of the State of North Carolina was ready to capitulate before a show of force, and from this place an expedition should be mounted that would fan out west, south, and north until Norfolk was entered through its back door, and Raleigh would surrender when New Bern, Washington, and other centers of the rebellion were taken.

Hawkins returned to Hatteras and, by no less authority than a Presidential order, to the command of his regiment and of the Federal forces assigned to the area. Nobody remembers what became of the fat favorite from Washington or what happened to Brigadier General Williams. And not only was Hawkins in command of all that he could see; he was directed and empowered to take over the most secret planning of a more massive invasion of North Carolina and southeastern Virginia. Norfolk, which commanded the south shore of Hampton Roads, would be taken from the rear.

But there had been mischief done during the colonel's absence in Washington and a great humiliation visited upon the triumphant invaders. The Confederates had captured the *Fanny*. This boat

was a son of glorified tugboat acting as troop transport and gunboat. She had a small cannon mounted forward, and on October
1, 1861, she was dispatched northward with thirty men of the
Twentieth Indiana and eleven men of the Ninth New York to be of
such assistance as she could in repelling any counterattack of the
Confederates from Roanoke Island.

As of that day the military situation was nebulous. There
were reports that Colonel A. R. Wright had two thousand men
marching down from Oregon Inlet to retrieve Hatteras Island
from the invaders. There were gunboats in the Sound and in the
sea offshore and there were about five hundred men, women, and
children, residents of the villages down the Island. They had got
that far in their efforts to get off the Island and to a place of some
tranquillity. It was an uncomfortable place for them to be: on the
east and the west sides of them, warships, and to the south an
advancing Federal army. From the north, reportedly, a force of two
thousand Confederates. The Islanders were caught in the middle of
what would, undoubtedly, become a fearsome carnage.

In the course of the day there was a considerable expenditure of
powder in every quarter, except from the north. The Confederates
were just not there. The Federals advanced with the utmost caution
from the south and the gunboats fired with great diligence. So busy
was the *Fanny* firing toward the huddled lot of Islanders just north
of the village that two small Confederate sloops, under sail, were
able to come upon her without being noticed. There was nothing
to do but surrender and they did. The Confederates took the
tugboat and its cannon and its crew hastily to Roanoke Island.
Three of the crew were converted to the Confederacy and so were
listed in the Ninth's roster as "deserted to the enemy." The *Fanny's*
boiler exploded during the battle of Roanoke Island the following
February but without killing anybody.

Chicamicomico's massive grunting and marching at any rate
disposed of a phantom army of two thousand Confederates and
retained for poor Johnny Barnes the distinction of being the only
human being dispatched by gunfire throughout the campaign

that began when the *Harriet Lane* fired her exploratory salvo into the builders of a fort back in July. When the huddled inhabitants were sure the firing was over they continued their dispersal. Some of them, by whatever means they could lay hand to, went across the Sounds. Others returned to their homes, and some of them signed the Oath of Allegiance, and there was a kind of peace on the Islands.

Peace, in so far as actual military operations went, but there was much running to and fro of men bearing messages, of men bearing commands and commissions. Arriving they found Colonel Hawkins engaged in literary statesmanship. He was engaged, in a house that still stands in Hatteras village, in the preparation of an "Address to the People of North Carolina." The peroration of the address, a copy of which still survives on the Island, said, "We come to give you back law, order, the Constitution and your rights under it, and to restore peace." The Islanders would have preferred a loaf or two of bread—and that the Colonel's red-pants soldiers desist from their thieving.

And to his superiors he reported, in a document that was not known on the Island, "I regret to be compelled to state to you that the conduct of the men and some of the officers of the Twentieth New York Volunteers has been that of vandals. They have plundered and destroyed. . . . I saw party after party come in, some of them headed by commissioned officers loaded down with the result of their plundering." Colonel Hawkins was not having an easy time, and in the midst of these troubles Marble Nash Taylor returned from New York.

When Hawkins was conferring with President Lincoln he set forward the suggestion that, from his observation, the majority of the people in eastern North Carolina were at heart loyal to the Union and that a provisional government should be established. Lincoln considered the proposal and afterward set down in writing the added suggestion that the post of governor of such a redeemed state might be a suitable job for "Seward's boy." Seward's boy took to the notion of being governor of the first redeemed state with great avidity, and there were communications from him to be read, considered, and acknowledged. He was all set to come down and take over when the unfrocked Methodist preacher from Virginia arrived. Taylor was accompanied by Charles Henry Foster, a native of Maine, a graduate of Bowdoin College and, apparently, a man of flexible convictions. He had edited a pro-slavery paper, but now he was all for the Union, and he aspired to be a Congressman from the first district to be redeemed. These were the first carpetbaggers to penetrate the South.

After looking the local situation over and hearing about "Seward's boy," the pair departed from New York, riding the crest of the wave of the great victory in the South. There was a mass meeting presided over by no less a man than the historian George Bancroft and attended by such notables as William Cullen Bryant, William B. Astor, and the merchant prince A. T. Stewart. Taylor was vastly eloquent and pictured the redemption of North Carolina as an accomplished fact, needing only the implementation of a little financial help to become a militant reality.

They appear to have got the money, largely from Astor and Stewart. They returned by way of Washington and no more was heard of Seward's boy. There was considerable ado about the convention of the people to be held at Hatteras on the eighteenth of November at which would be present the chosen loyal representatives of forty-five eastern North Carolina counties. The Navy Department gladly furnished Taylor and Foster with special transportation and their ship rounded Cape Hatteras on November 15. They graciously gave audience to Colonel Hawkins and permitted him to examine their credentials authorizing them to set up the liberated government.

Eight people attended the convention. Hawkins was not among them. Four of them were residents of the Island who had returned to their homes after the Battle of Chicamicomico and had, for convenience if not from conviction, signed the Oath of Allegiance. There were two people, J. W. Bailey being one of them, present from across the Sound in Hyde. There seems to have been little occasion for the making of speeches, and it was not until the next day that Taylor and Foster issued their proclamation, written in the best Bowdoin English by Foster.

Hatteras was proclaimed the capital of the redeemed State of North Carolina and Marble Nash Taylor the governor thereof. An election was to be held forthwith in a district containing Hyde County, of which the Island was then a part. The Honorable Charles Henry Foster would be the candidate for Congress. He was duly elected, apparently by proclamation, and presented with his credentials for admission into the sitting Congress. They refused also to issue him expense money and with that the matter dropped.

Taylor strutted and declaimed in the village for some while and insisted that Colonel Hawkins address him as Governor. The military commander had little time now for the amenities of civil affairs. He was excruciatingly busy with military matters, and by December he knew that early in 1862 the most formidable expedition ever put together by the government of the United States, until then and for long afterward, would sail from Hampton Roads under sealed orders, not to be opened until the expedition was one day at sea.

No amount of sounding the waters of local folklore, or examination of such records as exist, sheds any light upon the subsequent career and disposition of Marble Nash Taylor, Governor of the redeemed State of North Carolina. He appears simply to have become engulfed in what was to happen shortly, and after that it would have taken more than his frenzied eloquence and the gullibility of William Cullen Bryant to gain him much notice. North Carolina was just not yet redeemed, and there would be a good deal of killing before it was. Governor Taylor just vanishes.* Both

---

*This shadowy figure vanished from Hatteras Island and from history but lived out the rest of his life in North Carolina, as carpetbagger, as pracher, and finally as fruit tree salesman, and was burried in Moore County in 1894. I am profoundly grateful to Mrs. Rose Cochran McLean for an eyewitness account of his fantastic funeral. —B.D.M.

Methodist and Baptist denominations, under whose cloaking he had once preached, had repudiated him. The name does not appear in any record that survives on the Island.

These Islands, and much of the rest of the world, remember General A. E. Burnside, mostly for his whiskers, which have never become fashionable in the region in which the expedition that also bears his name was to operate. General Burnside's expedition emerged from Hampton Roads, after hearing a lot of band music at Fortress Monroe, on January 11, 1862, and in due season the orders were opened. The orders, as virtually everybody knew, directed the expedition to proceed to Hatteras Inlet forthwith and to return to Hampton Roads by way of Norfolk's back door, capturing the city.

General Burnside's whiskers became visible on Hatteras Island on January 14, and the resident wonder at their curious magnificence diverted, in some measure, the native attention from what was accumulating in the Bight of Hatteras. The General came ashore as soon as his flagship made anchorage in the Bight and established himself in quarters prepared outside the village and near a point, now marked with a cast-iron tablet, from which General Billie Mitchell took off to sink two battleships sixty-one years later.

No marker mentions the occupancy of the site by General Burnside, but it was there that the Islanders got their first sight of the whiskers that were as outlandish as the whiskers of the, by now, notorious Edward Teach in an earlier day. The General was among the first of his expedition's twenty-odd thousand men to come ashore, and he was greeted respectfully by Colonel Hawkins, whose own whiskers provided no competitive notice.

There was sound reason for Burnside's haste to be off his ship and to get dry land, such as it was, under his feet. It is remembered that such of his face as could be seen among his beard was greenish. He was seasick. It had been an exceedingly rough passage around the Shoals, and there were 20,000 other people not feeling at all well. So unwell did the General feel that signals were hoisted for a doctor to come ashore, and in response Colonel J. W. Allen of the Ninth New Jersey Infantry embarked, with his regimental surgeon, in a small boat to come in and minister to him.

General Burnside felt better after the administration of some paregoric, and Colonel Allen and Surgeon F. A. Weller began their return trip to their ship. Both were drowned and their bodies were not recovered. The sea's anger continued for eight days, and throughout most of this period it looked as if general disaster could not be avoided. There were eighty-two ships in the fleet, ranging from Erie Canal boats and Brooklyn ferryboats to ponderous battleships, and the sea was in a frightening mood.

Seventeen of the ships were smashed. The big transport *City of New York* was the first to be beached and broken up, a total loss. Her crew and troops reached shore without casualty, but their equipment was lost. The gunboat *Zouave* foundered and her one hundred artillery horses—and the General's saddle horse—had a bad time of it. Some of them made it to shore but sickened of pneumonia and died. There was not much of anything that anybody could do until the sea had been calmed, which did not occur until January 22.

An evil time was had by everybody. Drinking water gave out on every ship and there was none to be had ashore. Aboard they spread sail to catch rainwater, since it rained steadily for the week. Salt spray contaminated the water so caught, and the men got sicker and sicker, and there persists a certainty on the Islands that a good many of the ship-held troops, unable to take any more, went over the side and to death. There is nowhere any official confirmation of the story, but it is not wholly unreasonable.

But the weather calmed and the convoy began its back-breaking task of making port. The northeaster had played havoc with the channel, and the charts were awry. The wind and the tides had shifted a lot of sand around, and the first ship that tried to get through went aground in the Inlet. Whereupon Admiral L. M. Goldsborough invoked an expedient that is even now common practice when any kind of boat gets stuck—turn her propeller and let it scour out the sand.

Into the Inlet the Admiral sent the most powerful ship in his command. Her bow hit sand but her crew moved everything movable toward the stern while her paddle-wheels continued to thrash. While the wheels stirred up sand the ebbing tide moved it toward the sea, and after a day the vessel had burrowed her way into the relatively deeper water inside. Other ships, astern, were in line and continued to keep the water agitated. After five days of this the fleet reached harbor, sixty-five ships, all told, and the Burnside Expedition took a day off to recover from as savage a beating as the sea has given any expedition.

Three-quarters of a century must pass before Mr. Hanson Baldwin would enrich the language with the word "logistics" and editors almost everywhere, and radio announcers as well, would feel compelled to define the word, but the problem of logistics in this first long-range military operation undertaken by the United States raised its unkempt head inside Hatteras Inlet. Military usage, up to now, had been for invading forces to live off the country when and if they took it. The Federal fleet had these Islands but they couldn't live off them.

Most acute at the end of January, 1862, with the invasion already three weeks behind schedule, was a supply of fresh water for the boilers of sixty-five vessels and some dry wood with which to kindle a fire under them. Then, as now, the villages of these Islands, except that one lying along these ridges, depended for their domestic water on the rains. When rain fell it was piped down from the roof into cypress-walled cisterns, and that is still the procedure.

Enough rain had fallen in these past two weeks to fill every cistern in creation, but there were few cisterns left in the village. Twenty thousand men, thirsty after two weeks at sea, can drink a lot of water, and the cisterns were dried where they stood. And there was the added problem of some fuel that would convert water, if they had it, into steam enough to propel the invasion northward toward glory and the entrenched Confederacy on Roanoke Island. It was a gloomy business and it was thirteen days before any workable solution was discovered.

While some were detailed to tear any needed buildings apart and convert them into fuel, others were sent to learn logistics from the wild horses and the wild cattle that roamed the Islands, or such of them as had not been killed off for something to eat.

The horses especially had adapted themselves to need, and when they were thirsty they pawed a hole in the earth. The hole soon filled up with non-brackish if not very palatable water. . . . The horses remaining on Ocracoke Island still follow the instincts of their forbears—and the expedients of Burnside's troopers.

Much of the Island, in that day, was still covered with forest, but green, freshly-cut pine does not burn readily, and the invader's plans required fuel that would burn lustily. The furnaces under steam boilers had not yet been adapted to coal. In Hatteras village especially there were dwellings, warehouses, stores from which their owners had fled before the first wave of the invasion the preceding September. Most of them were occupied by Colonel Hawkins' people, but Burnside's people evicted them by the simple expedient of tearing down the houses and converting them into firewood.

There is nowhere any intimation that Colonel Hawkins protested. He would join the invasion force here and proceed northward, and it is not unlikely that his own men lent a willing hand to the destruction of the houses that had, in some part, sheltered them. The inhabitants, such few as had remained in residence after making a sort of peace with the invaders by signing the Oath of Allegiance, watched in numb silence out of which would evolve a bitter hatred that continued unabated, even down to the year 1936, when the native Southern Methodist churches, seven in number, refused flatly to be reunited with their Northern brethren in the Methodist Church of the United States and disavowed wholly the name of Methodist.

It is remembered on the Islands that General Burnside, defrauded of his saddle horse by the sea's distemper, kept mostly to his headquarters, and such as had matters for him to determine came to him. It was an inclement time, as it almost always is on these Islands at that season of the year. Although the thermometers do not show it, the weather can feel colder on that exposed beach than anywhere. I have been assured by my current neighbors among the

Seabees that the weather in Newfoundland, from whence a good many of them came here, is warmer with the thermometer at zero than it is here with the thermometer at forty degrees Fahrenheit. Considerable fuel was required to keep the General from feeling like he was freezing to rigidity, and his fabulous whiskers seem not to have warmed him noticeably.

And there was the feverish work entailed by the unscrambling of troop elements as they came ashore. The landings were made when and as they could be made. Altogether there were sixteen regiments and two added battalions, and they were considerably scrambled when they got off the ships that had fetched them to the Island. Massachusetts contributed five regiments, Connecticut three, New York three, New Jersey one, Pennsylvania one, New Hampshire one, and Rhode Island one. In addition New York contributed a battalion of the Union Coast Guard, and Rhode Island a battalion of artillery.

It was, as the Islanders remember it and describe it, a mess. The whole earth seemed to be swarming with a disordered mass of dirty, undisciplined people. At most there were never more than five hundred of the resident population of the village in that period, and even these seemed often to crowd it. But now there were forty times that many, added to the thousand or so men under Hawkins' command and the Twentieth Indiana Infantry, which appears from its records and the recollections of it that have become folklore to have been sort of housekeepers. Some of them were put to the task of repairing the Lighthouse, and a shipload of brick had been unloaded in the Bight for that purpose.

The village's harbor is not large. It was no larger in 1862 than it is now, and the fleet of the invaders found it an uncomfortable anchorage. The harbor faces north, and almost any day in winter, and sometimes in other seasons, the harbor "gets a shift." That is to say, the wind will whip around to the north and come sweeping across thirty-six miles of open, unobstructed Sound water. It can get very cold and very rough and immensely bleak.

General Burnside, who did not, as a matter of fact, originate a style of whiskers but borrowed from Prince Bismarck, whom he admired greatly, had with him on the expedition, as subordinate commanders, three classmates at the military academy, John G. Foster, Jesse L. Reno, who afterward had a celebrated town named for him when he fought Indians in the West, and John G. Parke. It is remembered and related on the Islands and may very well be true that by now the invaders had caught and subdued and saddled four wild horses, and that on the morning of February 5, three weeks and one day after he came ashore, General Burnside mounted the horse that was provided him and managed to stay aboard it until he reached the harbor one mile away. He was attended by his three classmate generals, also mounted, and as the party approached, the sixty-five ships waiting in or about the harbor used up some of their steam by blasting three times in concert with their whistles.

It was the signal of departure, and never had the ears of the Islanders heard so grateful and pleasing a sound. Only some fragmentary elements of the Twentieth Indiana remained, and they seemed to be glad to see the expedition depart, too. The generals boarded the flagships, General Burnside taking passage with Admiral Goldsborough, and sixty-five anchors were hoisted. The ships went northward and by noon even their smoke was scattered and lost in the haze above Pamlico Sound.

There was then peace in the village, and desolation.

And there was starvation. There was scarcely a boat left in the harbor that could make it across the Sound where the stores of corn were. There was also, across the Sound, uncertainty. And in any case, the Islanders had nothing left that they might trade for corn, or for other stores that might be eaten. The Islanders were now acquainted with hunger, and ahead of them lay years of privation, the remembering of which is acute in the fifth generation of their descendants.

There were tidings, the next day, from the north. The armada had passed grandly, with small, frisky gunboats running hither and thither and shooting off their guns in an abandon of merriness. There was the story, possibly apochryphal, of the small gunboat which approached the little settlement four miles south of

Chicamicomico and the boat's commander inquiring of his gunnery officer what its name might be. The gunnery officer looked at his rude chart and reported that it did not have a name.

And the captain said, "Give it a salvo anyhow," and it was done. The gunnery officer wrote down the name "Salvo" at the proper place on the chart, and the village continues now to be known as Salvo. The Islanders heard the little tale with wry humor and preserved it and then they remembered Johnny Barnes. . . . The invaders were gone but the memory of them remained greenly, and remains.

19

Across the Sound, in Hyde County, John Rollinson was learning to plow. He was thirty-five years old and, except by hearsay, he had no acquaintance with mule flesh nor with plowing. He was an able seaman, something of a scholar, and already something also of a philosopher, a quality that stood him in good stead. He had need of philosophy in dealing with unaccustomed problems concerned mainly with the necessity of feeding his children, his wife, and himself and, as time wore on, kinsmen and neighbors from the Islands who came.

There was also, and additionally, the problem of being a fugitive with a price, not specified, on his head. He was guilty, in the thinking of the military, of giving aid to and consorting with those in rebellion against the government of the United States. He was suspected of having counseled with people who called themselves privateers but who were denominated pirates by the provisional government set up in his own house in Hatteras village by an unfrocked clergyman. Life was not bright with prospect.

Hyde County, after the first rush of the invasion, was a place of relative quiet. It was off the traveled rivers, a lush backwater country, with no towns worth capturing. The invasion went past to the north and to Norfolk by midsummer, fanned out to take in all of the towns with which he had been familiar as Collector of the Port of Hatteras. Edenton, Elizabeth City, Plymouth, Washington, and New Bern succumbed to the invasion mounted from his own village.

In that era Hyde was the richest agricultural county in North Carolina. Its plantations spread widely and produced prodigally. There were slaves outnumbering their white masters three to one, and the black rich earth produced cotton and corn in abundance and without fertilizer or overmuch cultivation. Most of the able-bodied whites had gone off to the war, and it was with no difficulty whatever that John Rollinson found lands to rent. He knew little about farming. There were not, on all of his Island, five acres of cultivated ground.

He could learn. His learning came easily and rapidly, but there followed him home, when he came, a thing that had become a county-wide jest in Hyde—John Rollinson never could remember, when telling his mules which direction to take, to say "gee" and "haw" but admonished them with "port" and "starboard," even as later generations of Hyde County and other farmers were, in vehicular emergencies, to call their T-models to "woah."

But he learned, and there are occasional jottings of notes in the arithmetic textbook that became a journal that indicated his progress. Collaterally it is known that he had, when he became a fugitive and a refugee, some gold money that stood him in good stead and he, of course, had his journal with him. He even found the time, in winter, to conduct a school for such of the plantation owners' children as could be got together. The land responded nobly to his energy and he made a bountiful crop the first year.

Military authorities looked with a jaundiced eye upon any sort of traffic between the Outer Islands and the mainland, but a good deal of John Rollinson's crop of corn found its way back to Hatteras and to the other villages, and the second year some of his maritime neighbors joined him on the mainland, renting acreages for themselves and producing enough to live on. But they were, always, homesick. They wanted to be back on their own Island, back at sea, back in the Sounds fishing.

By 1863 and the second year of his exile John Rollinson was no longer fleeing from the government. He made no humiliating concession by signing the Oath of Allegiance, and it is a circumstance of some importance that when he applied to the military commander of the mainland he was accorded permission and safe-conduct to revisit his home village for a space of two weeks. He was depressed by what he found, not only in his own village but in Ocracoke, where he stopped off en route from Washington to the Outer Banks. He returned, not unwillingly, to his rented acres. The young corn needed weeding—and his neighbors on the Outer Banks needed corn. The windmills stood, somehow undamaged, in their villages, and idle.

King Pharaoh Farrow was dead and the invaders had, with a peevish sort of ferocity, broken his massive gravestone and tumbled it down in the sand. His goods and chattels were scattered, pillaged, and his half dozen slaves were taken, the men to be freed into an unrewarded new slavery as servants and the women to be put to such uses as they had not known when they were slaves. Only the Farrow land was left, scores of tracts of it, the title to which would, in another era, plague the land-title legal experts of the government endlessly.

Stagnation and hunger lay deep along the Islands, and in the northernmost of the villages young Bannister Midgett continued in an illiteracy that would, in time, become his boast and hallmark. . . . In the woods around the village that was called Trent young Abraham Midgett grew apace and became the marvel of all who knew him. Nobody could understand how any body could grow so much when there was so little for him to eat. Already his strength was a thing of legend.

There were fish in the ocean and in the Sounds, and the sea continued, in her wayward, often erratic fashion, to bring her strange gifts. There were, to be sure, soldiers about but they, like the inhabitants, had become listless, passively inert. They looked with disfavor upon the natives when they were restless; issued orders against their immemorial habit of walking the beach, especially after a blow of wind, to see if anything had washed up.

Sometimes there were things. Useful, edible things, and some days there would be gruesome, terrifying things. As on the morning of the third day of the New Year, some who walked along the beach came upon the water-grimed body of a man in blue clothes, what there was of them. And then, a little further along, above the Light-house which the Twentieth Indiana now had back in commission, another. There were five of them.

One among the dead men looked somehow familiar, and some of the older men of the village came. They knew him, indeed, and his body, there where the tide had left it, occasioned no sorrow. Some of his people were sent for and they declined to so much as come and look at him. For them he had died when he put on the Federal uniform. They had heard that he was a member of the crew of a strange and reportedly terrible new sort of a boat. They called it the *Monitor* and it had spread terror around Norfolk. There were some who had even seen the vessel, and what one Islander has seen, all Islanders have looked at vicariously.

Some men from a detachment of the Twentieth Indiana came from their camp in the lee of the repaired Lighthouse, half a mile back from the sea, and looked at what was there. It was not a sight to gladden anybody. The bodies had apparently been in the water for two or three days, and some of the soldiers speculated idly about where they came from. They remembered that, midafternoon of the last day of the year, they had observed, well offshore, a big ship towing something that lay low upon the water.

The weather thickened and the wind came in gale force out of the southwest as night approached, and the convoy was lost in the haze. Next morning, when the wind had shifted around, northwest, north, and then settled down steadily from the northeast, there was only the big ship, cruising around aimlessly, as if it might have been searching for something. And then she disappeared to the north and the sea was empty, in so far as anybody could see. . . . But not wholly empty. It held these five lumps of what had been men, and at high tide she rid herself of them.

Nowhere was there any sign of a wreck. Nothing that had been part of a ship or part of a cargo came up with the tide, though the villagers searched hopefully. They were hungry. They were cold, too, clothed as they were in tattered garments that had not been renewed since the beginning of the war. It may be that some of them would have stripped these bodies of what covered them, but the soldiers began preparation to take them away. But where?

Along the ridges that reached back from the sea there were graveyards where generations of Islanders had buried their dead, but none of these welcomed these dead. They were not their dead, not even that one who had been born on the Island. In all of the graveyards there were cedars, everlastingly green, standing watch over the dead, and this must have been in the minds of the soldiers when they cast about for a place to bestow these bodies. They fetched a cart and piled the dead into it, five of them.

When the cart was loaded the soldiers went away with it and the villagers watched them with uncaring apathy. They went west along the slope of the last ridge—this ridge—and after a while the cart came back. It was empty and the soldiers filled it with scattered stones that had been a part of the damaged Lighthouse. The stones were of no use in the repairing of it, since brick had been brought from some far place for this business. The cart went back along the slope of the ridge but nobody followed it.

The stones lay there, embedded in the earth, until I stumbled over the topmost one on a winter's day ninety years later. . . . Near by was, and is, the stump of a massive cedar tree and, in 1863, its branches must have hidden whatever was under it. But by now a dogwood, five inches through the trunk, was growing with its roots deep down among the New Hampshire rocks that General Henry Dearborn had brought here in 1797 to build Mr. Hamilton a lighthouse. Not knowing, then, what might be under the stone over which I had stumbled, nor for a long time to come, I did not disturb it too much. Afterward I came upon a single gold-faced coat button which, so experts have assured me, was in current use by the U.S. Navy about 1850.

By now the sea around Cape Hatteras had come to be very lonely. The war had gone elsewhere, and the ships had followed after it. Sometimes there would be sail, or the smoke of boilers, far offshore, bent upon some unimaginable mission, but they did not come any more to or through the Inlet. The soldiers remained, seemingly forgotten by those who made war elsewhere. They had little to do. Nobody molested them and nobody undertook to be friendly with them. Often enough they were as destitute as the Islanders when supply ships neglected to come to them.

More and more there was passage toward the mainland as one or another expedition of soldiers went looking for something to eat. They pillaged neighboring counties when they had to, returning sometimes with corn, which they ground in the windmills of the villages. There was no sharing, and it is a literal fact that no Island family then, or now, had any direct or indirect contact with them. No name on these Islands derives from any soldier who was stationed here throughout the bitter five years of the occupation. The Islands absorbed none of them.

For a while, after the mid-point of the occupation, Ocracoke returned to some measure of consequence. It lies more directly near where the up-State Tar River, after changing its name to the Pamlico, widens out into Pamlico Sound. Washington, sixty miles inland from Ocracoke, captured in the spring of 1862 in the invasion that fanned out from Hatteras Inlet, became the center of considerable Federal activity. There was no railroad, and the headquarters there, and at New Bern where another provisional government was set up with somewhat more success, used water transportation.

Wherever the armies went they spread disease after them, and a good many families at Washington, by special permission, were allowed to visit Ocracoke during the warm months, and it was there that Josephus Daniels, afterward to be Secretary of the Navy, caught his first glimpse of the sea. He was then an orphan. His father, as carpenter in a New Bern shipyard engaged in construction of vessels for the Confederacy, was taken prisoner. While a prisoner aboard a gunboat approaching his home town of Washington he was killed by a chance shot from a shore battery firing from within a block or so of his own house.

After the U.S.S. *Rhode Island* lost her fabulous tow off Cape Hatteras—nobody was ever quite sure where it happened, and the location given officially varies from "eight miles east of the lighthouse" to twenty miles off the point of Cape Hatteras—ocean traffic was ordered to give that area a wide margin for errors of navigation. The Lighthouse was denounced by Admiral David Porter as being useless because of its short-ranged visibility. He had also given that as an excuse for his own misadventure off the Cape in 1855. Shipping virtually disappeared from the Graveyard for a space of five years, and from 1862 to 1867 no ship is listed as having been lost.

It is commented on even yet, when elderly Islanders consider the weather and its vagaries, that during the period of the Civil War no hurricane approached Cape Hatteras. Why this was so none will venture any opinion beyond that of Martin Tolson who, in moments of truculence, is likely to say that mankind making such a fool of itself, the weather just didn't need to do anything but look on while they vexed themselves with their own foolishness. There were, from time to time, lashing gales but no hurricanes.

Since the sea was empty of sail, of steam, and of any salutary agitations of the weather, the Islanders turned more and more toward the mainland. In one way or another people again got themselves small boats and somehow found sailcloth for them, and they went back and forth, when they were permitted or when they had anything to take with them, to Elizabeth City, and to Washington. There was little to be had there and less market for what could be found to take to market.

Yoepon tea was again in good demand, and the womenfolks back on the Islands were busy with their tea ovens. There was no coffee anywhere in the South and, when they could spare it, they had to parch rye or corn and grind it for a simulation of coffee. Yoepon was a welcome addition to the depleted pantries of the mainland, and a bale of it could buy a good-sized shoat, which made excellent variation in the tame diet of the Islanders back at home. There was also an increasing market for salt or dried fish. But the Islanders looked no more to the sea for a long time.

No longer was there any sound of war. The cannon had long been silent, and the sound of them would not be heard again along the Outer Banks until a fateful afternoon in August, 1918, when four badly-aimed shells from the deck guns of a submarine belonging to the Imperial German Government whistled past their intended target and thudded harmlessly into the sand west of the Lighthouse.

20

Within three miles of this house there are five tons of gold valued at about two million dollars. The gold has been there a hundred years and it is not unlikely that it will still be there a thousand years from now, unless the sea, in one of those moments of derisive whimsey that she is so capable of, might take the notion to fling it up on the beach just to see what a wild scrambling there would be among her children on these Islands.

Nothing can be set down as improbable, or impossible, on these Islands where almost anything is rather more than likely to happen. From time to time, even within my own experience, the sea has had her playful days when she would reach down in her pocket, so to speak, and fling a coin or two landward. I carry in my own pocket a piece that the Islanders call a Spanish Dollar and that Mr. Robert Louis Stevenson made celebrated as a Piece of Eight. It was picked up within the shadow of the Lighthouse.

And not more than a month ago these labors were interrupted one morning when a very mannerly mess attendant attached to the Navy came with something that he had picked up. He had been scrubbing it with detergents and kitchen abrasives and he had made it so slick and, as he thought, pretty, that precise identification of it seems unlikely. But it was a gold coin, possibly the American gold dollar, heavily encrusted when he found it. This condition suggests that it must have been in a sand-buried locker and wasted little time reaching the shore. Otherwise the action of the tide would have cleaned it.

Since then most of this man's spare time has been devoted to walking that beach hopefully, and it is by no means unusual for him to encounter in his walking his gold-braided commanding officer. That is, they may bump into each other because each is walking with his gaze intently fixed on the sand. Or if not his commanding officer, almost any one, or any dozen, of the three or four hundred men in the outfit. They have been told, also, about the five tons of gold and each, very likely, is having a very wonderful time just dreaming about what he would do with it if he suddenly became a millionaire at the hands of this sea. . . . It keeps them, if nothing else, from other mischief.

But nobody can ever tell about this ocean. It is a matter of fact that Captain Benjamin Dailey, mentioned herein already and who is likely to appear almost anywhere in this text, picked up a peck-measure of assorted coins, mostly Spanish Dollars, on one beach patrol following a storm in 1883. He was officer in charge of the Coast Guard Station then, and when he came back he set the bucket of money under his bed very casually, and some of it disappeared sometime afterward when some shipwrecked sailors were given shelter in the Station until they could be transported.

When it pleases her the sea takes, and when it pleases her she bestows. Nobody ever has taken, and no Islander has ever thought of taking anything from her except a fish. When she has claimed a ship for her own, after perhaps casting ashore such things of it as she had no desire of, she has kept it until such time as it pleased her to dole out a little of her vast treasure hidden somewhere in the bottomless sands of Diamond Shoal. It is a matter of cold record that when she has taken a thing for her own, no man, in four centuries of trying, has ever laid hand upon anything that she has claimed.

This is The Graveyard. It covers, actually, about thirty square miles of shoal. It is twelve miles, normally, from the end of the Point to the seaward end of the Shoal, and it is from two miles to three across. In this narrow area, through four centuries, 382 ships have been sunk, and have been drawn down into the grave, and no man has seen them, or touched them, to this day. These are the ships that she claimed for her own. The others are ships that she has battered, has broken, and cast them ashore for such use as their owners or their finders could make of them or their contents.

There hangs above my fireplace here a massive enlargement of a photograph taken from the air on April 19, 1942. The *Empire Thrush* was a 5,000-ton English cargo ship and, the day before, she was set upon by a German submarine. One torpedo hit her low, piercing her hull amidships, which was immensely fortunate. In her cargo holds she carried 3,500 tons of TNT. Fifty feet forward or aft and there might have been little left that was familiar around here. This happened 2.8 miles from the crest of this ridge.

When she was photographed the next morning from the air she was sitting on bottom in about thirty-three feet of water, according to the chart. Her stack and some of her superstructure showed above water, and bunker oil was still pouring from her wound, slicking the sea to port. . . . Since then, beginning in 1945, I have explored the area many times from the air, and once from a boat. Fishermen who take their trawlers through that slough corroborate my observation: no trace of her visible above the sand.

How far down did she go? There is no knowing. Once I went that way on a Coast Guard 83-footer, and nothing in its battery of electronic gear gave any slightest reaction that would indicate where she is, or how deep down she is. She is just gone, utterly. Away from the center-line of the Shoal, where the water is deeper and the action of contending currents less pronounced, there are wrecks to be seen, strewn along the floor of the Bight and of the ocean above the Shoal. But anything that hits the Shoal, anything that the sea proposes to claim for her own, it is hidden away.

In 1856 the *Mary Varney*, San Francisco to New York, hit the Shoal not half a mile from where the torpedo hit the *Empire Thrush* on an April day eighty-six years later. In a specially reinforced and guarded area of the skipper's quarters there were ten heavy redwood boxes containing bar gold. She was, as her story is remembered and related on these Islands, a hundred days out of San Francisco and she had failed, by a little, of making port in New York in that space of time.

When she approached Cape Hatteras a spring gale met her, swung her shoreward in the great eddy, and drove her hard against the Shoal. She did not break up. The winds stripped such things as were superfluous, her masts, her rigging, and flung them to the Islanders, who saw very clearly what was happening. It was scarcely two miles from the Point. And then the sea took the *Mary Varney*, her pride and her gold, and she has kept them.

How deep does this ship lie in the sand of the Shoal and how deep the others that the sea has taken down, unbroken, into her keeping in these four centuries? There is no man who can answer with any certainty and no man has yet devised a gadget that will probe down so far. There have been efforts to get down to this or that ship, but the literal fact abides—when she has taken a ship for her own, no man's hand may ever again touch her.

She is not greedy, but she has little tolerance for weakness or laziness or carelessness. Eight thousand ships pass in a year, carrying every conceivable thing that mankind has bethought him to move from one place to another on the earth, and she has laid no hand upon any of it. And then in the night, any night, she will break a 15,000-ton tanker square in two, and so quickly and so neatly that there is not a second of time in which to send out any cry of distress. She has found a weakling, a ship too hastily designed, too inexpertly built.

What she wants for herself she hides away, and the rest of it is cast upon the beach whereon, immemorially, the law of finders-keepers has applied. It is an error to think that finding a thing made a thief of the finder. There are procedures under admiralty law, and under state statutes where there is an ocean, that make provision for the protection of an owner's interest in shipwrecked property. North Carolina still maintains an ancient fiction that there is need of a Wreck Commissioner, and one is solemnly appointed when the Governor thinks about it or is reminded of it.

Any beach cargo that happens on these Islands has to be salvaged quickly, preferably before the next tide, or it will be taken back to the sea. Wreck Commissioners and Owners' Agents, until recently, were confronted with a week's journey after they heard about the disaster that had befallen. It was not the custom on these Islands to wait for them. The sea didn't wait. Since the improvement of communications—the telegraph came to the Island in 1870—there have been occasional formal procedures in the matter of wrecks, and a thin sheaf of them is among the yellowing files of the Clerk of the Superior Court in the county. But most of them happened above Oregon Inlet and within sight of the courthouse.

Few of them have to do with untoward happenings on these Islands, and there is no mention of the *Flambeau* in them. For this one it is necessary to explore the files of the Military District Governor, who still reigned in North Carolina in March, 1867, and the reports made by troops who were continuing the occupancy of these Islands begun in August, 1861. On these Islands, and indeed throughout the entire region, it is still remembered with wry vividness. It is remembered as the Stovepipe Hat Wreck.

It is my continuing hope that someday one or another of my neighbors will come up with a Lincoln-model stovepipe hat, but it is not a very green hope. Still. . . . The Federal troops and the U.S. Marshals were pretty thoroughly aroused by the owner of these, by then, unfashionable hats. The tall beaver went out, sartorially, with the death of its most distinguished wearer, who was Abraham Lincoln. When the fashion changed and the silk hat appeared from France with the blessing and support of the Third Empire, the honest American beaver slid toward oblivion.

Dealers were left with vast stocks of them on hand, and then a pair of more than usually enterprising traders—their names as remembered on these Islands and mentioned in musty military records are continued in merchandising quarters even now— discovered that there was a ready and profitable market for these castoff hats in South America, especially on the West Coast of that continent. Whether the Spanish influence there had disavowed the French silk hat it is not possible to say very definitely.

But at any rate there was enterprise in North America and demand in South America, and so these very enterprising merchants bought, and cheaply too, every available hat left in the United States. With other merchandise they were loaded aboard the small steamer Flambeau and the voyage to South America was begun. The two merchants, in so far as it appears, did not go. They merely consigned. There is no suggestion, locally, that they were among the surviving passengers and crew who were washed ashore, eight miles south of the then location of Oregon Inlet. The Inlet moves south at the rate of eighty-two feet per year and has covered some distance since March, 1867.

The *Flambeau* was a flimsy little steamer and would likely not be allowed to clutter the sea in these times. When she hit the beach with her cargo of ten thousand beaver hats, Lincoln-style and even taller, she began to break up. The site is plainly marked, to this day. Nothing is left but the upper part of her boiler, and there it sits about fifty yards offshore. It is a favorite tying-up place for fishermen of quality. The former Comptroller General of the United States, Lindsay Warren, and his good friend Shepherd of the Marines, have often tethered to the *Flambeau's* boiler.

Presently the beach was littered with hats, and it was not long before every man, woman, and child on this Island had one of his own. Or at least he had one or more in his possession. Some among them, Southern Confederates in their sympathies, disdained to wear them and used them as objects of ridicule. But everybody had a hat, and the fashion spread north of the Inlet and westward to the mainland. The beaver hat, and the taller the better, was very general Easter wear that spring.

But not for long. The owners of the hats knew men of considerable potency in Washington and they entered protest at the pillaging of their hats. They were not, to be sure, pillaged. The ship by now had broken up and hats were scattered knee-deep for miles and were to be had for the picking up. But the military sent down stern word from Washington. The natives must be brought to book for this treasonable thievery against potent friends of the government in power in Washington. The property must be retrieved. . . . It was apparently believed that the cargo had fallen into the hands of one, or at most, a few men.

Orders are orders, even on remote islands, where there is military strength sufficient to enforce them. There ensued a house-to-house search and everybody—which was everybody—found with property in his possession was ordered into arrest. The hats were, of course, seized. They were collected and eventually were delivered into the hands of the owners by the Military Governor of the rebellious district of North Carolina which was no longer a state, and so passed the stovepipe-hat insurrection, if that is what it was. They called it the new rebellion in military circles for a while.

Captain John Allen Midgett used to say that he had heard Captain Bannister Midgett say that even the porpoises were wearing stove-pipe hats that spring and that Bannister Midgett had the time fixed in his mind because it was just thirty years, practically to the day, after the Flambeau that he was called upon to institute a new era. That would bring the time to March, 1897, but Captain Bannister resisted the era, and when he died in 1921 he was still of the belief that neither steam nor gasoline was intended to propel a boat. He believed in the wind and in the oar.

He refrained from belief in the efficacy of gasoline as a propulsive agent and, in 1918, when he saw the ocean take fire right in sight of his house at Chicamicomico, he was more than ever sure that it was of the devil.

21

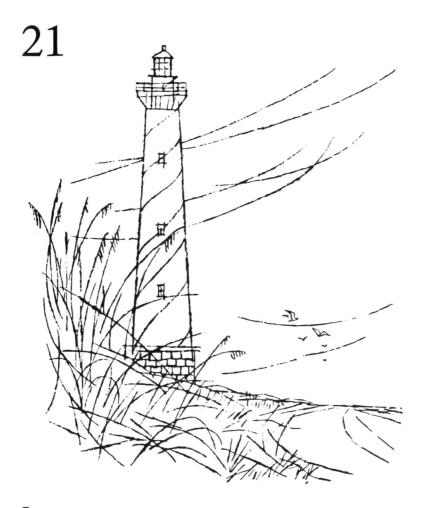

John Rollinson returned from exile in the summer of 1865 but went back to his rented farm in Hyde County that fall to harvest, with the help of some of his Island neighbors who accompanied him, the crop that he planted in the week that General Lee surrendered in Virginia. There was coin enough to sustain the Islanders throughout that winter, such of them as came slowly homeward from other places of exile.

There were no questions to be asked, no answers to be required of them, where they had been, what hostages they had given anywhere in order to survive. It had been a grievous time and a time in which a man's opinions, his allegiances, became secondary things. There was for the most of them the mere question of survival somehow in a time when they were again castaways in a civil upheaval. It did not matter any more whether a man had been a Secessionist or a Unionist.

But it did matter if he was hungry and it did matter whether he had held true to his allegiance to the sea, which gave strength and which required no less.

The house, staunchly built on the highest bit of ground in the village, which had known a brief glory as the capitol of a government that never was, which had sheltered the convention that was never a convention but the empty gesture of a sordidly empty little mind, was still standing but not much more, and it was two years before John Rollinson could bring down to it from Trent village his aging parents. It was a place for them to die, but that their death was hastened by the privations they endured in the occupation the son was able to think upon in sorrow without bitterness. They loved their Island.

Stagnation there still was, but there was also hope. The Islanders were at home again and the sea was there, wide and generous. She beckoned and promised new life, and there were brief comings and goings of ships. Not the ships that they once knew, their masters known to everybody, often from among themselves. These were strangers, sharp traders with goods to sell to a people who could not buy and eager to buy what they did not have. The last bale of cotton seen in the village was on that August day in 1861 when the forts fell and the invaders took away the shipload of it that was waiting.

There was no job for a collector of the port; there was no port. And had there been it must have gone to someone other than John Rollinson, or any other Islander. They were lumped together, now, as rebels, and the patrolling authority that represented the military provisional government knew them all alike. John Rollinson was no longer even a justice of the peace under the authority of the court of common pleas and quarter-sessions.

But there was little need of such and, indeed, there has been little in my decade on the Island. It is only recently that a justice of the peace and a deputy sheriff have been installed: it is a long way to the courthouse for one taken exceeding the speed limit.

On January 7, 1867, the brigantine *George E. Maltby* foundered and broke up on Diamond Shoals and three months later the schooner *Vesta* was wrecked as she approached Hatteras Inlet in rugged weather. These disasters were important to the Islanders, not for what the sea left for them on the beach, but because of the clamor set up by the owners. They inveighed bitterly against the government of the United States for maintaining so inadequate a beacon on the Cape. They pointed, also, to the fact that the sea had taken a total of thirty-two ships of war in the same area, whereas the enemy's guns had hardly so much as pinked one of them.

Shipping wanted a new lighthouse and by the end of the year about a hundred inhabitants of the Islands had jobs on the new lighthouse, and such of them as could qualify as bricklayers got the preposterously high wage of $1.50 per day, working from "can to can't," which is the vernacular for dawn to dusk. From kilns along the James River in Virginia scows brought 1,250,000 brick, somehow bringing them into Cape Creek, which afterward would be straddled by the preposterous wooden legs of Marconi's tower.

The work was under the direction of the U.S. Army Engineers Corps which, in the way of military elements in wartime, had expanded mightily and was eager for any work that would justify its continued bigness. It is a recurrent phenomenon, and even now there is a startling example of it in the presence on Cape Hatteras of a battalion of the Navy's Mobile Construction Force which, in more recent wars, has wrought with distinction. It is not unlikely that a contractor would have built whatever it is they are building for a vastly lesser cost but, as their very affable commanders assure the Islanders, "It is good training," but for what no one appears to know.

Earnest and helplessly superior young ensigns, and even sedate commanders, all of them instructed in the newer engineering practices in the best schools, look now with sometimes not quite urbane disbelief when any Islander, native or not, explains to them how the massive tower was designed and built. Its walls at the base are fourteen feet solid masonry, for one thing, and narrow to eight feet at the top. That, they will say, is rather wasteful, isn't it, when a little steel would have served admirably to give the tower strength, and they do not remember, if they ever knew, that Sir Henry Bessemer was only forty-four years old when the tower was designed and his manner of making steel had yet to find acceptance and use in America.

And the piling, now, they will inquire. There must be some massive piling under so formidable a structure weighing—they calculate quickly and possibly accurately: not even John Rollinson's homemade arithmetic has the answer—six thousand, two hundred fifty tons. (There is some granite used for trim and some cast iron in the housing for the lantern, which is a little heavier than mere brick and mortar.) Tell them now about the piling, how many pieces of it and how deep into the earth was it driven?

There is no piling under the Lighthouse, and if it is one of the elders whose father worked on the tower and handed down its lore, he is likely to say that it was built just like the Hamilton-Dearborn tower yonder and it must be a pretty good way to build a tower because the foundations of the first one are still there and this one has, in its eighty-odd years, taken a good deal of pounding one time or another. . . . But no piling? Why, in the new facility, so trifling a structure as a water tank, weighing a mere fifty tons or so, the specifications called for piling of such-and-such dimension. . . .

No piling. Perhaps for the reason that there were no pile drivers. Or, as the Islanders will tell you, wisdom and engineering science was not invented by Seabees or ensigns or put together in colleges. Take that General Dearborn, now. Maybe he was not much of an engineer, more the political type probably. But he had somebody around who knew how to build things. When he came to need foundations for a lighthouse tower he scooped out the earth down below the water—water table they call it now—and then he took oak timbers, hewn, twenty inches square, and laid them flat on the sand in the bottom of the hole. Then he laid another layer of timber, same size, crossways, making a 40-inch foundation. Then he built his lighthouse on it and it stayed there.

In no essential did the design and construction of the two light towers, seventy years apart, differ. Dearborn brought stone from New Hampshire and the Engineers brought brick from Virginia. Dearborn manufactured lime for mortar on the site, burning oyster shells, and the Engineers brought in commercial lime. The Engineers increased the size of the base timber from twenty to twenty-four inches square and for oak they used heart pine and when, eighty years after it was built and twelve years after it was abandoned for a steel tower set back from the earth-eating sea, the tower was minutely measured, it was found that it was not out of line by any measurable fraction of an inch.

Dearborn hauled his New England stones two miles from the shore of the Bight and the Engineers hauled their brick one mile from the entrance of Cape Creek—and both used oxen. Wooden rails were laid along the sand and rude flatcars were built for both towers, and this is as near as these Islands have ever come to having a railroad. Dearborn contracted far the use of slaves in off seasons from their mainland plantation labor but the Engineers hired, when they could, native workmen. There were few versed in the art of bricklaying on the Islands, but they learned quickly. And they needed work.

No need was apparent for new quarters for the keeper of the light and they used the house that Dearborn erected, putting on an ell when it was found to be inexpedient to install the cellar the contract called for. The rugged walls of this house, built entirely of brick when all the stone in hand was used in the first tower and brick were easier come by than New Hampshire granite, are still intact and presently house the National Park Service resident ranger and his brood. Unsightly wooden additions mar the clean lines of the original.

In the while that men worked the sea watched, and in the year that the new light was commissioned—the date was January 1,

1870—two steamers were broken to bits within sight of it. Neither was a wreck of such proportions as to leave any residue of folklore on the Islands. On the twelfth of September, 1869, when the tower was within sight of completion, the sea raged under the whip of a hurricane that tore away more than a hundred feet of the beach before going on to New England to lash Puritans, and there were some among the Islanders who believed that here was portent of her displeasure.

When they were finished with their building the Engineers had a distinction that had not, and has not, been matched in the world. Here was a brick tower, 196 feet from base sill to the top brick. The iron superstructure added another dozen feet, and the whole of it cost $155,000. Even now when these young engineers look at it, its height, its thickness of wall, its cast-iron stairway anchored in massive masonry, they hesitate to say whether they could do it and at what cost. Their own relatively unimpressive achievement has cost, up to now, about forty times as much.

After the walls were finished they were painted and there was, as the Islander remembers with remote glee, a confusion in the design. Somebody somewhere got the papers mixed up, and the spiral striping that was intended for a new light tower fifty miles southwest on Cape Lookout was applied to the new Cape Hatteras tower, and the diamond-shaped figures, suitable for warning traffic away from Diamond Shoals, went to Lookout. It is still so. Tourists call it the Big Barber Pole and point their cameras at it. The Islanders have no such facetious name—it is The Lighthouse.

On the thirty-second day after the new lantern was lighted the Engineers buried some kegs of black powder at the base of the southwest facet of the eight-sided Hamilton-Dearborn tower, and the tower came rumbling down. I have known those on these Islands who heard the dull roar the black powder made when the fuse reached it, and the rumbling of the stones as they crumbled. It seemed an unnecessary piece of vandalism. There were those now who understood good brickmasonry when they saw it, or stonemasonry, because they had learned it in the new tower yonder.

Afterward, when the brickmasons returned to Virginia, there were some among the Islanders who went after them and got good-paying jobs in Richmond, which was in process of being rebuilt after the war. But none remained there for long: the Island called them back home, not to brickmasonry but to being Islanders. There were no more bricks laid, save for an occasional chimney, on the Island until the middle of the next century when one Islander, wishful to build a fancier tourist court than anybody else had built, summoned bricklayers and ruefully paid them thirty dollars a day.

This man, if he had remembered what he heard his grandfather say, might have remembered how to lay brick and saved himself a prodigious sum of money. Or it would have seemed prodigious in 1869. It was not any longer much of a sum: not that the Islanders had become rich, but that money was not of any great consequence. In 1869 a day's wages as a bricklayer would buy a forty-pound side of good salt meat or three bushels of corn, provided you had a bugeye to sail across the Sound and get it home. . . . In 1955 a bricklayer's wage for a day could scarcely do as much.

It was not a good sight to see the Hamilton-Dearborn tower come rumbling down. It was wasteful, somehow, and the Islander is a thrifty man, of necessity. In time to come the brick that were brought to repair the damaged lighthouse in 1861 were salvaged as one or another Islander had need of a few brick for a stove-chimney, but the stones were let lie where the black powder had laid them, and they were not disturbed until Mr. Byrum came, in 1935, to repair what the sea had done to the land in another sixty-five years.

22

Other seasonal employment was to be had.

Not only was there a new lighthouse, twice as high as the one it replaced, but the government of the United States, rankled in its memory by the beating its ships took at the hands of the weather—more Federal warships were sunk by weather off Cape Hatteras than by all combined Confederate cannon everywhere— had determined to do something about weather in general and in particular about the local meteorological product.

While some of the Islanders learned to lay brick and others to tote brick and mortar near two hundred feet into the air, yet others learned to set poles in the earth and to stand admiringly by while elements of the Signal Corps of the U.S. Army strung wires from one pole to another. On the day that the Lighthouse was completed the first and longest telegraph line, wholly owned by the government, was completed and a little instrument hooked on to the end of the wires.

Altogether it was pretty mystifying, the things that these aliens could think of, and this telegraph line was the ultimate in necromancy. Latter-day scientists in weather who fatten themselves on such resounding and generally meaningless phrases as "synoptic isobaric analysis" smile with remote disdain upon the procedures of that remote day when all they had to telegraph about was the amount of moisture they found in a tin cup, and how hot or how cold it was, and which way the wind blew.

Although Leonardo da Vinci had designed an anemometer four-hundred-odd years before, there was none in practical use in the United States in 1870 when the first weather station was established on Cape Hatteras. The duties of the lighthouse keeper were combined, for a time, with those of the observer, who was put to the inconvenience of learning how to make the little instrument tied to the end of the wires click intelligibly. It was a task of some arduousness.

Often as not the observer, when he did not feel quite up to the task of making the thing click sensibly, would report, by letter, that the wires were awry, and that entailed maintenance, which in turn, entailed employment, which became more than merely seasonal. For a while the military continued in residence and the line was solely their duty, but as the years wore on it was turned over entirely to civil servants.

To get on the payroll, for any sort of public employment, the first requisite, usually, was to be able to exhibit a certified Oath of Allegiance, indicating that the applicant had been a loyal adherent to the republic. The Republican party continued in power in Washington, and there are remembered instances, on these Islands, where whispering campaigns were instituted against one so employed, the substance of the whispers being that his Oath of Allegiance was faked and that the man was, in reality, a treasonable fellow. Or, in effect, a fellow-traveler. There was not, of course, room enough on the payrolls for even the loyalists or for any substantial proportion of them, and a considerable bitterness ensued, a feeling that is reflected graphically enough in a brief note in John Rollinson's book. He reports the result of an election very briefly. Thus—"Tildern, 82. Hayes, 37." At that time John Rollinson was superintending, for a wage of $30 per month, "Colonel [Jonathan] Wainright's porpus factory." Colonel Wainwright was the only Federal soldier to return, industrially, to the Island after the end of hostilities. His name is preserved in the records by a nephew who became a general.

I have mentioned that it was possible, and often practicable, to mail a letter to the Weather Bureau in Washington which said that the telegraph line, extending from the Virginia capes to Cape Hatteras, was not in working order. There were, now, post offices. As late as the beginning of the Civil War anybody with a letter to be mailed on these Islands took it or sent it to a post office in Hatteras. Before that time, it was necessary to send it to Ocracoke, and there is in the Hooper cheesebox a receipt for postage paid on a letter dispatched from there in 1836. There were no postage stamps. The postage charge was forty cents.

But now there were post offices and postmasters and a contract carrier of the mail. For reasons that continue to be obscure the Department, when it established post offices, changed the names of the communities. Chicamicomico became Rodanthe for no reason that I have been able to discover. Salvo became Salvo by virtue of having been the target for a badly aimed litter of cannonballs. The two Kinnakeets were lumped together and became, just as obscurely, Avon. Cape became Buxton, Trent became Frisco, and only Hatteras retained its original name. Ocracoke, of course, had its own post office.

And here is a divergence that for a long time drew the two Islands apart. Ocracoke's post office was served then, as now, by a mailboat that sailed from the little mainland village of Atlantic, or from New Bern directly. The Hatteras Island villages were connected, by mail as well as by telegraph, with communities to the north. A steamship line between Elizabeth City and Manteo on Roanoke Island carried mail, and there was direct contact with Norfolk, also by boat. The mail came three times a week to Roanoke Island.

Thence sailboats came down the Sound, stopping first at Rodanthe which continues, by most Islanders, to be called simply "Chicky," and from that point, south and west, the mail was taken aboard a horse, in saddlebags, and fetched down the Island. The mail-rider left Rodanthe upon the arrival of the mail boat, which depended on the wind. He rode down the Island, fetching letters, sometimes as many as a dozen, and an occasional newspaper. It required the whole of a day to make it from Rodanthe to Hatteras, and the whole of the next day to make the return trip. He carried also messages, verbally entrusted and verbally delivered. He also dealt in leisurely intelligence of a more general nature.

There exists nowhere, in so far as my searching discloses, any official record of these operations, and it is not possible to determine who had the job of mail carrier in any specific year. It is tolerably certain that Bannister Midgett carried the mail from his native Chicamicomico-Rodanthe for a while, despite the fact that he was unable, as he maintained, to read and write. There are some who maintain that he was admirably equipped for the duty because he never tarried along the way while reading post cards.

Abraham Midgett had the post for some years and it is reported that on one occasion he toted on his shoulder, while leading his mail-laden native horse, one barrel of flour from Avon to Buxton. That I am disposed to doubt, though it is established by eyewitness accounts that he once toted such a burden from his small sloop, aground on a shoal a mile off Buxton, and that he did not set it down in his own kitchen until his wife had come and cleared away a place for it. He just stood there waiting until she cleaned out the place.

But every village has its recollection of some improbable feat he performed there. It is related that on one trip down he found the little post office at Avon off its foundations because of the previous night's high tide and that he amiably took the building by one corner and set it back upon its blocks. . . . Of this there is no record of an official kind, and the most impressive thing produced by the Hooper cheesebox is a receipt for a registered letter issued there in 1874.

These post-war Federal benefactions, this distribution of largess in the way of employment for strange works, was not wholly new on these Islands. Federal authority and patronage began to touch the Islands as early as 1848, when it was lawful for a man who needed a job, or could qualify for it, to organize a lifesaving crew which concerned itself with the saving of lives of shipwrecked persons. A man had to have a good surfboat, and a small building from which to operate in season, and his crew were required to be on call when there was emergency requiring them.

This arrangement was devised under a patchwork of Congressional enactment dating back to the organization of the U.S. Revenue Cutter Service under Alexander Hamilton in 1790. Whenever there occurred anywhere on the coasts of the United States a wreck of sufficient horror, a new patch would be added to the structure of the law, and by 1848 most exposed areas had their lifesaving crews. The procedure was not complicated: a stout boatman would organize a crew, present it to the authorities in Washington, usually through the means of a revenue cutter—such as the *Harriet Lane* when it visited a port of entry in the course of its cruising.

Total annual cost of such a crew would never be large. The head man, or Surfman in Charge, got $20 per month for not more than six months. He had eight surfmen, serially numbered—a man could work up from No. 8 to No. 1 by—well sometimes but not always by being an able man with an oar. They worked through the hurricane season, usually from August to February. After which the crew was disbanded, or off active duty—and payroll—until the following season. The total cost, seasonally, for such a crew, would be less than a thousand dollars.

These men owed their first allegiance to the sea, and their pride was in their craftsmanship as oarsmen, as surfmen. There is a special science in launching a boat through the surf, and it is a science that cannot be put down in a book, nor learned from a book. Through all the years of my knowing him one of the greatest of them, John Allen Midgett, with gentle patience, undertook to enlighten me in such matters as how to know the precise instant in which to commit the boat and, returning from the sea, the precise instant when it should be beached without harm to the boat, its crew, its passengers.

Never was his patience and gentle courtesy quite exhausted with me, but sometimes he would say that he guessed a man, to really understand about it, had to be born to it. Captain Johnnie, as the Island remembers him, was born to it, as were the generations of his race before him. Whether the almost occult science has perished from the Island I am not now quite sure. There are now Coast Guardsmen, even Island-born who, when they stop by to see if there is still breath in me or merely to ask if there is a letter to be mailed, look at the faking rack above this typewriter and solemnly ask me what it is.

These men were born to it and their allegiance was to the sea and to the oar in hand. There were, on these Islands and away from them, those who said that these men, in organizing such crews of lifesavers, were actuated more by the impulse to be in on the ground floor, so to speak, when a wreck occurred than by any devotion to the preservation of human life. There were jealousies born that continue. Affiliation with one or another of these crews became a family matter, an inherited, a transmitted estate. Even now there are families born into the Coast Guard that the lifesaving crews became—and those who never get anywhere in it.

But whether or no, between the year of 1848, when the first of them was organized and mustered into service, and the mid-seventies, when they were displaced, these crews performed a memorable service to ocean shipping. They were, of course, displaced wholly during the years of the Civil War and immediately thereafter. Three of these locally-organized and part-time-employed crews were active on the two Islands in 1870. There was

the oldest of them at Chicamicomico, manned wholly by the Midgetts, a second at Cape Hatteras, with the names of residents of
four villages—Miller, Meekins, Scarborough, Stowe, and Dailey—
enrolled, and on Ocracoke Island a third, with Wahabs, Howards,
Gaskills, and—among the greatest that ever lived on the Islands—
the Garrishes.

Among these was born, perhaps feebly at first, a sense of
allegiance to the sea and to the oar that grew into one of the proud
traditions of America. First they were able seamen-surfmen. They
knew how to put a boat through the surf, knew every whim and
vacillation of the sea. And they knew how to bring her back again,
with whatever she had saved from the sea. There was, of course,
a healthy rivalry among the three crews, a rivalry that persists in
handed-down instinct among their descendants in the fifth and
sixth generations of what are now called seamen on duty at the
remaining lifeboat stations.

And there is a tremendous surviving pride, never vocal nor
boastful, but a thing that expresses itself in the mere way of a man's
walking along the beach, in the way that he glances down at the
surf curling in upon the sand. They have few words in them. At
one time or another I have examined, in their own words and in
their own lame handwriting, the reports of every major disaster in
which they have had a hand since official reports were first required
in 1877. Nowhere in written language is there such an economy
of word.

Earliest of them is that set down, when his hands grew some
new skin, by Captain Benjamin Dailey in 1884, after he and his
five men had rescued the crew of the *Ephraim Williams* in seas that
looked death when they put their surfboat through the breakers
five miles north of the Lighthouse. Official inquiry and the ensuing
reports use reams of paper and many thousands of words, ecstatic
and incredulous words, in describing the sea of that day. Captain
Dailey used precisely 209 single-syllable words. No man was lost
that day, but the surfmen were unable to sit, or to pick up so much
as a spoon to feed themselves, for many days. They had worn the

hide off their bottoms and off their hands in the mightiness of their effort.

But they must have suffered much less than did Chief Warrant Officer James Henry Garrish, Keeper of the Lifeboat Station at Ocracoke fifty years further along, when he was commanded by two admirals to get up and make a speech about some exploit that resulted in the bestowal of two medals. Garrish was a massive man, and gentle as only the enormously powerful can be, and he was among the first of his breed that I came to know three decades ago. His surfmen said of him that his voice would carry three miles against a gale of wind and that, if he was a mind to, he could get out there on the beach and yell down any hurricane. But his voice was, most of the time, soft and gentle.

This night, in an inland city, there was a vast dinner, with two admirals and a scattering of Congressmen and one governor. They were making an occasion of the presentation of two medals to this massive man. He came, fearful and apprehensive, to my room in the hotel a little while before it was time to go down to the banquet. He was uncomfortably magnificent in a very costly uniform he had acquired for the occasion, and for the first time in my acquaintance with him he had on shoes. Normally he patrolled the beach and commanded his station barefooted. But now he looked like two complete admirals. He was six feet and four inches high and, naked, would have weighed 205 pounds. He shook with sheer fright. From a fruit jar, fashionable container of contraband in that day, and from which two admirals and one governor had drunk modestly a little while before, Jim Henry Garrish poured an iced-tea glass to the brim and downed it. He continued, however, to sweat cold sweat. He wondered if I couldn't get him out of this mess, somehow. He just didn't want to go down there.

But he went, after fortifying himself with another pouring to the brim of his glass, which he downed, as they say, neat. There were speeches by people who like to make them and, finally, there were two honors pinned to the massive chest of the outwardly calm surfman. He towered above everybody. And then from around the banquet hall there arose cries of "Speech." It became an over-powering tide of clamoring, and finally the senior admiral quieted them and turned expectantly to the newly decorated master of the sea. Garrish did not budge, and he looked helplessly around, finally at me.

And the admiral said, partly coaxing, partly ordering, "Just get up and tell us what happened, in your own way, Mister Garrish." Mistering him had an ominous, official sound. Garrish got to his tremendous feet and looked around. He was utterly terrified, utterly helpless. Two stubby fingers found their way down the in-side of his immaculate collar. And then the collar, the neat black tie, ripped away. And he said, "Well, we just seen 'em out there and went and brung 'em in." He sat down.

There was the surfman incarnate. There was, also, James Henry Garrish, great-grandson of a man who had, a long time before, organized one of the earliest lifesaving crews. There was the great tradition.

23

There are names on these Islands that are not remembered, and are not mentioned. Good neighbors they may have been, and good fathers. They did no evil, paid their debts and their preachers, lived uprightly in the sight of their God and their fellow-Islanders, were ready ever to give whatever they had to any who lacked. But they are not remembered and are not mentioned. It would have been, would be, a kindness to forget them utterly. These are the men who refused the sea.

It is not a law written down in a book. It is not a judgment measured in words spoken. It is sensed, sometimes, if unwarily you pronounce a name that is proscribed, and the men who may hear you will not look at one another, at you, or at anything. Unless, to be sure, it is where you can look to the sea, and their eyes have a stillness in them when they look to the sea. No syllable has been spoken but the silence has in it an eloquence that could not be framed in all the words in all the books.

And the worst judgment that can be put into words about any man is a simple, "I'd not like to have him in a boat with me." It is not an easy thing to assess, this final and irrevocable damnation. It does not mean that the man is banished, that he is thereafter no fit man to associate with in matters that have to do with other things than the sea. He may be a good carpenter or skilled in the use of all manner of tools and beloved of womenkind. But he has refused the sea.

It has seemed to me for a long time that these who have refused the sea, who have quailed before her wrath, are especially esteemed by women. The women of these Islands hate the sea and but rarely go near it or look toward it. It is, indeed, only quite recently that any woman of the Islands has ever put on suitable garments and gone swimming. So recently as a decade ago the sight of an Island woman on the beach, except possibly as a gatherer of seashells, would be a matter of such scandal that it could not be spoken of except in privacy and in unmixed company.

Except as a passenger engaged upon a necessary journey, no woman, in so far as I have been able to discover, has ever committed herself to the occupancy of a boat. No woman could possibly pull an oar, nor bend a sail, and her presence aboard any sort of a boat is a menacing nuisance. And, besides, the sea does not like women any more than women like the sea. There is here an immemorial jealousy, and no woman has ever felt secure in her possession of any man who had already committed himself to the sea.

They say of the men of these Islands that they make poor husbands and good sons. The sea is the mother of all things that live; life came out of the sea a billion years ago. There is an atavism here that is beyond any explaining of mine but it is so. Did not the sea bring these men here and has she not brought them strange, sometimes terrible, gifts? She is their mother, and after these years I have become able to accept the analogy as something that is natural and that is good. Any Island man may be less than faithful to a wife but few among them have been less than devoted to their mothers—to both mothers.

It is by no means a thing that should astonish anybody that the women of these Islands hate the sea with a compelling jealousy. Too often she has robbed them of their men. They go down to the sea and they do not return again, or when they have come back it is after the sea has shown them strange and sometimes terrible things and great beauty and they can not ever again think undividedly of mere wifely charms and graces.

Among the Islanders I have known there was one who lived to be ninety. His third wife survives him and a moderately gracious woman she is, too, but it would afford her no pleasure to be mentioned more precisely so close to quoted words of her husband's when he would say, "I've seen a lot of pretty things in my life and I've had me three wives and all of 'em I took because they were good to look at, but all of 'em put together, all the women I've ever seen in my life, were not as pretty as a clean barkentine with all sails set in a fair wind."

Conjugal heresy, to be sure, but there it is. This man provided well for three successive wives, and in addition to this widowed third is survived by ten children. His father was also of the sea, and his grandfather and great-grandfather, in 1818, were castaways on these Islands. They returned again and again to the sea but came back to wives and families they had acquired in due season. No one of their descendants has ever refused the sea—and no one of them has ever been completely possessed by any wife.

But there are compensations, even if they, in the aggregate, set up a strange paradox. These Islands, and the villages on them, are a pure matriarchy. The wives stay at home and keep the house, bear the children. And they rear the children. On land they are mistresses of whatever there is, of their houses, of their children and, when they come home, of their husbands. No man who has given himself to the sea is quite ever the master of his own household. It is a price that he must pay and he pays it with such grace as he can contrive.

Often enough the arrangement is a not unhappy one. In their own fashion, women can be as contrary and temperamental as the ocean ever dreamed of being, and the men appear to like it, or at least to make the best of it. For the most part, though there are enough tales to the contrary to make life at least diverting, the wives are not inconsiderate and only at times abandon themselves to tantrums. But they raise the children and they do their ablest to wean them from their father's other love who is, in a fashion, a stepmother to them.

When she becomes pregnant, as likely as not, an Island wife will begin, perhaps not quite consciously, to hope that it will not be a manchild. Not this time, anyway. They are instinctively fearful about having a son—the sea will in her time snatch him away and make him her own. I have inquired discreetly into not less than seventeen instances where the birth of a son has so disturbed the mother that she denied to herself and to the world that it was a boy at all. She would raise him as a girl and persist in the delusion until nature would take a hand and dispose the lad into his proper place. Usually he then runs away to the sea at a very tender age and it takes a long time for him to accommodate to the veneration that most male Islanders have for their mothers—both mothers.

Women are the arbiters of domestic life, and often enough the only recourse left a wife-handled husband is to get somewhere and become hell-roaring drunk, and it is my personal observation that nowhere else in the known world can a man address himself to the business of getting drunk with such complete and absolute abandon. So, and not unnaturally, the women are against alcoholic indulgence, a polite euphemism they use. They are against liquor, against beer, against wine and all else by which a frustrated husband might find some alleviation of the boredom entailed in that state.

At one time in my residence on the Islands there was held a plebiscite on the selling of beer, and the vote was overwhelmingly against it. Especially unanimous was one of the villages, where a good ninety-nine percent of the votes were counted against beer. It was reported that one militant wife appeared at the polling place with a tombstone in her arms and voted her grandfather against beer, after hectoring the registrar, male, to look back in his books for a generation until he came to where the deceased had been qualified to vote.

The tale is, of course, apocryphal. The votes registered for beer were cast by a handful of not-yet-married motherless young men who were just being contrary. The men voted dry because they had to, but they drink wet because they want to, provided they are out of sight, out of hearing, and out of smelling of their homes. And one of the most delightful spectacles I have witnessed on the Island was my favorite among the merchants on a weekend when his wife departed the Island to visit their grandchildren somewhere. The merchant got two cases of beer and set them on the counter of his store and an excellent time was had by everybody, including neighboring wives who strolled past storing up hideous details with which to agitate his wife when she got home. They, however, overed the crisis and live together contentedly.

But few Island wives will "go for broke" in their ruthless over-riding of their husbands' natural inclinations. They know, most of them, that they are at best only the second choice of their lords and that they can, and assuredly will, return to the great love of their lives. They know, or most of them do, that they cannot too long flout the sea, and some of them, I think, must be a little fearful of her. They—and here again is an atavism—know that the sea may punish a man for his wife's jealousy, and then they would not have any husband at all.

But there are those who have refused the sea, perhaps from their tuition at the hands of their mothers. There are others, whose names are not mentioned, who have given their names to the sea and then quailed before her wrath. It is not held against a man. He will make a good, faithful husband, but he may not again walk in the company of those who have trusted themselves to her.

The time of the testing comes when the sea has laid her hands upon some man, some ship, and unless some of these her children will come to intercede for them, they will die. The great era, the Time of the Surfman, began to dawn in the murk at the end of the Civil War when ships again spread their sails thick against the horizon off the Cape. There grew up along these Islands the great tradition of the surfman that was epitomized in the now legendary retort of one of the greatest of these men with an oar when a member of his crew quailed.

That day the sea had the look of death. She had taken a great clipper in her hands and had broken it apart as if it had been a match and men were about to die. The redoubtable Captain Pat Etheridge had his surfboat on the beach, in the shadow of the new Lighthouse, and was ready to launch out into a maelstrom that offered little but the certainty of dying. One of his crew hung back at the word to put the boat into the surf, and then he said that if the regulations said go he would go—but he couldn't see that they had a chance of ever coming back.

Captain Etheridge impaled the man with a sulphurous gaze and said, "The regulations don't say a damned word about coming back—they say you go. Are you going?" The man's name is not remembered on these Islands, but the surfman's blasphemy is embedded in the tradition of his service. The men aboard the fragmented clipper were brought ashore and not much harmed.

24

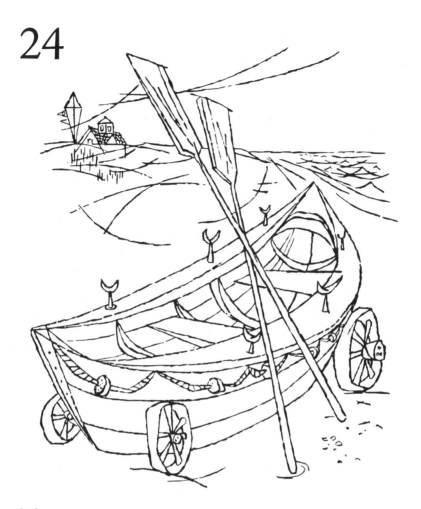

Thomas Nast has no monument on these Islands, or elsewhere that there is any local knowledge of, but now and then, among yellowed papers that somebody may fetch you out of an attic, there will be a print of the cartoon. It is, very possibly, doubtful that Thomas Nast ever heard of these Islands but, next to Alexander Hamilton, he stands preeminent as the shaper of their latter destiny.

It was an event that happened off the Island, to the north, that motivated America's most effective cartoonist. Except for Nast's reaction to it, the disaster that befell the U.S.S. *Huron* a dozen miles north of Oregon Inlet on a December night in 1877 had little impact on Hatteras and Ocracoke. Among the kegs and jugs that littered the beach there were the bodies of 103 members of the crew of this newer of the Federal fleet's gunboats.

It was not a pretty story. It is not yet a pretty story, no matter how much effort is devoted to not setting down the whole of its ugly detail. The Islands' womenfolks will still tell you that it was the judgment of God sent upon them because they were all drunk. They use very plain words about intoxicants, these women do, and the findings of the board of inquiry, generally not mentioned in the more recent accounts, tend to justify the women of the Islands.

Not that the hushing-up has anything very directly to do with the consequences of the disaster. It was enough that 103 bodies littered the beach where summer people now romp and that some of them were the bodies of the ill-organized and unequipped semi-volunteer lifesaving crew that undertook to save them. Here was the most deadly marine disaster that had happened to the United States Navy since it was put together a hundred years before by a fugitive Scot who had come to North Carolina through the port on Ocracoke Inlet.

Here in this heap of 103 bodies of dead men was material for America's first and greatest cartoonist, and the most feared in an era when men were beginning to be terrified by their own cupidity. Nast lashed the Congress and the Administration for its criminal negligence, and the makers of law staggered under the impact of his attack. There is not now in America, and there has been none since Nast, one who wielded the power that he made his own and which he used, always, against abuse of power. Most Americans, in these times, remember him as the originator of the Republican elephant and the Democratic donkey or as the man who destroyed the colossal Tweed Ring in New York.

These Islands remember him as the man who restored the Hamilton concept of a guarded coast, and there was a time when a print of the most graphic of his cartoons hung, framed, on the walls of every Lifeboat Station between Oregon and Ocracoke Inlets. They are gone now, these prints and, in most instances, these stations that came into being when Congress made haste to establish the U.S. Lifesaving Service as an independent branch, coequal with the Revenue Cutter Service, in 1878, and the old patchwork quilt was thrown away.

Along the whole of the Atlantic Coast the now displaced part-time rescue service had served as a training period for men who came, ready with experience, into the service. They knew the sea, they knew how to launch a boat through the surf, and they gloried in their strength and sea-wisdom. They brought a tradition with them that was already in its third generation. . . . The youth who poked his head in a little while ago to see if I were alive and to say, cheerfully, "How's it goin' today?" is of the eighth generation. He will be twenty years old in June. . . .

There was need now, in 1878, along the whole of the coast and more especially athwart these Islands for the service contemplated in the new legislation. The country was recovering from the bewilderment of war. Ships had come back to the sea. In the North especially there was a wide and urgent demand for building material, and the two Carolinas and Georgia had become the center of the lumber industry. These states were cutting down their virgin long-leaf forests, mostly drained already of their sap, the turpentine of commerce.

Steamers were more numerous than they had been but their operation was costly. Most of the billions of feet of lumber that were shipped out of the ports of Wilmington, Charleston, and Savannah were, for reasons of economy, carried in schooners. There evolved a type of vessel that was especially designed to accommodate such cargo. It was a booming time and I have heard men who were active in the Lifesaving Service in that era say that they had seen as many as fifty sail past in a single day.

At sea shipping boomed but these ships were too big for the shallow inlets of the Outer Banks. Times never again became what they were before the Civil War, though a measure of commerce came back, in small ships, that went out through Oregon, Hatteras, and Ocracoke Inlets to the West Indies. The timber of the mainland counties served by these Inlets had been long ago cut. It began as early as 1680, and by 1880 there was not much left and what there was found passage on expanding lines of railroads, which carried the region's products to deeper harbors and larger ships.

Some among the Islanders, equipping themselves with larger boats, two-mast barkentines mostly, ventured out into world trade, and it was the boast of the late Captain Jefferson Davis Hayman, whose father introduced the sweet potato that bears his name into American agriculture, that he sailed the *Ocean Bird* out of Hatteras Inlet light, went down to Trinidad and loaded his vessel with asphalt "which stunk so nobody else would haul it," and carried it to Washington, D.C., where it became the first asphalt paving laid in that capital.

But Captain Hayman departed from Hatteras, where his father had been captured, with his ship, in 1861, when the *Ocean Bird* was crippled by a hurricane that left her stranded high and dry. Afterward he was elected sheriff of the county. His father hated Yankees mightily and when he heard, in a Federal prison, that a man-child had been born to him, he sent back word that he was to be named for the President of the Confederacy. The good captain was exchanged and afterward commanded a successful blockade runner.

Small coastwise sailors trafficked in molasses and, so long as it was a lawful import, in rum and other West Indian items of export, but more and more the vessels got too big for these shallow Inlets and trade centered, for North Carolina, in Wilmington, which had a railroad and reasonably deep water in its river harbor. Shipping as a business along these Islands languished and men who had been employed in it shifted either to the bigger ships or into the Lifesaving Service.

Under the enactment of 1878 three Lifesaving Stations were authorized on Hatteras Island and two on the shorter Island of Ocracoke. It is difficult to establish now which of them was first to be activated, since they were all authorized in the same appropriation, but it seems reasonable to conclude that it was probably the station at Oregon Inlet. Alpheus W. Drinkwater, the county's most notable contemporary citizen, was born there in 1875, while his father was keeper of the station. This, of course, antedates the enactment of 1878 by three years, but, as indicated, there were already loosely integrated, part-time stations, with rudimentary buildings.

Work began on Chicamicomico Station before the end of 1878, not unnaturally under the supervision of Bannister Midgett, who was full grown now, and avowedly illiterate. When he finished the station the next year he became the keeper of it and he continued in that capacity until he was retired after the formal merger of the Cutter Service and the Lifesaving Service into the U.S. Coast Guard in 1915.

And here is as good a place as will occur to record the fact that in the seventy-eight years of its existence as a Lifeboat Station Chicamicomico had three keepers, or, as they came to be known, officers-in-charge. Bannister was succeeded by John Allen Midgett and he, in turn, when he was killed in a traffic upset—mighty boatman though he was he never quite mastered the automobile— by Levene W. Midgett, who was in command when the station was decommissioned and handed over to the National Park Service. Neither of the three admitted or claimed relationship to the others. The original building, considerably expanded, still stands.

Work began about the same time on the replacement for the crude housing of the part-time crew at Cape Hatteras, but the station was not completed and occupied until 1880. I have possessed, after salvage from a bonfire that was made of the old station and its litter, the property book which was kept from the opening day and have observed with wonder that among the properties issued and signed for were "12 sheets of foolscap paper, one lead pencil, four envelopes," among other things. . . . If the youth whose head was visible in the partially-open door a little while since should have to go to Norfolk, to have a tooth pulled, it will take thirteen sheets of paper to get him there officially and "in the public interest."

If for no other reason the old hands in the Lifesaving Service practiced laconic narration out of necessity: the government of the United States did not furnish them paper in quantity to encourage wordiness. They had a pint of ink issued also and that lasted, in so far as the book indicates, beyond the life of the station. There is no further entry recording the issuance of ink, though pen-staffs and points came about quadrennially. And an occasional lead pencil. . . . John Rollinson must have used it as a copybook maxim in the 1840's since, when it was apparent that he had sharpened a new goose feather into a pen he would write, testing, "A man of words and not of Deeds, is like a garden full of weeds." It recurs twelve times in his journal. . . . These were not men like weeds. Pulp paper was not known and the good rag paper that was used was expensive and not wasted idly. The station logbooks are austerely brief. If there was nothing to report, and for long months at a time there was nothing but idleness, they wasted no paper in saying so.

It was 1884 before there was anything much out of the ordinary to set down. By then there were seven stations on the two Islands: Ocracoke, Hatteras Inlet, Creed's Hill, six miles west of Cape Hatteras, then Cape Hatteras, Big Kinnakeet, Chicamicomico, and Oregon Inlet Stations. Except for Creed's Hill all stations took their names from the locality, and I have not been able to determine for whom the Creed's Hill Station was named. Eventually there would come to be stations at six-mile intervals from Cape Lookout to Virginia Beach, a total of twenty-seven. Eight of them were left in 1955—and it has been a decade since sail was descried from the lookout towers of either of them.

Each station was manned by a keeper, a cook, and nine able-bodied men with an oar. The station was equipped, first, with a lifeboat, propelled by eight oarsmen with the keeper at the sweep oar in the stern. There was a cart upon which to haul the boat from the station to where it was needed on the beach, and the station stable housed at least two native horses, each selected because of his strength and staying power. They may not have been animals to attract anything but derision at a horse show, but when they bent into the collar of their cart-harness, the cart, and its heavy lifeboat—weight 2,600 pounds—moved. The cart's steel tires were very broad.

That was all, in 1884. Afterward there would come to be all manner of specialized gear, the Lyle gun, the faking rack for its line, and the beach-anchored breeches buoy. But in the beginning the men went out in a rowed lifeboat and brought in the shipwrecked. It was as simple as that—and very rugged. A man had to be strong of back, he had to know the sea, and he had no fear in him. He had, also, a deep, a compelling pride. He was paid a wage of $20 per month, plus his uniform, when the Service came after a while to have a uniform, and his keep.

Every man lived within sight of his own house, and he could go home one night in nine. No woman ever approached a station, and it is only this year that I have seen the wife of a member of any crew come in and sit down at the dinner table. It is my belief that it will not recur. I have sat also through the very dismal silence that falls if the impatient wife of a crewman drives to a station, expecting her husband's liberty to begin, and honks the horn of her vehicle to let him know that she is waiting. . . . A second blast of her horn, I like somehow to imagine, would be calamitous and her husband might, not unreasonably, expect to be transferred to a weather ship shortly. Here again, tradition.

Tradition, in the formative stage for thirty years and more, crystallized in the U.S. Lifesaving Service five miles north of the Lighthouse four days before Christmas Day in 1884. There had been, to be sure, shipwrecks and men saved from them from the time ships begans to pass Cape Hatteras. But since the establishment of the Service as a separate agency nothing of very notable consequence had happened. What needed to be done had been done and it could have been done by anybody with any knowledge of the sea. The capabilities of the Lifesaving Service had not been tested.

Captain Benjamin Dailey, Keeper of the Cape Hatteras Station, sighted the *Ephraim Williams* on the afternoon of December 18, 1884. She was schooner-rigged and through the powerful glass—bought by the government, one of three, for use in the War of 1812 and issued, when they were commissioned, to Lifesaving Stations—

she had a heavy deckload of lumber. She was apparently having difficulty as she approached Cape Hatteras from the southeast. The wind was north.

Throughout that afternoon and the next day the ship was still in sight, tacking groggily in the roughening sea. Sometimes she was hidden in mist that hung over the Shoals, where cold north and warm south currents met. By now she was alone out there, too far out to signal, not close in enough to be in difficulty. But still she made little progress. The weather worsened. The thermometer dropped, that night to 23 degrees, and sleet pitted a man's face when he faced into the wind, which had freshened into gale force.

For a day the schooner apparently turned her bow away from the wind and she was not visible for some hours. Captain Dailey wondered and remained himself in the watch tower, massive glass in hand. (Extended it is 71 inches long and it takes all of a man's arm to hold it steady in calm weather.) At daybreak of the twenty-first the ship was again in sight, with a part of her deck load missing. The beach patrol had brought in word that some lumber was beginning to wash up. The sea was, as the Beaufort Scale measures its violence, No. 7, and the sleet had some rain mixed in with it.

After breakfast Captain Dailey called Captain Pat Etheridge at Creed's Hill Station six miles away and asked him to come and bring his best oarsmen in case they were needed. And, of course, his boat. The two crews set out along the beach, moving at a slow pace, even though the wind had shifted now into the southwest and was blowing a gale. The ship was making a groggy progress northward. The crews paced its progress northward, watching every minute to see if any sign came from the schooner five miles offshore.

At eleven o'clock the crews were four miles north of the Lighthouse. They were joined on the beach by the crew of Big Kinnakeet Station and they waited there. The sea was in a fearful uproar. The southwest wind was driving against the inshore Labrador Current which, for two days, had had a 41-knot gale behind it, and between the shore and the laboring ship there stretched five miles of as rough water as is remembered, with only occasional eddying lulls close inshore that were comparatively calm. The ship's signal became visible. The crew, six men, asked to be taken off. The *Ephraim Williams* was beginning to disintegrate and her small boats were smashed.

There was no word spoken on the beach. Captain Dailey looked at Captain Etheridge silently. They understood each other. Captain Dailey would command. He looked around the three crews gathered and when he looked at a man the man answered with his eyes. One by one, four men were silently selected. They moved over to stand beside Captain Etheridge. These details I have set down are from the recollection of two of the crew whose lives extended into my acquaintance with these Islands. . . . Nine men would have been better, but there were six men out there to be brought back and fifteen men would have overfilled the lifeboat.

When he was able to write, nine days later, Captain Dailey set down in his report the simple statement—"After a hard struggle we got to sea." That is all but there is implicit in these eight words eight generations of seamanship. They rowed five miles to the schooner, by now falling apart, approached through waters wildly hazardous with floating timbers. They took six men into their boat and brought them ashore. They were gone from the beach two hours and thirty-five minutes.

In the words of the Congress ". . . medals of honor, with suitable devices . . . for service above and beyond . . . ." These six men were the first to be accorded the Congressional Medal of Honor for Lifesaving. Only at one other time, for an exploit in 1918 and twenty miles north along the beach, was the entire crew of a lifeboat awarded the honor. In two instances father and son, each in his generation, were awarded the medal, and in one instance, that of Captain Baxter Miller, it was twice awarded and to a man so gentle-seeming that his voice could scarce be heard across the room. Beginning with Captain Dailey it has been the custom, when the recipient died, that a likeness of the medal, with its crossed oars, be graven upon his tombstone. The tradition was set, fixed. It continues.

In the serried ranks of the Annual Reports that range along the shelf above this fireplace there are scores of chapters that would fill many books reciting the rescues that have been made within sight of this ridge that looks down upon the sea. Choosing among acts of heroism which is the greater . . . because those who were heroes were never aware of it . . . is an unprofitable business. I have, over the years, assembled the citations and a roster of men to whom the awards were made. They appear at the end of this text. The list is long.

These two men, that day, set the stakes that plot generations of behavior, and it should suffice to say that from that day, down until this day, no crew has refused the sea. There have been, to be sure, individuals, but when there has been need there have been men. It is an attestation of their courage that no crew has refused the sea and it is no less an affirmation of their rugged seamanship—they prefer the word surfmanship, but it is not in the dictionary—that no regular crew, no member of any crew, has ever been lost when he committed himself to the sea to save a life of another. The sea loves her own.

Since the citation that accompanied his medal achieves a terse brevity that would do credit to the keeper of a station driven by regulations to set down an account of his own heroism, I am disposed here to expand a little, from native sources, the exploit by which Surfman Rasmus Midgett, in 1899, won the award, single-handed and alone. He was the father of Arthur Midgett, who, in 1918, was a member of John Allen Midgett's crew which rescued the survivors of the *Mirlo*.

Before the advent of the Great Storm, as the Islanders speak of it, the hurricane of August, 1899, another station had been erected six miles south of Chicamicomico and named for a neighboring island—Gull Shoal Station. No trace of it remained past the '44 Hurricane, which set a new mark for violence in this century. Rasmus Midgett was a surfman attached to Gull Shoal Station when the three-day West Indian storm set up a record that endures for violence and persistence. It began on August 16 and it blew, with winds at 150 miles, for three days.

In the record books there is mention of nine vessels wrecked between the Lighthouse and Oregon Inlet, but in the native account the number is fifteen. It was a very terrible time, with the Island, except at its highest points, as this ridge, under water. There was no loss of life among the Islanders and the material damage was not great. But the damage to shipping was enormous and more than a score of lives were lost. Every man in the Lifesaving Service was doing round-the-clock duty with only one man left at each station to receive new reports. The telephone lines—the telegraph was no longer used—were down.

At four o'clock on the morning of August 18, Rasmus Midgett, alone at the station, went out and bridled his native horse, remembered admiringly on the Island as having been named Gilbert. The sea was still breaking across the Island but the wind was somewhat abated. Midgett got aboard his horse—saddle-animals are not mounted hereabouts, but boarded—and set out to patrol the beach in search of whatever he might find. He went a little way northward and turned south, past his station.

Two miles down the beach he reined Gilbert and listened. He thought he had heard, above the roar of the wind and the surf, the cry of a human being. There was not, that he knew of, any wreck in that immediate area. He listened. Unmistakably, now, it was a human cry—and a woman's. Rasmus Midgett considered what to do. No need to go back to the station, since there was nobody there, and it would take an hour. Nor was there any sort of equipment left there, all of it being out at the scene of other wrecks.

Nothing was visible through the murk, and the cries were but dimly heard above the wind. Gilbert did not hesitate when his master turned his head toward the sea and clucked to him. Rasmus Midgett rode through the seething break of the sea until, in the growing dawn, he could make out the lines of a three-master, by now beginning to break up. She was close in, and when the sea went down, she would be high and dry, what was left of her. But now, the water was belly-deep on Gilbert and well up Rasmus Midgett's legs. When the sea broke it engulfed them momentarily.

There was no hesitating. The cry came again and Gilbert and Rasmus went toward the disintegrating ship. Now they were alongside, and in the lee of the sea. Midgett called to the woman to jump but she held back, and her half-grown son was pushed over the breaking rail. Midgett gathered him up under his arm and rode shoreward and left him there.

Nine times more Rasmus Midgett rode Gilbert through the foaming tide and each time brought another of the shipwrecked ashore and dropped him without waiting to get off the horse. Then he went back and brought the bodies of three who had not survived. A fourth washed up and they were buried at the north side of the station. The grass above the grave is, even now, a little greener than the grass around it, and that alone marks the burial place of the captain's family. . . . Locally the ship, the *Priscilla* out of Baltimore, is known as the flour-and-lard wreck. The beach was littered with barrelled flour and tubbed lard, and in the Mariners' Museum at Newport News there are photographs of the ship, the lard, the flour, the crew that survived. But not of Rasmus Midgett. The medal is graven upon his simple gravestone, the emblem of a tradition.

25

Throughout the whole of his life Bannister Midgett maintained, for his own convenience, the fiction that he was unable to read and write. As the occasion required he blamed his condition variously on the prevalence of Yankees on these Islands when he was of an age to learn to read, or upon the treasonable neglect of the Southern Confederacy to maintain schools during their rebellion. When, in mixed company, some South and some North, it was inexpedient to charge either with his illiteracy he would blandly state that "the hawgs et up the schoolteacher."

As a matter of fact and of record Bannister Midgett read widely and wrote fluently, but in privacy. It was only in public and in the

discharge of official duty that he assumed the posture of an un-
lettered man. It saved him a lot of such bother as is inherent in
the keeping of records, the carrying on of official correspondence,
and the like. These he ignored, and when a harassed official would
finally come down to inquire of him why he had not observed such
and such an order, or replied to urgently official letters, he would
say that he had not been able to read them.

There will be tales told of Bannister Midgett for generations
to come on these Islands, and of other generations of Midgetts—
what mighty men they were—and are—but for the present the
climax of the telling will come with the consequences of Bannister
Midgett's public illiteracy, which delayed the development and
adoption of the internal combustion engine in an important branch
of the government of the United States for the space of ten years.
Bannister Midgett was a mighty man with an oar.

There have been, apparently, Midgetts on these Islands from the
beginning of time. Where they came from—there are thirty-five
separate and distinct families currently living on the two Islands and
none admittedly related to any other—none can or does say. They
were here, outnumbering all other names, when the government
first counted its citizens in 1790, and they continue with unabated
fruitfulness in each decennial enumeration.

It is my surmise, and a good many of them agree with me—but
whether out of neighborly politeness I cannot say—that the name
very likely is evolved from an ancient jest. Every generation of them
has produced giants. They are men of imposing stature, with, to be
sure, an occasional runt to prove the rule, and it is conceivable that
the first one to land on this Island must have been such a fellow.
More than once in the long tale of these Islands a man has come
ashore from a wreck, forgetful, for one or another reason, of his
own name.

There is no way of knowing for sure, so it is not unreasonable
to conjecture that a long time ago, very likely in the latter half of
the seventeenth century, a formidable figure of a man came ashore,
naked even of a name. Of my own knowledge it has happened

as late as 1903. He stayed, as many since have stayed, and the Islanders, here before him or arriving subsequently, wryly spoke of him as "that midget" because of his great stature. This inverted sense of humor is a native characteristic and derives directly from the British habit of understatement.

And so they called him Midgett. This admittedly is a surmise and not history, but it will do until a better answer as to the origin of the name is worked out. The name is not encountered elsewhere. There are, to be sure, other spellings of it. Some of the tribe wandered off the Islands, again for one reason or another, and changed the spelling of their name. As for instance the Midyette family, which has for some generations been of considerable prominence on the mainland.

These and others trace their origins back at least to the west bank of Pamlico Sound, in Hyde and other counties of the mainland. It is a matter of record that some of these mainland families, being adherents to the Southern ideology in 1861, fled the Island before the onward sweep of the Yankees. They replaced the *g* in their name with a *y* and added an *e*, and there is record also of an Island-born fellow of this generation, migrated to a small inland city, carrying the native spelling with him.

But he became relatively prosperous, married a lady with an excellent soprano voice who sings in the most fashionable choir in the town, and when her name appears in the papers, as it frequently does; it is carefully spelled out: M-i-d-y-e-t-t-e. When a copy of this journal penetrates the Islands it is read with appropriate chortles, and it has been many years since her husband ventured down among what were once his own people. The inverted humor of these Islands would be something to face.

The Islanders spell it Midgett. I have found it in forgotten graveyards along the Island, rudely spelled out with a knife's biting into heart cedar, grave-markers that have withstood two centuries and more of the elements. Heart cedar, as a grave-marker, will outlast marble. I have many times examined the reassembled fragments of King Pharaoh Farrow's tombstone, and no syllable of its legend has survived the blasting of wind-driven sand.

Where the first Midgett came ashore and settled down is as uncertain as when, but it is a reasonable conjecture that it was toward the north end of the Island, in the vicinity of the village that was, or became, Chicamicomico. The name is Indian in origin and the town is no longer known by it: the Post Office Department calls it Rodanthe, but no native Islander so denominates it. Even the U.S. Coast Guard, so long as it maintained a station there, called it by its native name. For convenience some Islanders sometimes wryly speak of it as Midgettown.

There are a lot of Midgetts there, three-quarters of the population, and those not of the name married into one or another branch of the race, and so also with the next two villages to the south. There are Midgetts in every village on the two Islands except Kinnakeet—for no reason that I can discover—and in other parts of the surrounding country, even as far as Norfolk in Virginia, there are scores of them. It is a fecund breed and a rugged one.... Of the thirty-seven Congressional Medals of Honor for Lifesaving extant on these two Islands, nineteen of them were awarded to men of this breed.

Rugged they are, and proud, and disdainful of any kind of earthly pretension. They can with a straight face pretend that they can't read, but not one of them has ever pretended that he was important enough to name so much as one small creek after himself, or a channel through the shifting sands of the Sound. And here again there is this same inverted sense of ironic humor that runs from generation to generation.

A long time ago, in the settlements across the Sound on the fringe of the mainland, there was, and there continues to be, a family of considerable consequence named Payne. Some of them spell it Paine. As early as 1850 they had started naming things after themselves— Paine's Creek, Paine's Shoal, and the like. Altogether there are a good half dozen points charted and so named, and most of them lie directly across the Sound from these three upper villages.

Such pretension sits uncomfortably upon the Island neck, and along about 1830 or 1840—the first chart is based on the 1850 survey—Islanders returning from the mainland whither they had gone to trade dried fish for corn or pork, started naming places. Come down the Sound-side from the village of Salvo, third in line from the north end—and even now the traveler will encounter No Ache Creek, No Ache Slough, and No Ache Bay. . . . Sometimes a man, if he used a certain creek for tying up his own boat, might give his first name to it—but never a creek is named Midgett.

Bannister Midgett was a lad when the Civil War surged northward from the lower end of the Island, and I have heard that it was his custom to point to a double-page spread in *Leslie's Weekly* depicting the terrible battle of Chicamicomico, and when he had impaled a harassed figure of a half-grown boy with his forefinger, he would say, "That's me." I now possess the tattered paper and often have recourse to it. The area around the boyish figure in the picture is worn thin with finger-smudging, and it may well be that it was Bannister Midgett himself. I am disposed so to hope, anyway, since I have not yet found a photograph of him after wide searching.

As depicted by Leslie's artist it was a time of gruesome confusion when a thousand inhabitants of the Island, Southern in sympathies, were crowded along the narrow strip of sand above the village. From the ocean on the right and from the Sound on the left, looking at it from the south, which was the direction of the victorious onrush of the Yankees, vessels of war rained confusion upon the Islanders with cannon. Bannister Midgett, if indeed it is he, faced the south and the enemy intrepidly, small though he was.

Actually it was not such a deadly battle, but the victory-hungry Yankee press made a good deal of it as a sort of poultice for the ignominy of Bull Run. More extended notice of the campaign has been given elsewhere, and for the moment it will suffice to recall that Bannister Midgett survived, as did all the others in the harassed company. Perhaps never in history was so much ordnance discharged with so little hurt to the target.

Nobody at all was so much as scratched, but the picture made good copy in New York, and for the time being it was set down as a great victory.

Bannister Midgett survived unscathed but, as he invariably pointed out when there was need in later times, he was deprived of book learning, which did not hinder him, seventeen years or so later, from becoming the building contractor when the federal government began the construction of a Lifesaving Station at Chicamicomico. Nor did it impede him when he applied, not in writing, for the post of Keeper when the station was presently activated. He held the post against all challengers until he was retired in 1916.

And a mighty man he was with an oar. He needed to be, here above Wimble Shoal which, next to Diamond Shoals, is as dangerous a place as there is on the whole of the Atlantic coast. Scores of ships died there—and because Bannister Midgett had an instinctive knowledge of the sea, hundreds of men were saved. His logbook, often set down in private by his own hand, is a marvel of heroism, told with a simplicity and directness that was never conscious of his own heroism. He was a man not afraid of anything in the sea or out of it.

The tales they tell of him would, and perhaps should, fill a thick book, but one will do. They remember of him that there was nothing that anybody else had done that he would not try. Members of his crew were aware of this aspect of his make-up and they devoted a good deal of time to devising ways to test him. There was, they remember and recount with glee, the day he took two of his men and went ducking, rowing well out into the Sound to an anchorage on a reef.

One of the crew had brought a newspaper with him, a New York newspaper left by some visitor at the station. He read while Bannister Midgett kept lookout for any passing duck. He brought down only the larger, fatter ones, and there were already some in the boat. The crewman read his paper, addressing himself to his fellow crewman. The Captain disdained reading and pretended never to hear anything that was read in his hearing.

The crewman read with low ejaculation out of the paper. There was a man, it said here, who could take a raw duck, fresh killed,

slit him open and eat him raw. The other, as planned, expressed
disbelief. He said no man could do it. And the other, after reflection,
said that it didn't sound reasonable but he would bet that, if he was
of a mind to, Captain Ban could do it. The other, remembering his
lines, said that he didn't believe that even Captain Ban could do it.

After a while Captain Ban laid down his gun and said, "Hand
me one of them ducks—the biggest one." They handed him a duck,
the biggest one. Bannister Midgett calmly took out his knife, slit
the duck down its back, dumped its viscera over the side, and ate
the duck. Afterward he rowed back to the station, disdaining the
proffer of aid, and saying that not since he was a boy had he felt so
strengthened, and he believed that hereafter he would require all
members of his crew to eat their duck raw.

But evil came. It came in a box, together with a book, which those
of his crew who confessed an ability to read said were instructions
for use and operation. The box contained what was called a naphtha
engine, and the papers which came with it said that the engine was
to be installed in such and such a boat and, after the directed tests
were had, a full report was to be submitted. In writing, of course.

Bannister Midgett was filled with disgust and dismay. He had the
Islander's inherited distrust of steam, though he had not long been
born when the Horn of Gabriel sounded first above the Sounds.
But he had seen enough of steamboats during that war which left
him illiterate to last him a lifetime. He remembered, with gleeful
chortling, that day when the Yankees gave out of steam, and a lot
of Confederates, with sailboats, surrounded the steamless craft and
took every man jack of the crew prisoner and maybe took them off
down the Sound somewhere and drowned them like they should
have done. . . . Give him a man with an oar in his hand. . . .

It is not unlikely that if Bannister Midgett had had only the
orders from afar off, from Washington itself, to contend with, he
would have, as was generally his custom, ignored the box altogether
and at a suitable time dumped it into the ocean. But there was his
crew's curiosity about what was in the box, and what was in the
accompanying book. Every day, among themselves and just within

his hearing, they discussed the engine and the book, and they wondered what it would do if they installed it in a skiff, like the book said, and started her up.

When these tactics got them nowhere and the box and its baleful content just stood there, they shifted into a tack. They began to wonder, privately and among themselves, of course, whether Captain Ban was afraid of it. Bannister Midgett had, it is remembered, uncommonly keen hearing and his ears were, even in the Leslie picture—if indeed it is he—astonishingly big. They protruded widely beyond the reach of his impressive black whiskers.

There came a day when this passive resistance and this not wholly passive insistence could stand no more. Bannister Midgett bellowed very loudly and blasphemously and the crew took up the box, the book, and the skiff, and they went down to the Sound shore. They put down the skiff with its stern protruding into shallow water. The Keeper was a handy man with tools and he had directed the building of the station house, and the installation of the propeller, or wheel, was no problem.

Bannister Midgett worked alone, and near by the crew sat with the book. This was one of the very earliest naphtha engines, made in an era in which the word "gasoline" had not been contrived. It was a very crude engine, gearless and reversible. It had a single cylinder, and the directions in the book were as simple as the mechanism itself. The crew sat on the bank and read out of the book, beginning with Instruction One, and continued down the roster of procedures. It took most of the day, and the only comment Bannister Midgett had to make was, "What does it say next?"

Toward the middle of the afternoon the installation had come down to that section, "How to Start Naphtha Engine." Foul-smelling fuel was decanted into the opening appointed to receive it and the engine was, in so far as they could know from reading in the book, ready to be started, when Bannister Midgett asked the final and critical question, "What does it say now?" They read to him out of the book.

And then the engine started with such a roar as had not been heard hereabout since the unlethal bombardment at the Battle of Chicamicomico thirty-five years earlier. Somewhere or other Bannister Midgett must not have been paying full attention to the scholarly members, the reading members, of his crew. The engine started in reverse and the propeller bit hungrily into the water. Before he had time to consider what was happening, the boat was plumb out of the harbor, plumb out of range of his mentors on the shore.

Ahead, fifteen or so miles, lay the dimly outlined shore of the mainland, over about Paine's Creek, and the skiff was headed there, stern-first. Ashore the crew ran hither and yon, some wading out into the water as deep as their knees, and all shouting. Their words were shredded by the counter-roar of the godless, implacable engine that was hurling him westward, Paine's Creek–ward, at a fearful velocity. He was unable to determine what he should do next, or what the book would have recommended. But somehow the damnable piece of evil had to be silenced, stopped.

Even now, sixty years after the ill-starred advent of the naphtha engine, no prudent Islander will get wading-distance from the shore in a motor-driven boat without an oar handy. There was an oar in the skiff and Bannister Midgett knew the uses of an oar, even new and not-yet-tried uses. He took up the oar and with the butt of it, about half a mile outward bound, he beat the engine into submission. No vestige of it remains, but it is doubtful that even its designer and builder could have ever induced it to run again.

The oar survived practically intact, and with it Bannister Midgett rowed himself back to the shore. He beached the skiff and spoke briefly to his crew before he strode away toward the station, which he had built and which he commanded thirty-six years. "Some of you that can write, write them a letter and say the damned thing is no good for this country. And get the damned thing out of that skiff and plug up that hole you made in her to get that there through." He pointed disdainfully to the virtually unhurt propeller shaft.

His eventual successor in command made heroic history with an engine-powered surfboat when the sea took fire in 1918.

26

When an assassin's bullet found lodgment in the interior of President James A. Garfield on the second day of July, 1881, the unfortunate happening became of common knowledge on these Islands the same day, and the inhabitants became aware, for the first time, that the telegraph worked both ways. It could fetch tidings of tragedy as well as carry news of disaster or reports about the weather which, often enough, portended disaster.

Farrow Scarborough's cow calved that day, delivering herself of an uncommonly fine bull, or as his womenfolks put it, "boy" calf. Farrow Scarborough had been hoping that it would be that way:

the family ox was beginning to be elderly and would, within a year or two, need replacement. There was some ado about a name for the new calf, some of the household maintaining that it ought to be called Telegraph. Farrow Scarborough settled the matter without comment. The calf was named Garfield.

In due time the President succumbed to his wounds and in due course his namesake became an ox and his wound healed. Garfield was a sturdy calf and he grew lustily. He was docile enough and by the time he was two years old he was ready for the yoke. He became the biggest and most powerful ox remembered on these Islands, as tall as a man at the shoulders and broad of beam as any wife on the Island. He was a very noble ox, indeed, and his massive horns are preserved by Kit Midgett, who grew up, an orphan, in the Scarborough household.

When he was grown up Kit Midgett hired himself out to the Lifesaving Station as cook and continued in that employment for near fifty years, and in that service he saw the telegraph become the telephone, and he thought, sometimes, that they ought to have named the ox Telegraph so the era would not be wholly forgotten. Garfield's horns are kept in the attic of the house Kit Midgett inherited from Farrow Scarborough, and sometimes he will get them down and let you look at them. Not everybody, to be sure. I have heard him say, with the utmost composure, to some ill-manneredly insistent tourist that he never heard of an ox by that name, not that he could remember right then.

When the tourists have been repelled, and very likely without remembering to ask if Kit Midgett had ever heard of these Islanders being cannibals when they were shipwrecked—that one persists but I have nowhere found any tincture of truth in it—Kit Midgett may get to musing backwards and forwards, as he says. Although he has not in his eighty years ventured to project his voice on a telephone, the matter of communications rests near the surface of his thinking. Not very long ago he ventured out to the station where he had cooked for upwards of half a century. He had not been near it in ten years.

Afterward he came up this hill, arriving without any shortening of his breath, and he tarried awhile in detached wonder. Over there he had seen, for the first time, a thing they called a teletype, and in another place they had a transmitter over which even the younger members of the crew were able to talk directly with airplanes flying so high they could not be seen and with ships off yonder on the other side of the horizon, and they spoke casually to people in Norfolk, which used to be three days away by sailboat and even by steamer.

For an interval Kit Midgett considered these matters in ruminative silence, and then he said that it struck him as being sort of queer—they have every kind of machinery to talk with and nothing to talk about, nothing to report. There was nothing about any President being felled by an assassin, no ship being wrecked. But he did hear, when that O'Neal boy just picked up that thing and held it to his ear, somebody out yonder on the lightship reporting that the water under the lightship's keel, at that moment, was 68 degrees and the wind was twenty-three southwest. . . . But that thing they called the teletype, it kept a sight more noise than any telegraph ever did and he couldn't see how the crew could stand living with it.

. . . Yes, yes, he had seen that one they called Marconi. Came there to the station one day—he was cooking dinner at the time— and wanted to get them to send a telegram to somebody. There was a man named Edison with him. They said he had invented a thing called the electric light, but nobody around here had ever seen one of them. That was, yes, he was sure of it, about 1902. The one named Mr. Edison sat down at the table and clicked off the message himself. There was another man, but Kit Midgett is not able to remember his name.

It was, in all likelihood, Reginald Fessenden, and the trio had come to Cape Hatteras, as it turned out, to make some history that for the most part was little noticed on these Islands. They changed, here, the history of the world. They heard, from a hastily contrived tower on Kings Point, halfway between Buxton and Frisco, the first transmission of the human voice by wireless telephone, transmitted from a like tower fifty-two miles away on Roanoke Island. It was the belief, and the experience, of all of these electronic scientists, in 1902, that a radio wave could not be transmitted above dry land.

That was Marconi's idea and that was why he set up, within a thousand or so feet of the sea, the first wireless tower to be erected in the Western Hemisphere. He was not concerned with the transmission of the human voice by wireless telephone. He controlled, by patents of his own inventions, the wireless transmission rights for the whole earth, and a station of unprecedented strength, located on this projection into the sea, would be able to communicate with any ship on the ocean.

. . . It has been convenient for those who compose the history books of the electronic era to ignore the fact that long-range wireless transmission in the Western Hemisphere began on Marconi's tower on Cape Hatteras, and to forget an April ten years after the station was installed. That night the wireless operator was young Richard Dailey, a great-grandson of the English schoolmaster who was washed ashore on this Island nearly a century before. He was, that night, astonished at the clarity of reception and he had just finished taking down, and transmitting by normal telegraph to New York, a message of some urgency from a ship off Panama.

And then the wireless instrument began to click wildly and young Dailey stared at it unbelievingly. There must be some hoax here. The whole world knew that the *Titanic*, then midway the Atlantic Ocean on her maiden voyage, was unsinkable. But the instrument clicked away, insistently urgent. The station here was picking up the doomed liner's frantic dying message. Dailey dazedly took down the message and transmitted it immediately to the office in New York and was instantly reprimanded for cluttering the wire with foolishness. Didn't he know the *Titanic* was unsinkable?

Later that night the world believed it when a station in New York, manned by a youth named Sarnoff, picked up the message from the near-by *Carpathia* saying that she was going to the aid of the *Titanic*, sinking twenty miles away. That message was also received and recorded on Cape Hatteras, but the young operator did as he had been sternly told—he did not clutter the wires. He was still in Marconi's service on Cape Hatteras when the station was taken over by the U.S. Navy, as a precautionary step in neutrality, after the outbreak of war in Europe. He continued in Naval service until the end of the war and transferred to the Weather Bureau. . . . A crudely contrived switch, dating from Marconi's day, serves jointly with the half of a chain-shot as a paper weight at my elbow.

. . . The Fessenden–Edison–De Forest experiment in voice transmission to Cape Hatteras developed into radio, and Sarnoff became the head of one of the larger of its corporate manifestations. . . . Richard Dailey lives in comfortable retirement a mile down the road from the house in which Kit Midgett muses upon a remembered day when these Islands made a discovery that was of as great import to them—the telegraph could fetch as well as carry . . . and two stupendous epochs of war have not, in their drama, surpassed that. There is no longer a cow on these Islands and no calves come, requiring names. . . .

In the year that saw the final exile of the cow from Hatteras Island—the year of the Cattle Tick War—yet another invention came upon the earth, an invention that was to affect more profoundly the destinies of these Islands than any that preceded it or have followed it. Elsewhere it was a mere milestone, quickly past, as quickly forgotten; on these Islands it became, and continues, a landmark, the Great Divide between times that were and times that are. Advertisements of the day spoke of it as the Balloon Tire and little note of it was taken along the Outer Banks.

Despite the initial beating it had taken at the hands of Bannister Midgett, the internal combustion engine had persisted and had, in some measure, proved itself. Eighteen years after the first calamitous experimental installation at Chicamicomico, and by the time the Lifesaving Service was merged with the Revenue Cutter Service to form the U.S. Coast Guard, almost every station had its engine-powered lifeboat, though prudent surfmen always carried an oar or two with them when they ventured away from land. They still do.

Marconi had brought the first internal combustion engine to be successfully operated on these Islands, but he shipped it in by sailboat and set it up on a concrete foundation. It was used to generate electricity for the operation of his wireless machinery. It was evil-smelling, noisy, and cantankerous. A windmill would, many thought, have served him better, but most of the windmills had been razed by the Great Storm of August three years before. Meal instead of corn was brought in now, except for the Bateman Miller grist mill, wind-powered, at Kinnakeet.

As early as 1906 a gasoline engine had been installed in a 36-foot converted sharpie by Dr. J. J. Davis, who practiced medicine on the Islands for a time, eventually retiring southward in the face of the persistent and unrewarding healthfulness of the inhabitants of these Islands. He remembered that he was never, in fifteen years, called upon to treat a case of pneumonia on the Outer Banks, and the disease continues to be virtually unknown. But the Islanders remember his boat, though none has yet admitted having traveled in it, and just yesterday a visitor—a Midgett, of course—gleefully recalled how, in 1910, the gas boat under contract to carry the mails broke down and how he hitched onto it with his bugeye, towed it plumb to Manteo, and was back home before bedtime.

Internal combustion engines made little headway until the world was engulfed in war and there came to these Inlets a species of boat called the submarine-chaser that had two enormous engines and could—well, they very likely could have outdistanced the *Harriet Lane* with her steam engines. The Islanders never committed themselves to steam and, indeed, I have been unable to find any record that a boat powered by steam was ever owned on either Island, though many Sound boats so powered called at the deeper-watered harbors.

Travelers to outlying parts of the world brought back reports of a strange vehicle called the automobile, and there were reports, especially appealing to the young, that some of them had attained speeds of a mile a minute, which was somehow a sacrilegious thing. Only the wind ought to travel that fast and when she gets up that high she can be tolerably dangerous. None of these vehicles was seen on the Islands until 1917, when one of Mr. Ford's improbable Model-T's achieved the Island.

How it got here is obscure. The folklore of the event is confused, reflecting very likely the confusion that it precipitated among its beholders. It is not clear, even, who owned it, but that it was here, in 1917, seems reasonably established. It managed, with some equine help and a vast deal of pushing, to traverse the Island and departed by freight schooner. It was observed that its engine was utterly eccentric and that when it consented to run, the tires, especially those on the back wheels, promptly dug in. The only way to make it work was to let the air out of it and that destroyed the tire.

Engines, however, showed a continued and impressive betterment, and in 1921 the sight of a man named Billie Mitchell landing on any hard place on the beach at low tide in an airplane called the De Havilland had become nothing unusual. There were some, even, who had committed themselves to flying with him. They suffered no discomfort and were, they felt, in a more secure situation than they would have been out in the middle of the Sound in a boat that had only an engine in it. Another of these flying people was named Pat Bellinger (Vice Admiral P. N. L. Bellinger, USN Ret.) who had a kind of boat with wings and an engine.

Bellinger, as everybody knew he would be, got forced down halfway across the Sound in rough weather and was lost for some days before a sailboat, a bugeye, came upon him and retrieved him. They tried also to tow the disabled flying boat in but it sank. Only Mitchell—some called him a colonel but generally they settled for just Billie and that seemed to suit him completely—was immune to mishap.

And then on a day in August, 1923, Billie Mitchell again flew in. It was not ducking season, nor goosing season, and he never seemed to care much about mere fishing. He had other things on his mind and these things he communicated to everybody. He hired men and horses and carts, and when Shanklin Austin, aged six, presented himself and his horse for employment, Billie Mitchell hired him right off. He was to haul sand from the beach and fill up some holes on the flats. Shank got three dollars a day for himself and the stocky little native horse got three dollars. The cart seems to have been for free.

Nobody doubted that Billie Mitchell could do and would do what he proposed to do. He would sit on the counter of Shank's father's store of an evening and tell about it. When they got the holes filled up there would be a lot more aircraft, big ones with two engines, which could carry bombs weighing as much as a thousand pounds. There were going to be two battleships tethered to their anchors, or maybe turned loose with their engines going, and Billie Mitchell was going to drop these bombs down their smokestacks and cause them to sink.

It was as simple as that and nobody doubted that he could do it and would do it. When the holes were filled up the aircraft came, thirty of them, flying in a long string, like migrant geese, low over the beach. There came also barges loaded with drums of fuel, with tents and stores and bombs. Shank's cart was busier than ever and he began to believe that it was this and not the sand that he was hired to haul. He thought it was nice of Billie Mitchell to pay him off every night after supper, when the grownups waited until the end of the week to get their money. Shank Austin preserves some of the pieces of money he received at the hands of one of the most controversial figures of his generation.

It surprised nobody that Billie Mitchell sank the two battleships within twenty minutes after the bombers were in the air. There is an eyewitness account that has no exclamation point in it, set down for me by a then youth who was sitting on the deck of the Lightship, a quarter of a mile away, chipping paint. He continued his paint-chipping. It was all very casual and businesslike and nobody was surprised. They knew Billie Mitchell and they speak, now, of him as if he might have been in the village not longer ago than day before yesterday and be coming back this coming week end.

How profoundly the man impressed himself upon the Islanders can be measured, perhaps, by a small thing that happened over at

the Station some while back. It was on the usual Sunday, and at
the upper end of the table, where the senior crewmen, and guest,
were, there was mention of the then current MacArthur upheaval
when the general was relieved of command in the Far East. There
was shading of opinion. One or two of the older men had been in
the Pacific theatre.

Down at the far end of the table was the very junior member of
the crew, newly enlisted, who lacked a dozen years of being born
when Billie Mitchell came to the Islands. What he knew of the man
he had inherited. A lull in the talk caught Johnnie's muttered "Hell
with MacArthur—the so-and-so was on that court that kicked
Billie Mitchell out of the Army." Nobody rebuked him but his face
became very red. The Islanders do not forget one they have taken
for their own.

Not one of Billie Mitchell's engines failed him when he brought
in what amounted to the entire bombardment equipment of the
virtually moribund Air Service. It was not yet become the Air Corps
and lacked a generation yet of being the Air Force. He established
a confidence in the internal engine, and taken with the invention
of the balloon tire, changed the course of life and of living on these
Islands. The year was 1923, and the month was September.

Nowhere else, in so far as I know, is the low-pressure automobile
tire called the balloon tire. The name persists on these Islands, and
as soon as the tire became available the automobile appeared to
stay. There were no roads, beyond movable trails in the sand, but a
low-pressure tire could go almost anywhere. If the going got bad,
all that a driver had to do was to let out some air, letting the tire
down to its minimum, and the engine would move it. You carried a
pump, of course, and when you got unstuck you put the air back in
the tires to save them from being rim-cut.

As the Cattle Tick War grew in intensity the cattle and the
horses vanished from the Island, but the automobile, as a destroyer
of grass, took their place. It was too much bother always to let out
some air and put in some more. Quicker and simpler to drive where
there was some grass to give traction to a normally-inflated tire. It

was easier on the driver—but it was hard on the grass. In twenty-five years there were still less than a hundred automobiles on the Island, but even that few can destroy a lot of vegetation. The Islands were, as early as 1935, beginning to feel the wear—and the sea is very jealous of her grass. A car could destroy as much grass on one traversal of the Island as a cow could eat in a year.

But the Islands were committed to the motor vehicle. The small fishing boats traded their sail and centerboards for engines. For long there was controversy among the dwindling race of fishermen about restrictions that should be imposed on sail-powered and engine-powered oystermen with dredges. Government had moved so far inland that there was never any equitable supervision imposed, and fishing and oystering became a cutthroat piracy. There are few oysters left in Pamlico Sound, and since the world discovered that shrimp are not unclean or poisonous, fishing has also virtually disappeared from the Sounds. To take a pound of shrimp it is necessary to kill off nine pounds of small fish that, next year, might have been marketable trout. . . .

It is always prudent to look for paradox on these Islands before it creeps up behind you and bowls you over. The balloon tire came loaded with its own vintage of paradox. Here was a wide-ranging, freedom-giving vehicle—the automobile, perhaps because of Billie Mitchell, is somehow associated with the heaven-roving aircraft-replacing the sailing boat, and even the powered boat, and at once it began to saddle the Islanders with an inhibited feeling. There was no freedom in it at all. There was nowhere, after all, that anybody could go in it, except maybe to the next village.

Of course the thing could be taken out on the beach, when the tide would be low and the beach smoothed over by a mild sea. Then it was possible to drive the vehicle for every ounce of power it had in it and even I, perhaps foolishly, in 1938 and on a visit here, drove the thirty-eight miles between the Lighthouse and the Inlet in thirty-two minutes. There was no need whatsoever but the thing very likely is infectious. Here a reasonably efficient vehicle in good running order and here a road, a hundred yards wide and as smooth as pavement. Why not?

Most did. But having done that there was not anything else to do but do it again and most did, as long as their fuel held out. And as long as their womenfolks would let them. A boat is tied up down at the dock, out of the reach and the authority of women, but a car you have to bring home and there it enters into the dominion of women. In so far as I have been able to determine there was not, in 450 years, a woman on this Island who could, or who was allowed to, sail a boat.

But a car now, a vehicle that sat docilely in the back yard and within the range of the housewife's authority, that was something else. Women began to drive, and they began, as well, to say when the man, or the men, of the house could drive. Women on these Islands think very highly of the automobile. They can and do command it, most of them, certainly all of the younger ones, and from my apprehensive observation, as I creep modestly along now paved roads, the wildest driving I have encountered on this earth is that performed, on occasion, by native females. They terrify me, and the automobile has not liberated the male of the Island.

Astonishingly few of them, male or female, mangle themselves very seriously and there is not, among the natives, any record of a death on the Island in what the papers call a traffic accident, but unaccustomed visitors depart the Island with shudders. I have said of Johnnie Williams, sometime crew-member at the Station, that he must be the only man on this earth who could drive an automobile sideways along the half mile of road that connects this hill and that station and not do himself hurt. Sometimes he would turn it over and one day, seeing him in a reasonably well preserved vehicle, I inquired whose it was. He said that it was his and I demurred that it couldn't possibly be—there was no dent in the top of it.

Liberation from the hemmed-in state that the automobile engendered began in 1926 and as the result of a very severe storm that raked the Sounds. Toby Tillett, a Roanoke Islander, had just put his life's savings, about $5,000, into some pound nets and two boats with which to fish them. The storm wiped him out, save for one power boat. He contrived a rude flat, and with the remaining boat to haul it, instituted ferry service across Oregon Inlet.

Across the Inlet it was possible, at low tide, to drive the whole way into Norfolk, Virginia, in one day. Toby Tillett charged them one dollar to get them across the Inlet.

Business prospered amazingly and a larger flat was needed, and then a ferryboat that could carry six cars at the time. It grew to ten, and in 1940 the State, prodded by the now wandering Islanders, subsidized the ferry, freeing it of tolls. In 1950 the State bought outright and the talk now is of a bridge.

The Islands were free of their isolation but, in inescapable paradox, they had to share their freedom with their women, and that is not, to a man of the sea, anything but a new kind of slavery, one that he had, in a dozen generations, freed himself of. A man has to ask his wife if he can have the car.

Sometimes an over-wifely wife has been set back upon her heels so to speak by being converted into a widow when the sea would lay hands upon some recreant fellow. A dozen times that there is here a record of, a man would be driving abandonedly along the beach, playing tricks by seeing how close he could come to the thrust of the surf and get away. Twelve times, as I say, the sea has lashed out and taken the car, or the truck—the fish-truck has replaced the old-time buy-boat that came and bought fish—and twice the man with it. Once the sea has mauled a vehicle, salted its engine, it is not again an automobile. It is junk and usually is left where the sea hits it.

But there is a paved road the length of the Island now, and from most miles of it the sea can not even be seen and, since the tires leave the grass alone, the country turns again green and small trees venture to grow. . . .

27

Rather than endure the indignity of being called a Chief Boatswain's Mate, Bannister Midgett departed from the station which he had built and which he had commanded for more than thirty-five years. He withdrew from his native Island and took up residence among foreigners on Roanoke Island, about twenty-five miles away, and continued there until his days were ended. Until the last hour of his life he continued to denounce the occurrence in Washington on January 28, 1915, as a shotgun wedding.

No redeeming glimmer of satisfaction penetrated the enveloping gloom, not even the retention of Sumner Kimball, in a somewhat reduced capacity. He was no longer Superintendent of the U.S.

Lifesaving Service, the post he had filled since the beginning not long before Bannister Midgett built Chicamicomico Station. Of course Bannister Midgett had had his ups and downs with Sumner Kimball, but he was not a bad man. None of the Midgett young were named for him, but there were other families on these Islands that were not above such diplomacy, notably the Scarboroughs.

For half his lifetime, when his name was signed to a piece of paper, a chore that some member of the crew usually performed for him, there appeared, immediately under the signature, the words, "Keeper, Chicamicomico Station." There are, in his Wreck Report Journal, a total of 112 such entries where human life was saved, and no one of them indicates that he ever became a Chief Boatswain's Mate. He was a Keeper and not a mate. It is remembered on these Islands that he denounced mating as a practice suited to the nature of rabbits, muskrats, geese, and mere sailors.

Bannister Midgett was no sailor. He was a surfman.

This shotgun wedding which occurred in Washington on January 28, 1915, was the passage by the Congress of the act merging the U.S. Revenue Cutter Service and the U.S. Lifesaving Service and the naming of the ensuing result the United States Coast Guard. Instigator of this outrage, as it was esteemed along the Outer Banks, was a man named Josephus Daniels, and he did it with a covetous eye. Mr. Daniels concedes as much in his volume, *Our Navy at War*, published after he was retired as Secretary of the Navy in the Wilson cabinet. The admission is watered down considerably in the fourth of his five-volumned autobiography.

Daniels had proposed the merger to William Gibbs McAdoo, Secretary of the Treasury, who had agreed to it with disarming alacrity, up to a point, and beyond that he outsmarted his fellow cabinet man. The U.S. Coast Guard remained an agency of the Treasury Department instead of becoming a part of Mr. Daniels' Navy. Left in the organic law, to be sure, was Hamilton's proviso that, in times of war the organization would, automatically, become a part of the Navy. Daniels did succeed in having his own man placed in the Assistant Treasury Secretaryship in charge of Coast

Guard, and newspaperman Byron R. Newton's name appeared where Sumner Kimball's name had always been.

Secretary Daniels could attain command of the new Coast Guard only by having a war, and Bannister Midgett was sure that the country would soon be so engulfed. There were those, and they continue, along these Islands who share such an appraisal of the sequence of events. Within three years Bannister Midgett's old station and the crew that he had hired into the service and had trained in the minutest intricacy of surfing, had performed a feat of lifesaving that brought the admiring awe of two continents to Bannister Midgett's native village.

And whether he liked or not, the government of the United States continued to think of Bannister Midgett as a Chief Boatswain's Mate, Retired, and at satisfyingly regular intervals there arrived a Treasury Department check, signed by Mr. McAdoo, which, in conjuction with his life-long thriftiness, enabled Keeper, Chicamicomico Lifesaving Station, to live in secure comfort, even in exile. His son was drowned while serving aboard a Coast Guard cutter, at his own choice. It was a grievous blow, but the old man's pride sustained him: he had not in his lifetime committed himself to the sea with anything but an oar to sustain and uphold him.

War came back to the Islands.

It rose up out of the sea, far offshore, on a morning in May, three years after the shotgun wedding in Washington. The transition from Treasury to Navy Department had come smoothly, and men in the eleven stations dotting the 65-mile length of the two Islands remembered what their fathers had told them of the coming of the *Harriet Lane* in 1861 with the Navy's pennant replacing the Treasury Department's flag. An ancient shared pride was rekindled, and there were some who were sure, as they gazed into the horizon's mist, that the *Harriet Lane*'s trim hull and rigging sailed there again.

But it was no trim-lined cutter that John Allen Midgett, the second keeper of Chicamicomico, saw on an August afternoon in 1918. There had been portents of strange things offshore, and as long as a year before there had come telltale litter on the beach when there had been no storm to tear a ship apart. In Washington the people who had such matters in charge were silent, and when it became necessary to say something they admitted briefly that some ships had had the misfortune to hit mines that had been set adrift mysteriously in the western ocean.

This theory appears as a fact in the Daniels postwar book, written in 1922, and is amended to read "submarine" in his later accounting of the era. But it needed no admission from Washington, and denials of it made no difference: these surfmen knew a submarine when they saw one, and they knew the flash of a gun in the night, the thrusting whine of a shell when it moved, with an incredible muzzle velocity, through still air. They would come to know again the dull thudding of a shell against resilient sand.

Some of the debris that washed ashore showed evidence of fire, and some of it smelled of powder, and along the Islands the surfman knew that there was risen up from below the surface of the sea a new threat, that the ocean was no longer a guarding element to the shores of the continental United States. The threat was accepted calmly. Its form had changed, it might be, but the sight of a hostile invasion was not new to these Islands. It had begun, a long time ago, when the first chain-shot, fired from a primitive cannon, landed on this shore. . . . The red, Spanish-iron fragment of it will, in a minute or so, let down its weight on the sheet of paper that has these words on it. . . .

It surprised nobody who watched, though the rest of the United States, when they heard about it, would recoil in shocked panic—the enemy at our very shores, within sight of land, with their guns pounding and their torpedoes weaving a white wake of foam as they rooted their way just below the surface of the sea. It was natural enough that submarines should come. Where else was there a condition so made for them? Here were the ships crowding the sea's lanes, and here were protecting shoals where a submarine might lie in ambush, waiting.

It had begun in May, 1918, and the schooner *Hauppauge*, built

in Wilmington and launched that spring, was set upon off to the
northeast. She was loaded heavily with lumber destined for the
erection of troop cantonments in New Jersey, but the lumber,
when the ship disintegrated, eddied for a while in the ocean until
it was caught by the south-flowing Labrador Current and piled
above Wimble Shoal, which juts out from Chicamicomico. Their
surfman's instinct told the watchers at the eleven stations that this
was no storm's doing. There had been no storm.

There were submarines and there were tankers. Tankers were
something new to this sea. The world had turned, almost overnight,
from coal to petroleum for power, and no day passed without one
of these new ships spreading black smoke along the sea. Southward
they rode the Labrador down, and northward, after the menace
came, they came closer inshore than is the normal custom for ships
on that course in the region above Cape Hatteras. It was the tankers
that became the chief quarry of the hunting submarines, though
they would expend a shell or two on anything that appeared. The
Germans had no friends on this side of the Atlantic and anything
was fair game to them.

Even the Lightship. . . . It was a very businesslike performance
the submarine put on that afternoon at 1:30 when it arose a little
distance away and signaled Captain Walter Barnett to keep his
fingers off his radio or the submarine would shoot it off. Captain
Barnett paid them no heed. He was halfway through his alarm
message when the Germans made good their threat and a shell
ripped away the antenna. They were good marksmen. There was an
immediate following message: the skipper and his crew had fifteen
minutes to abandon ship, after which it would be sunk. There
being no alternative Captain Barnett and his men took to their
oars and rowed home. It was twenty miles and it took them eight
hours to make shore, landing almost precisely on the spot from
which Etheridge and Dailey got to sea after a hard struggle to bring
off the crew of the *Ephraim Williams* thirty-four years before. The
Germans came closer inshore and took a half dozen precautionary
shots at the telephone lines. . . .

During the night the submarine cruised northward and lay to in the lee of Wimble Shoal, not a mile from where John Allen Midgett and his crew kept watch. It was not until afternoon that the raider stirred from its hiding. Up the sea from the south came the black smoke of a tanker, lying low against the horizon. She was heavily loaded, and against the thrust of the Labrador ten knots was as good as she could do. Captain Johnnie kept his eyes on her and he was looking directly at her, five miles offshore and directly abreast the station, when the submarine's guns flashed.

This Midgett literally tumbled down the stair to the tower without waiting to see the smoke well up from the tanker. He had expected what would happen, though there was no precedent, in any sea, for it. The same thing was to become commonplace one war later, when torpedo hit tanker. The ship virtually exploded, and a vast pillar of smoke rose up, and the sea itself seemed to take fire, oil spreading out on the surface from her bunkers and burning. The boat was ready, at the water line. It had been kept ready for many weeks, and before the pillar of smoke had reached zenith in the lazy stillness of the air, the lifeboat was through the surf and headed outward.

On the seaward side of the sinking tanker the flooding tide washed against the hull, keeping it clear of oil and of fire, and the lifeboat, taking a short cut through the fire, approached on the clean side of the ship. Thirty-eight of the forty-four men aboard the vessel were taken off. The others had perished already, and the comparatively small lifeboat, with towed craft, containing members of the crew for whom there was not room in the lifeboat, headed back to land, again taking a short cut through the surface fire ... service above and beyond.... Tradition was become entrenched....

There were here implicit lessons that nobody learned, none except the surfmen who went out that day and in the days to come and who handed down to their inheritors, the native surfmen, two things: the way of a surfman with the sea, and the way of a man who has not fear of the sea. Out of it the makers of military strategy took nothing. They spoke misleadingly of "mines" when the text read clearly "submarines," and they comforted themselves with the belief that here was the war to end wars when it was but a prelude to a war that might well end not only war but a civilization that has not learned a better solution for its perplexities.

This prelude to war ended, and not more than twenty-four dead ships found lodgment in the sea's graveyard. On a day in March twenty-four years later I rode, as a mere passenger, with a little formation of seven A-20 Air Force attack-bombers above this cemetery of man's aspiring. This little flight was based at a field 250 miles inland which had been left there, simply as a hopeful precaution, by a man who foresaw not only the inevitability of war's coming but also the certainty that the Germans, when they were ready, would strike here at the most vulnerable, and wholly undefended, point in all the western ocean.

What came to be called the Battle of Torpedo Junction was at its height. A few weeks before I had ridden in this same ship when it flew in joint ground-air maneuvers and we somewhat hilariously dropped 24-pound sacks of flour on jeering infantrymen. Even though a civilian, I was allowed to drop a flour sack along with the rest of the crew, and I undertook to aim it at the command tent of a lieutenant general who, not many years before, had bitterly opposed Benjamin Delahauf Foulois in urging the development of an aircraft that became the B-17. The flour sack missed, but by not very much, and Hugh Drum afterward reviled me.

Flying that day at an altitude of seven hundred feet the crew were able to count eleven pillars of smoke each marking the death of a freighter or a tanker, all of them within a radius of twenty miles of the Lighthouse. There were no sacks of flour aboard, but down in the belly of each A-20 was a bomb taken from the mysterious canvas-covered heaps that grew, week by week, at one side of the field back deep in the mainland. Henry H. Arnold knew a war was coming, knew that something beside flour sacks would be needed, and that they would be needed above the Graveyard of the Atlantic.

Two of the ships ahead of ours peeled off from the formation and climbed a little and then went along a new course. Within a moment their bombs dropped, and the silhouette of a submarine rose fleetingly into view. It sank, and the formation, in what the Navy would have called a line-of-ships, circled for a little while oil bulged up from below. . . . That evening, back at the base, there were orders for the Squadron to move on to where the war was happening, and within a week they were in Europe. It was five years before I again saw the Graveyard.

There were no surfmen, as such, on the beach that rimmed the Graveyard that day. They were gone, as afterward became clear, to the Southwest Pacific where, manning rude landing craft or any small boat that was handy, they put the Marines ashore at Guadalcanal and, after a while, put ashore two divisions of U.S. Infantry to replace them. And after that they brought off what remained of the Marines—and of themselves. Four of them remain on active duty on these Islands into an era when, no longer ago than last week, a young Coast Guard ensign, who is an uncommonly able helicopter pilot asked, wonderingly, "What is a surfman?"

And while his enlightenment was undertaken he looked, perhaps admiringly, at a great photograph that hangs above the fireplace, the picture that shows the British freighter *Empire Thrush* sitting on bottom, with only her superstructure showing and a jet of bunker oil pouring, underwater, from the wound that killed her, and the nearness of her grave to this house alone accounts for the selection of that picture to hang where it hangs. The grave is exactly two and one-half miles beyond the window at my left elbow.

There are 107 other pictures, of other ships, in the set, all sunk within sight of this hill in a six-month period beginning on January 18, 1942. Although, for most of the time, I was half the continent away from Cape Hatteras, the record reports that I took them, but there is an accompanying letter filed with them, or should be, which confesses mere theft in the Service's interest. In the period of transition after that war, when the Coast Guard was about to pass back into the hands of the Treasury Department, leaving its records, I merely swiped the negatives, kept them until the transfer was effected, and turned them in to Coast Guard Headquarters intact.... Ten years have passed, and it is not unreasonable to hope that the statute of limitations has taken absolving hold upon the matter.

It is less than fortunate that none of the photographs show some of the things that the older surfmen, those who were too old to risk the hazards of landing on North Africa or the islands of the Southwest Pacific, remember very vividly. They do not show the bright yellow sands that rim the ocean when they turned black with the accumulation of 400,000 tons of crude petroleum. They remember that it was leg-deep for a distance of thirty miles on both sides of the Cape, northward and westward, and that it was three years before it cleared wholly away.

Nor were there pictures of any of the 1,056 men and women and children whose bodies were, most of them, committed to the Graveyard. Some of them washed ashore, and when it was not possible to dispose of them otherwise they were buried in a little cemetery off the road and hidden among bordering pines between this hill and the Station yonder. It was a grim time but, now, it is not a talked-about time. Sometimes a phrase, or a sentence, will get back to it, but it needs a perceptive ear to register the minor tones of it.

For the traditional surfman it was a bewildering time. Most of them had been called to far seas and in their places here came unschooled recruits, willing youths but not schooled in the use of the oar or lettered in the way to launch a boat through the surf when it is in a bad mood. Actually the rating of surfman was dropped from the lists of the Navy not long after the Navy lost the most of its power in the middle of the Pacific Ocean, and it has not been, and will not again be, re-established.

Perhaps wisely, the strategists, when they had recovered themselves after Pearl Harbor, elected to attack the menace at its source, or nearer its source, and after the mid-year the Battle of Torpedo Junction waned. For the most part the shore-based crews along these Islands had to content themselves with gathering up the litter of dead along the beach, and a messy business it was. To get to the ocean it was necessary to wade in oily muck that was often knee-deep, and the approach to the enemy was better made by air.

Coast Guardsmen, flying out of the newly-completed Air Base twenty miles up Pasquotank River, mostly in antiquated and hopelessly outmoded aircraft, patrolled the area. They actually destroyed submarines, and there are eyewitness accounts of it. But they have never become official, any more than there is official admission in any important quarter that offshore fishermen, operating out of Hatteras and Ocracoke Inlets, were accosted by pleasant-mannered submarine crews who rose boldly in daylight beside their slow-moving boats and entered into polite negotiation for any coffee, any sugar or condensed milk the fisherman might have aboard. . . . After a while the Government put short-wave radios aboard the fishermen and designated their skippers as intelligence operatives. But the submarines were no longer around.

And the Islanders chuckle reminiscently now about Pinky Wade, whose name is not set down in the history books, nor in any roster that names the accredited wearer of medals. It was the first story that came to me afterward, and if Pinky Wade should sometime come back to the Island he would have a sure, wholly undemonstrative, welcome. In his way Pinky Wade is the Island's principal hero of that dark and confused time. . . . He would have made a good surfman if he had been born at a different place, and in a different time.

He comes from my own county and he remembers, though I am unable to recall it, that it was at my hands that he got his first ride in an airplane. He was, and perhaps still is, a fool about flying, even though he is, by now, not too far from a time when young people will address him as "Hi, Pop." He must be all of thirty-six or thirty-seven, but he was just a youngster, pink-cheeked and redheaded, when the Islands came to know about him. It was his ambition to become a fighter pilot in the Air Force but they would have none of him. Pinky Wade was color blind.

But he could fly and when, nothing else appearing, and no other defense being in sight, the Civil Air Patrol was assigned patrol duty along the Outer Banks, Pinky Wade came with them. They were a motley crew and eager. They came and brought whatever they could get into the air with. And they flew their sputtering courses above shallow offshore waters. They were not armed. Their only weapon was the noise their engines made.

But that was not enough for Pinky Wade. Borrowing whatever he could and tinkering with any tool that he could lay hand to, he contrived a bomb. It weighed about twenty-five pounds, and Pinky Wade flew diligently up and down, every morning and afternoon. The window of his beat-up cub was always open and the bomb lay threateningly in his lap, ready. And there came the afternoon when he sighted an actual submarine basking on the surface about two miles offshore, its crew sunning themselves on the deck.

It may be that if he had made his approach with a muted engine, with his throttle back, he might have been able to slip up on them, but Pinky Wade exuberantly came with wide throttle. Some of the Teutonic sun bathers, reportedly quite naked, made as if to man their deck gun but thought better of it. By the time Pinky Wade's cub was overhead, about fifty feet in the air, they were closing the hatch. Pinky Wade chunked his homemade bomb out the window. It made a fearful splash, and a column of water rose up when it exploded.

The submarine disappeared. It may have merely submerged, but Pinky Wade's grandchildren, when he achieves them, will grow up with the certainty that Grandpa Wade sunk a submarine. The Islanders may be less sure but they remember him for trying and they hope that sometime he may come back and let them look at him. He landed once on the beach near a station, his tanks dry, and took off in a flurry of blown sand as soon as they had doled a little fuel aboard him. Anyhow he tried: he did not refuse the sea and he is remembered for that. He would have made a surfman. And he is part of the Island's folklore.

There is more, much more, of it and some of it is preserved by—
and here again, paradox—the very silence in which it is embedded,
something to be sensed rather than heard, known. The submarines
were gone, the tide of war and its black oil ebbed, and the defense
of the Outer Banks became less tense. Out yonder in the world the
headlines suddenly were alive with a vast uproar when, eight hundred miles from Cape Hatteras, another submarine, approaching
the shore of Long Island in the night, landed, not shells or bombs,
but a crew of spies.

These were taken, and Coast Guardsmen like to remember
that it was a youthful recruit, patrolling the beach, who discovered
the first clue to their presence. The secret service men and the
newspapermen led the populace in a mounting hysteria that
demanded both vengeance and protection. The men were herded
to the nation's capital, tried amid great clamor, and some of them
executed. . . . Mention that on these Islands and there will fall an
utter silence. A curious thing at first, with its implications hidden,
this silence.

Nowhere does there exist a shred of written-down evidence
to buttress the story, but there were two of these expeditions of
spies with orders to sabotage, to kill, to burn. The second landed a
little distance from Oregon Inlet and they are buried not far from
there. I have not ventured to approach the spot, but it could be
found without undue searching. I am not sure how many bodies
were put into the grave but there were six or seven. Such of their
equipment as was useful and salvageable was retained and the rest
of it destroyed and nothing said about it.

There are in the world, very likely, people who would make a
vast and shocked outcrying at the notion that a detachment of spies
would be, or could be, so summarily dealt with. But they are no
deader than those that were executed amid such commotion, and
I am not unduly disturbed at the thought that whatever money
Germany supplied its agents with, and the amount in the Long
Island case was considerable, may have been equitably distributed

among such as may have had a hand in an effective, and very tidy, resolving a matter that, in the end, could have had but one answer.

That, also, is the way of these Islands, and of these Islanders.

***

War was gone, at any rate for the time being, from these Islands, and it is not improper to reflect that if the rest of the country had, proportionately, sent a like numerical representation to the armed services, the number of men under arms at the height of the war would have approached fifty million. There are three thousand people on the two Islands, and 912 of them were in uniform, in every branch of the service and in every theatre of war. . . . Shank Austin spent his days sweating on the Burma Road, remembering sometimes his friend Billie Mitchell, by now dead, and by night sweating over a moving picture projector, since he had developed a moving picture business back home on his Island. He hauled dirt for the Burma Road, and was not paid three dollars a day. And he missed his sturdy beach horse. . . .

A restlessness came home with him, and with the others who came back from far places. The Island was changed and it was not changed. The surfmen who went off to the wars came home no longer surfmen, and the Stations were virtually abandoned in the loose interlude of transition back to the Treasury Department. Some said that the Coast Guard had died and would not be brought back to renewed life. . . . They even read it in the papers and it was a shocking thing to think about. . . . A good three-quarters of the population, directly or indirectly, knew nothing else.

There came a day when the first Governor of North Carolina to formally appear on the Island came down, not to visit the Islands especially, but as a guest-in-chief of a vast corporation who hoped, possibly on that specific day, to come upon oil in the improbably deep hole they had drilled into the plain below this hill. There was a great company. On the way down R. Gregg Cherry, Governor, saw a light and he added a new paragraph to the speech that he made at the schoolhouse and was tremendously applauded.

... Seventeen miles of pavement, connecting four of the Seven Villages of the Island—"and the next man, the man after me, can finish it for you. . . ." That day there were only two members of the Coast Guard left who could attend, in uniform.

But a little more than a year afterward, in the second week of my residence here, a not wisely counseled road contractor, whose bid on the first pavement to be laid on the Outer Banks had been low, decided that he would do like he had seen the Islanders do— drive straight down the beach with about $250,000 worth of road-building machinery. It made a massive procession, graders, tractors, the like of which had not been dreamed about on these Islands.

From beyond the Lightship the sea looked upon this monstrous procession and recoiled. When the convoy was within a mile or so of the Lighthouse she hit it, and within a quarter of an hour it looked as if the Islanders' dream of a road had vanished. And then a kind of miracle began to happen. Surfmen who had left the service, and the handful at the Station—numbering three—got themselves together, plunged into the seething surf, compelled engines to run, and before dark the man's machinery was safe behind the protecting dyke that Mr. Byrum's miracle, with the help of the wind, had erected there. The road was safe, and within a month's time the Coast Guard had reactivated all of its stations, and yet another era began on the Islands.

APPENDIX

CHRONOLOGY

1497   Amerigo Vespucci touches, for the first time, continent named for him, anchoring in the Bight of Hatteras abreast native village, capital of Hattorask Indians.

1547   (Traditional) English and Spanish crews fight in Bight of Hatteras. English ship, not identified, sinks. Some of crew escape capture and make shore.

1585   Raleigh's expedition passes offshore, continuing northward.

1650   Evidences of expanding population on Hatteras and Ocracoke Islands reported. The word "mustee" appears.

1685   Settlement on south side of Ocracoke Inlet charted as Portsmouth. First ships from Albemarle province use Inlet for egress to the sea.

1700   Portsmouth described as the largest port on Atlantic Coast south of the Virginia capes.

1706   Six "mustees" baptised into the established church in Hatteras (Indian) village, missionary rector protesting their lack of souls.

1712   Total of 154 persons baptised, many of them mustees and some few Indian. Minister still protests their admission to sacraments, but church authorities in England adamant.

Chronology

1718   Battle between Captain Maynard and Captain Teach in Ocracoke harbor. Teach killed, with twenty-one others. Some of crew escape to land and go "underground."

1723   Windmill for grinding corn established at Kinnakeet.

1737   Ship with cargo of Arabian horses, traditionally "about 100," wrecked off Ocracoke Island. Horses and native attendants make it to shore.

1746   Five members of the crew of British merchantmen killed when they come ashore to rustle cattle about two miles north of Cape Hatteras.

1755   Charter for town of Portsmouth proposed in Provincial Council sitting in New Berne. Members of incorporating commission named but no record exists of its functioning. None were residents of the town.

1757   Provincial Assembly repeals law laying a special tax on mustees, levied apparently about 1720. Since they were neither slaves nor poll-taxable whites a special impost was provided. After the repeal of the "Mustee Tax" men of white and Indian blood were regarded as taxable citizens.

1773   Alexander Hamiltion, aged seventeen, passes by Cape Hatteras, narrowly escaping death when *Thunderbolt* catches fire.

1790   First U.S. Independence Day observed at Ocracoke, the celebration being combined with the annual roundup of yearling wild horses. Both are continued.

           The First Congress approves Alexander Hamilton's request for authority and funds for erection of lighthouse on Cape Hatteras, August 4.

Chronology

1796   General Assembly of North Carolina grants permission to the federal government to buy four acres of land as site for lighthouse on Cape Hatteras.

1797   Construction of lighthouse begun by Major General Henry Dearborn.

1799   Lighthouse on Cape Hatteras and beacon at Ocracoke Inlet activated.

1806   Congress directs survey be made of hazards to navigation in Cape Hatteras-Ocracoke area. Lightship proposed.

1827   John Rollinson born at Trent.

1836   First steamship, *William Gibbons*, wrecked on Hatteras Island, thirty miles north of the Cape.

1837   The *Home*, steamer, beached and breaks up on Ocracoke with loss of ninety lives, most deadly disaster in the record of the Outer Banks.

1849   Lifesaving Stations at Oregon Inlet, Cape Hatteras, and Ocracoke.

1856   Wrecked *Mary Varney* establishes Oden family on the Outer Banks.

1860   "Lincoln 43—Douglas 43."

        Inbound tonnage through Hatteras Inlet sets new record.

1861   Volunteer troops arrive to erect forts at Inlet, May 9.

        Harriet Lane shells forts on July 11.

        Federal fleet appears off Hatteras on August 25. Bombardment begins on August 27. The forts surrender on August 28 and Union occupation of the Outer Banks begins. The Islanders flee to mainland.

Hatteras village proclaimed capital of "retrieved" State of North Carolina on November 18 by "convention" meeting in Rollinson residence.

1862   Federal fleet, numbering eighty-two ships, appears off Hatteras Inlet in heavy weather, January 14. Seventeen ships of fleet founder and break up before armada effects passage through Inlet eight days later.

Invasion of eastern North Carolina fans out from Hatteras, February 5, commanded by Burnside. Dwellings razed to provide fuel for remaining sixty-five ships of the expedition.

Lighthouse is restored to use after mysterious damage.

1863   Burial refused by remaining Islanders for native member of the crew of the U.S.S. *Monitor* washed ashore north of Lighthouse on January 2.

1867   Construction begins on new Lighthouse. Many repatriated Islanders learn bricklaying.

1870   U.S. Signal Corps completes telegraph line from Virginia Beach to Cape Hatteras.

New Lighthouse activated. Hamilton tower razed by explosives.

1874   U.S. Weather Bureau establishes station in new Lighthouse August 8.

Four Lifesaving Stations on two Islands serve without pay due to lack of appropriation by Congress.

Chronology

1877   U.S.S. *Huron* wrecked ten miles north of Oregon Inlet with loss of ninety-eight members of crew. Five members of Lifesaving crew lost in effort to assist.

1878   Thomas Nast's series of cartoons lashing the Congress for niggardly support of Lifesaving Service begin.

1880   Lifesaving Service revitalized and placed on established basis. New stations ordered built, five on the two Islands of the Outer Banks.

1884   Crew of *Ephraim Williams* rescued at great hazard and first Congressional Medals of Honor for Lifesaving are awarded. John W. Rollinson becomes superintendent of Colonel Wainwright's "porpoise factory."

1894   "The Terrible Winter" sets in.

1897   Bannister Midgett tests first internal combustion engine.

1899   The "Great Storm" begins on August 16 and lasts for three days. Fifteen ships wrecked within 40-mile reach of beach. Rasmus Midgett decorated for rescue of crew of the *Priscilla*.

1902   Guglielmo Marconi begins construction of first wireless tower in Western Hemisphere. Thomas A. Edison and Reginald Fessenden test transmission of voice by wireless on King's Point.

1912   Only direct contact with sinking liner *Titanic* is made by Cape Hatteras Wireless Station.

1915   Congress combines U.S. Lifesaving Service and Revenue Cutter Service into U.S. Coast Guard. Bannister Midgett retires rather than be called "mate."

Chronology

1916   U.S. Navy takes over Marconi wireless station as step toward neutrality. Developed into first radio compass station.

1918   German submarine sinks Diamond Shoals Lightship and, two days later, British tanker *Mirlo*, whose crew is rescued at great hazard by John Allen Midgett, successor to Bannister Midgett in command of Chicamicomico Station.

Submarine sinkings off Outer Banks total twenty-two ships.

1920   The Balloon Tire makes its appearance on the Outer Banks.

1921   "Cattle Tick War" begins when Department of Agriculture decrees dipping vats for cattle and horses. Dipping vats dynamited.

1922   First obstetrical case evacuated from the Island by air, in U.S. Navy flying boat.

1923   Colonel Billie Mitchell brings bombardment wing of Air Service to Hatteras and on September 5 sinks two battleships off Diamond Shoals.

1926   Ferry service instituted across Oregon Inlet. Cattle Tick War ends when authorities agree to buy and exterminate cattle.

1928   Balloon tires replace cattle as destroyer of grass, and erosion of beach is accelerated.

1930   Phipps interests buy large acreages on both Islands for investment and recreational use. Cape Hatteras area included in purchase.

1933   The year of the storms. April and August bring heavy seas, which cut down the beach. Lighthouse is believed in danger. Last four-master is wrecked at Gull Shoal during August hurricane.

1935   U.S. Army Engineers fail in efforts to check erosion, and plans are developed for removal of light to new tower 6,000 feet inland.

        Phipps interests donate Cape Hatteras acreage to State of North Carolina for recreational area. Unit of Civilian Conservation Corps arrives to begin conservation measures. The Byrum miracle begins.

1937   President Roosevelt signs Cape Hatteras National Seashore bill.

1938   The light is moved to new location and U.S. Coast Guard abandons Cape Hatteras Station for a new site.

        Hall Roosevelt, examining CCC's work in sand fixation, predicts that light will be brought back to old tower, which had been ceded to National Park Service as part of the National Seashore proposed by Congressman Lindsay Warren.

1940   Ocean pushed back nearly 1,000 feet by Byrum dykes.

1942   Battle of Torpedo Junction begins on January 18 with the sinking of the first of 108 ships lost off Cape Hatteras within the following six months.

        Old Lighthouse is used again as lookout tower. Radio Compass Station is decommissioned.

1945   Standard Oil Company begins drilling exploratory well south of Lighthouse after leasing three million acres of land in eastern North Carolina.

Chronology

1946   Governor R. Gregg Cherry allocates $350,000 for building first seventeen miles of paved road on the Outer Banks, connecting Kinnakeet with Hatteras.

1948   Governor Cherry speaks at celebration marking completion of first link of Outer Banks Highway, and U.S. Coast Guard announces intention of moving "the light back home."

1950   On January 23 the light is returned to the Lighthouse.

PROPOSALS* for Building a Lighthouse &c on the Head Land of Cape Hatteras on the Coast of North Carolina of the following Materials, Dimensions and Description:—

The Form is to be octagonal, the Foundation is to be of stone to be sunk thirteen feet below the bottom of the water table or Surface of the Earth and to be commenced of the diameter of twenty-nine feet from such commencement to the height of four feet. The Foundation to be laid solidly: and from thence to the bottom of the water table the Foundation Wall is to be nine feet thick and nine feet high.

The diameter of the base from the bottom of the water table to the top thereof (where the octagonal pyramid is to commence) is to be twenty-eight feet, four inches and the wall is to be seven feet thick. The wall of the octagonal pyramid is to be six feet thick at the base thereof on the top of the water table. The height of the building from the bottom of the water table and from the surface of the earth is to be ninety feet to the top of the stonework under the floor of the lantern where the diameter is to be sixteen feet and a half and the wall three feet—the whole wall to be built of stone.

The water table is to be capped with sawed stone at least eight inches wide, sloped to turn off the water. The outside of the wall are to be faced with hewn or hammer-dressed stone, having four windows on the north east and five windows on the southwest, the sashes to be hung with hinges and each sash to have twelve panes of glass, 8 by 10 inches.

On the top of the stone work is to be a framed pair of joists bedded therein planked over with oak plank extending one foot and one half beyond the wall thereby forming an eave which is to

*This document from the National Archives is the first proposal for the erection of a permanent building undertaken by the Government of the United States. Difficulties encountered in the purchase of land for the structure delayed the undertaking, and the Cape Hatteras Lighthouse is not, for that reason, the oldest. The Islanders, even then, parted with their land reluctantly.—B. D. M.

be finished with a cornice, the whole having a descent from the center sufficient to throw off the water and to be covered with copper. A complete and sufficient iron lantern in octagonal form is to rest thereon with a complete set of lamps constructed according to the plan and direction in the annexed draft. —

The eight corner pieces or stanchions of the Lantern are to be built into the wall to the depth of eight feet where they are to be secured by eight large iron anchors passing through the wall, the ends of which are to be secured into an iron band on the outside which will be in contact with the conductors, these stanchions to be 3 inches by 2 1/2 inches in diameter—the lantern to be six feet six inches in the smallest diameter: it is also to be eight feet six inches high from the bottom of the floor to the dome or roof and to have a dome or roof four feet in height.

The whole space between the posts or upright pieces at the angles is to be occupied by the sashes which are to be struck solid, the sashes to be constructed for receiving panes of glass 14 by 12 inches. A part of the sash on the southwest side is to be hung on hinges for a convenient door to go out on the platform. The rafters of the lantern are to be framed into an iron hoop over which is to be a copper funnel through which the smoke may pass into a large copper ventilator in the form of a man's head capable of containing sixty gallons. This head is to be turned by a large vane so that the hole for venting the smoke may be always to leeward. Eight dormant ventilators are to be fixed in the roof, a large curved air pipe is to pass through the floor and a close stove [?] is to be provided and fixed in the lantern. There is to be a strong railing to form a convenient balcony round the lantern and eight pairs of stairs to ascend thereto. The entrance to the lantern is to be by a trap door covered with copper. The building is to be furnished with two complete electrical conductors, or rods with points. The floor to be laid with planks of at least one and an half inch in thickness. The entrance of the Light House is to be well secured by a strong door hung upon hinges with a strong lock and latch complete.

An oil vault is to be built 20 by 12 in the clear and arched over and covered with earth or sand over which a shed is to be built. It is to be furnished with nine strong cedar cisterns with strong covers, each capable of containing one hundred gallons of oil. These cisterns are to be sunk in clay which is to be well rammed round them. The space above the cisterns to be sufficient to accommodate an equal quantity of surplus oil, the entrance to the vault to be well secured by a strong door with latch and lock.

Also a frame house to be 34 feet in front and sixteen feet deep with a cellar under it, the cellar walls to be 18 inches thick and seven feet high. The first story of the house to be eight feet, the second seven feet high. The floor to be laid whole length and nailed through. The stack of chimnies is to be furnished with two plain fire places on each floor, one of them large for a kitchen, two windows below and three above in front and rear, each sash to have 18 panes of glass 10 by 12 inches, the doors to be hung and finished completely. The ceilings and sides of the house to be plastered with two coats; all the wood work inside and out to be painted well and the whole finished in a plain, decent manner. A well is to be sunk at a convenient distance and furnished with a curb, bucket and rope complete.

If it is impracticable on account of the flow of water or any other insuperable cause to sink the foundation of the Light House to the depth of thirteen feet or if the soil at that depth from the surface be deemed too unstable to support the weight of the proposed building the foundation is to be underlaid and properly secured by timbers of large dimensions.

THE SUBSCRIBER will find all the materials, labor and other objects of cost and expense and will execute the before described work (viz—the erection of a Light House on the Head Land of Cape Hatteras) in a good and workmanlike manner for the sum of Thirty Eight Thousand Four Hundred and Fifty Dollars, to be paid in the following manner:—

Eight Thousand Dollars at the first to provide materials, Etc. Six thousand dollars when the first story beams of the

Light House are laid.

Eight Thousand dollars when the Lantern of the same is finished.

Remainder when the whole work is finished and he further engages providing of materials and the commencement of the work shall be immediately begun and the whole work finished with all possible speed.

HENRY DEARBORN

Pittstown, [Mass.]
August 21, 1798.

Approved September 21, 1798.
JOHN ADAMS
[President]

JOHN ROLLINSON'S listing of ships entering the Port of Hatteras during his term as Collector of the Port, beginning in 1859 and ending with the onset of the Civil War.

A list of vessels from the West Indies, 1859

Jan.	9	Sch.	*Rough & Ready*	S. H. Beasley, Master
"	9	"	*Melvinia*	James Cahoon, Master
"	17	"	*Baltimore*	V. A. Knight, Master
"	21	"	*Champion*	Robert Monroe, Master
"	21	"	*Mary*	Silas Blount, Master
Feb.	17	"	*Virginia*	John King, Master
"	19	"	*Rio*	James Hobbs, Master
"	19	"	*Lydia & Martha*	W. Ballance, Master
"	25	"	*Harriet*	William Kinston, Master
"	27	"	*Debro*	Spencer Midgett, Master
"	27	"	*Davenport*	W. Davis, Master
"	28	"	*Julia Ann*	G. E. Sampson, Master
Mar.	3	"	*I. W. Hughes*	William Howard, Master
"	13	"	*Baltimore*	V. A. Knight, Master
"	16	"	*Sally Smith*	Daniel Hayman, Master
"	16	"	*Loriccinth* [?]	John W. Partredge, Master
"	24		*Mary Louise*	B. F. Gautier, Master
"	31		One was Th. Hayman he came in while [I] was gone to Portsmouth.	

Second Quarter, commencing April 11, 1859

[By inference Mr. Rollinson must have been called to Portsmouth, headquarters of the Revenue Service for the area, for conference. Subsequent entries are in more detail. Dates are not always set down, but the entries are by successive numbers.]

Sch. *Rough & Ready*, Samuel Beasley, Master, from Martinique bound to Washington. April 13th. 30 tons stone ballast. $650 American gold. Ship's stores.

Sch. *I. F. Davenport*, Warren Davis, Master, April 15. From Barbados bound to Elizabeth City, N.C. 35 bbl sugar. One tierce sugar. 5 tons stone ballast. Small stores.

Sch. *Crinoline*, I. F. Craddic [sic] Master, April 20, from Nevis, W. I. bound to Edenton, N.C. 40 tons stone ballast, two puncheons of molasses, 4 barrels of sugar.

Sch. *Caroline Casey*, John Cudworth, master.

Sch. *Rio*, James Hobbs, Master, from Vaeques [?] bound to Elizabeth City. 34 puncheons of molasses, 10 barrels of sugar, 160 gallons of rum.

Sch. *Haretrine* [?] William Kitson, Master. May 7, from St. Kits bound to Edenton. 20 tons of ballast, 10 puncheons of molasses, 2 barrels of sugar, 1 bundle of letters, $50 in gold.

Sch. *Loucinth* [?] John W. Pateridge, master, June 3. 2 puncheons of molasses, 2 barrels of sugar, 30 tons of stone ballast. Bill of exchange $1500. Ship stores, ½ barrel flower, ¼ barrel sugar, ¼ bread, small stor from Trinidad bount to Elizabeth City.

Sch. *Debra*, Spencer Midgett, master, June 19, from St. Kitts bound to Plymouth. 13 hogsheads of molasses, 8 barrels of sugar.

Sch. *Soloman Andrews*, E. M. Putnam, master, June 25, from St. Kitts bound to Washington, N.C. Fifty five hogsheads of molasses.

Sch. *I. F. Davenport*, Warren Davis, master, June 26, from Trinidad bound to Elizabeth City. Fifty hogsheads of molasses, four cags [sic] of [illegible] 40 cocernuts [sic] and other small stores.

Third Quarter, commencing July 11, 1859

Sch. *Cronoline* I. F. Craddock, master, July 5th, from Nevis bound to Edenton. Five hogsheads of molasses, 40 tons of stone ballast, 2 boxes of bay water, one case of Jin [sic]. Ship stores, one barrel of sugar, 2 demajohns [sic] of Jin, other small stores.

Sch. *Baltimore,* V. A. Knight, master. July 6. from Port or [sic] Prince, W. I., bound to Elizabeth City. Ballast & ship stores.

Sch. *Haretrain* [?] from St. Kitts bound to Edenton. 20 tons of ballas, 10 puncheons of molasses, 1 bundle of letters, $800 in gold.

Sch. *Mary T. Parmley* [Parmalee?] David Gaskins, master. July 14 from St. Kitts bound to Washington. Cargo 80 puncheons of molasses.

Sch. *Lady Antrim,* Thias Hayman, master. From St. Thomas bound to Edenton. 30 tons of stone ballast, 1 barrel of beef, one barrel of pork, 1 barrel of pilot bread, 1 barrel of flower, one case of Jin.

Sch. *Corrine,* John Brown, master, July 31, from Turk's Island to Plymouth. 10 barrels of sugar, 4,572 bushels of salt, 22 pounds of perserves [sic] 1 barrel of bread, part of a barrel of flower, part of barrel of pork.

Sch. *Harriet Ryan* [which seems to be the indicated spelling from the entry of Sept. 12, 1859] William Hickson, master, from Barbados to Edenton, 30 tons of ballast, 1 bundle of letters and $1000 in gold.

[September 16, 1859, the entry reads:] The Three-master come in about 1 o'clock P.M. then over the swash and then got collared and lay about half on. Did not speak her.

Fourth Quarter Commencing Oct. 1, '59

Sch. *Sophy*, Callan Perce master, Oct. 4, from Barbados to Plymouth in ballast.

Sch. *I. F. Davenport*, W. Davis, master, October 5, from St. Martin's to Elizabeth City. 1100 bushels of salt, 13 barrels of sugar, 6 tons of ballast.

Sch. *Lady Antrim* Thias [Matthaias?] Hayman November 16, from Barbados to Edenton. 20 tons of ballast, ½ barrel beef, ½ do pork, ½ do flower 10 pounds of coffee, 1 case of Jin, 1 dimajohn of Jin.

Sch. *Harriet Ryan*, St. Tomas to Edenton, 30 tons of ballast, 6 puncheons of molasses, 1 bundle of letters, $500 in gold.

Sch. *Crinoline*, I. F. Craddock, master, November 28, from Point Peter, Guadaloupe, bound to Edenton. 50 tons of ballast, 4,000 oranges.

Sch. *Colremine*, I. Brophey, master, Dec. 4th, from Turk's Island to Plymouth. 4662 bushels of salt. ½ barrel of flower, ½ do of bread, ½ do of pork, ½ do of beef, 100 lbs sugar.

Sch. *Baltimore*, V. A. Knight, master, Dec. 18, bound to Elizabeth City from Inauga. 995 bushels of salt.

Sch. *Sally Smith*, Daniel Hayman, master. Dec. 19. from Barbados to Edenton, 35 tons of ballast, 3 puncheons of molasses, 3 barrels of molasses, 900 oranges, ship stores, part of a puncheon of molasses, 1 barrel of yams, 4 bottles of Jin, part of a barrel of sugar.

Sch. *Pawline* [Pauline?] G. Bradstreet, master, Dec. 29th from Point Peter, Guadalupe, bound to [illegible]. Fifteen thousand orranges, 28 tons of ballast, ship stores.

No. of vefels borded in 1859 was 66.

Quarter commencing January 1th, 1860

Sch. *Rio,* John Pew master, Jan. 18 from St. Thomases bound to Elizabeth City. 36 tons of ballast, ½ barrel of flower, ½ do beef, 1100 dollars in gold.

Sch. *Lydia & Martha,* Jan. 20, John Burgess master, from St. Martins bound to Elizabeth City. Three thousand bushels of salt, three thousand arranges, five hundred pines [pineapples?] cost $3 per Hundred. Stores 1 bb of flower, ½ do of pork, ½ do of sugar, small stores.

Sch. *Devenport,* Warren Davis, master, Jan. 26 from Guadalupe to Elizabeth City. 30 tons of ballast, 2000 orranges, and ship stores.

Sch. *Harriet Ryan,* William Hickson master, Jan. 31 from Turk's Island to Edenton. 2766 bushels of salt, 1 bundle of letters, $800 gold.

Sch. *Deborah,* Spencer Midgett, master. February 20. From Barbados bound to Plymouth. Ship stores and ballast.

Sch. *Charles Robert,* Stephen Fowler, master. Feb. 22. From St. Martins bound to Washington. 3800 bushels of salt. Stores, ½ barrel of bread, ½ do pork.

Sch. *Pacific,* James Farrow, master. Feb. 24. St. Martins bound to Washington. 10 puncheons of molasses. 527 bbls salt, 3 bbls sugar. $800 in gold.

Sch. *Baltimore* J. W. Cox, master. Feb. 26. from Antigua to Elizabeth City. 953 bushels of salt and small stores.

Sch. *Champion,* John Douphy, master. March 18 from Guadalupe bound to Washington. 760 five-frank pieces, 195 gold pieces, 20 francs each and small stores.

Quarter Commencing April 1th, 1860

Apr. 4.— Sch. *Sally Smith*, Daniel Hayman master, tonage 106 35/95 from Trinidad, Port of Spain bound to Edenton. 9 puncheons of molasses. 7 barrels of sugar, 30 tons of ballast, 200 coconuts. Ship stores, a part of a puncheon of molasses, i barrel of sugar, i case of Jin, 6 bottles of pepper.

Apr. 5.—Sch. *I. F. Devenport*, Warren Davis, master, 114 36/95 tons, from Antigua, W. I. bound to Elizabeth City. 2028 bushels of salt and small ship's stores.

Apr. 16.— Sch. *Lydia & Martha* M. A. Burgess master, 114 36/95 tons from Antigua bound to Elizabeth City. 30 tons of sand ballast 11 puncheons of molasses, 1 puncheon of rum, 10 barrels of sugar.

Apr. 22.— Sch. *Pacific*, James Farrow, master, 80 18/95 tons. From St. Kitts to Washington. 40 puncheons of molasses, 2 barrels of sugar, 200 dollars in specie. Ship stores ⅔ barrel of pork, do of flower, do of br ad, small stores.

May 10.— Sch. *Baltimore*, J. W. Cox, master. 58 66/95 tons from Anaugua bound to Elizabeth City. Cargo 952 bushels of salt, 58 bags of coffee. Small stores.

May 10.—Sch. *Isabella*, G. W. Wallace, master. Tonage 86 32/95 from St. Martin's bound to Newburn. Cargo 1650 bushels of salt, 800 pines [pineapples] 20 bunches of bananas, ship stores, ½ barrel of flower; do of br ad, ½ do of pork, i do of fish, 1 do of cugar, 1 do of molasses.

May 27.— Sch. *Loucinth*, G. E. Sampson, master. Tonage 95 39/95 from St. Pierre, Martinique bound to Elizabeth City. Cargo, 30 tons of ballast, 10 half basket of champain [champagne] five cags [illegible] ship stores, i barrel of flower; 1 do of brad, ½ do of beef.

Jun. 3.— Sch. *Devenport*, Warren Davis, master. Tonage
11436/95 from Antiger bound to Elizabeth City. Cargo
ten puncheons of molasses, 4 cags [illegible] 40 pines,
15 tons of ballas and small stores.

Jun. 10— Sch. *Pacific*, James Farrow, master. Tonage 80 18/95
from Nevis and St. Kitts bound to Washington. Cargo
46 puncheons of molasses, small ship stores 1 bbl beef,
½ do pork, ½ do bread.

Jun. 10— Sch. *Harriet Ryan* William Hixton master. Tonage 106
35/95 from Barbados bount to Edenton. Cargo 20 tons
pork, one bundle of letters.

Jun. 10— Sch. *Sally Smith*, Daniel Hayman, master. 106 35/95
tons from Barbados bound to Edenton. Cargo 4 bbl
sugar, 1 puncheon molasses, 30 tons ballast, 250
cokernuts ship stores, 7 pounds of jelly.

Jun. 12— Sch. *Mary Louise* B. F. Gautier master. Tonage 144. 21
puncheons molasses, 5 bbl sugar. Stores, 1 bbl beef, i
do bread, 1 do pork, 1 do sugar. Coffee and tea. From
Barbados to Washington.

Jun. 10— Sch. *Lydia & Martha*, John W. Patteredge master.
Tonage 11. From Barbados bound to Elizabeth City.
Cargo 30 puncheons of molasses, 3 bbl sugar, 14 cags of
Tammons, a col [Colonial?] Bank bill $1310.42. Stores
½ bbl flower, ½ do pork, ½ do beef, box of fish, coffee,
tea and other small stores.

Jun. 14— Sch. *Southern Star* W. T. Dough master. Tonage 105
89/95 from Barbados & Rum Cey [Key?] bound
to Plymouth. Cargo 50 puncheons of molasses, 20
barrels of sugar, 1744 bushels of salt, 2 puncheons of
molasses.

Jun. 15— Sch. *Crinoline*, James Craddie master. Tonage 94 11/95.
Cargo 12 puncheons of molasses, from St. Kitts to

Edenton. Ballast 40 tons. Stores 1 bbl pork, ½ do beef, ½ do bread, ½ do flower, 1 case Jin, 2 demajohns of Jin, 1 cag of tammons, 2 barrels of sugar.

Jun. 16— Sch. *Hugh W. Fry*, E. I. Marshall master. Tonage 132. From Mantan Island Cuba to Baltimore. Cargo 116 boxes precipitate copper, 133 ½ tons copper ore. Ship stores.

[Later entry at bottom of page:] December 19th, 1870. I caught 119 Big talors on the same day as the steamer Birbank [Fairbanks] came in at Hatteras Inlet and Burned. [A "talor" is a bluefish.]

Jun. 16— Sch. *I. F. Devenport*, Warren Davis, master. Tonage 114 36/95. From St. Vinces [St. Vincent?] bound to Elizabeth City. Cargo 20 puncheons of molasses, 20 pounds of nutmegs, 12 tons of Ballas.

Aug. 7— Sch. *Marinah H.* John Dough, master. Tonage 90. From Barbados bound to Washington. Cargo 26 puncheons of molasses, 9 barrels of sugar, 2 puncheons of rum, ship stores 1 bbl sugar, do of flower, ½ do beef, ½ do of pork, small stores.

Aug. 16— Sch. *Harriet Ryan*, William Nixton, master. Tonage 91. From St. Kitts to Edenton. Cargo 20 tons of ballast, 10 puncheons of molasses, 1 bundle of letters, 300 dollars in gold.

Aug. 16— Sch. *Lydia & Martha*, James Patteredge, master. Tonage 111 77/95 from [blank] to Elizabeth City. Cargo 30 tons of ballast, 500 oranges, A colonial bill for $1410.60, 2 letters.

Sep. 5— Sch. *Devenport*, Warren Davis, master. Tonage 1]436/95. From St. Vincen bound to Elizabeth City. Cargo, 24 tons of stone ballast, small ship stores.

Sep. 7— Sch. *Resolution*, William Gales master. Tonage 62, from Turk's Island to Plymouth. Cargo 7 hogsheads of molasses, 1744 bushels of salt, 1 bbl of molasses, ship stores, 10 gallons of rum.

Quarter Commencing October 1th, 1860

Oct. 5.— Sch. *Wm. T. Henden*, Charles Layton master. Tonage 72 from Long Cay to Richmond, Virginia. Cargo fifty to fifty-five tons of guano.

Oct. 15.—Sch. *George Henry*, C. G. Fields, master. Tonage 111 90/95 from St. Martins bound to Newburn. Cargo 3289 bushels of salt, 2000 oranges, 6 cags tammons, ... i demajohn bitters.

Oct. 19.—Sch. *Planter* James Robs, master from Turk's Island to Plymouth. Tonage 97 59/95. Cargo 2560 bushels of salt, 3 barrels of sugar, 730 lbs, 1 puncheon of molasses 110 gallons.

Oct. 20.—Sch. *Baltimore*, J. W. Cox master. Tonage 59 from St. Martins bound to Elizabeth City. Cargo 204 barrels of salt. Small stores

Oct. 23.—Sch. *Harriet Rian* Wm. Noxton master. Tonage 91. From Nevis to Edenton. Cargo 11 puncheons of molasses, 20 tons of ballast, 1 bundle of letters, $500 in gold.

Oct. 31.—Sch. *Lydia & Martha*, Wm. H. Patteredge, master. Tonage 111 77/95 from St. Martins bound to Elizabeth City. Cargo 2535 bushels of salt, $480, 5 letters, ship stores.

Nov. 21.— Sch. *Isabell* G. W. Wallace master. Tonage 86 33 /95. From St. Martins bound to Newburn. Cargo 2250 bushels of salt, 1250 dollars in gold.

Nov. 27.— Sch. *L. T. Johnson,* Thomas C. Wallace master. Tonage 149 from St. Martins bound to Newburn. Cargo 1800 bushels of salt. 1000 coconuts, 500 pineapples, 300 oranges. Ship stores, 15 gallons of rum.

Dec. 21.— Sch. *M. C. Etheredge* G. W. Price master. Tonage 144. 67/95. From Point Peter Guadalupe bound to Plymouth. Ballast and ship stores.

Dec. 21.— Sch. *San Juan* V. A. Knite master. Tonage 105. From Trinidad bound to Elizabeth City. Ballast & ship stores.

Dec. 30.— Sch. *Lydia & Martha* W. H. Petteredge master. Tonage 111 from Damico bound to Elizabeth City. Cargo 40 tons ballast Colonial Bank bill #2291.25, 156 letters.

Whole number of vessels borded in 1860 43.

Quarter commencing Jan. 1th, 1861

Jan.   8.— Sch. *Harriet Rian,* Wm. Norton master, 91 tons bound from St. Wincen to Plymouth 30 tons of ballast and 500 dollars in gold.

Jan. 14.— Sch. *Five Boys* Wm. Jones master come while we was at Portsmouth.

Jan. 16.— Sch. *Isabelle* George Wallace master was not spoke on account of it being foggy.

Jan. 27.— Sch. *Planter* James Hobbs master. Tonage 97 59/95 from Salt Key, Turk's Island, bound to Elizabeth City. Cargo 2596 bushels salt, 1 puncheon of molasses, 1 barrel of sugar 1 cag of Tammons.

Jan. 28.— Sch. *Debro* James Simmons master. Tonage 114 40/95 from Turk Island bound to Plymouth. 2555 bushels of salt.

Jan. 28.— Sch. *Baltimore* James Cox master. Tonage 59 from St. Pierre, Maetinik bound to Elizabeth City. 59 tons of ballast & small stores.

Jan. 28.— Sch. *Rio* J. S. Day master. Tonage 87 from Rum Key bound to Elizabeth City. Cargo 2110 bushels of salt and small ship stores.

Jan. 28.— Sch. *Onpeak* E. C. Davis master. T nage 67 59/95 tons from Anquiller to Elizabeth City. 1500 bushels of salt, ship stores . . . 20 pounds of coffee, 20 pounds of sugar.

Feb. 10.— Sch. *San Juan* Warren Davis master. 105 62/95 tons:. From Anquiller bound to Elizabeth City. Cargo 2457 bushels of salt.

Feb. 25.— Sch. *Mary Louise* B G [illegible] master. Tonage 144. Cargo 16 puncheons of molasses, some ballast. From St. Kitts bound to Washington.

Feb. 25.— Sch. *Catherine* J. W. Latham master. Tonage 99 from Antiger St. Martins bound to Newburn. Cargo 11 demajohns of rum, 1100 oranges, 443 barrels of salt, 5 HHD molases.

Mar. 1.— Sch. *George Henry* James Fields master. Tonage 112 from St. Martins bound to New burn, Cargo 656 barrels of salt, 1 cask of molasses, ship stores beef, pork, fish, 2 cags Tammons.

Mar. 17.— Sch. *Charles C. Mecleese* [McClees?] Daniel Irland master. Tonage 113 from Denanah [?] bound to New Burn cargo 44 hogsheads molasses, 3 do of sugar, 44 barrels of sugar and small stores. 7 barrels of mullets.

Mar. 29.— Sch. *San Juan* W. Davis master. Tonage 105 from Barbados bound to Elizabeth City. Cargo 15 puncheons of molasses, 5 barrels of sugar, 1000 oranges, 1 cag of tammons, 4 bunches of menanners [bananas] 1 barrel of sugar, do of pork, do of beef and other small stores.

Mar. 29.— Sch. *Baltimore* J. W. Cox master. Tonage 59 from Gordilupe bound to Elizabeth City, 20 tons of ballast and small stores.

Quarter commencing April 1th, 1861

Apr. 3.— Sch. *Rio* Josephus Davis master. 87 90/95 tonage. From St. Thomas bound to Elizabeth City. Cargo ship stores.

[And the record ends:]

Hatteras, July 4th, 1861 . . . John W. Rolinson, Achsah Rolinson and Mifourri Rolinson was at the Fort and went over to the camp and took dinner with Cornel Stark. The first battle at Hatteras was fot [fought] by an Northern steamer. She commenced bombarding the fort about 3 o'clock on Wednesday July 10th, 1861. The first gun was fired from the Fort by Capt. Cahoon commander. Thar [there] was no damage done to the fort.

J. W. ROLINSON

[And then, more hurriedly, in an unsigned entry:]

The Bombardment of Fort Hatteras commenced Wednesday August 27 and surrendered August 28th, 1861. . . .

***

Afterward, apparently from memory, Mr. Rollinson set down the following account of the events of that period:

"The Bombardment of Fort Hatteras commenced August 28 and surrendered August 29th, 1861. John W. Rolinson and his wife and three children left home on the 28th of August and went to Bate Williams on the Cape on the 29th of August went to Kennikeet. From thar went to Middle Creek, landed thar August 30th, 1861.

"State that about three weeks in the house known by the name of Kit Spencer House. From that moved to Bysocken to the house belonging to Dr. M. Selby known as the Midgett House. State thar untill January Ith, 1862 then moved to Dr. Selby's overseer's house. State thar until 14th of March 1862 then moved back to Middle Creek to the Ben M. Gibbs house. State thar until August 14th 1862 then moved to Nebraska to the Oliver Gibbs House, and was there March 29th, 1864.

"I left Wysockin May 16th 1864 and came to Ocracoke and on the 20th day of May 1864 came to Hatteras, and on the 8th of June Christopher RoHnson Sen. and Reddin R. Quidley Sen. moved my family back to Hatteras and we moved in with my wife's father and Mother and stade thar until July 12th, 1864 and then moved back to the house I formerly lived in and on the 13th of September my wife had a son Borned and we called his name

Samuel Milton Selby.

And at the foot of this page is the notation, in another ink: "I put my Bill Smith boat on the Beach February 11, 1874."

Elsewhere, in obscure corners of pages otherwise filled, there are two entries from the Civil War period:

"Went back to Hatteras on a business March 9, 1864 and returned to Hyde county March 18th, 1864. . . . I planted my western cut of corn April 22. Planted my lower cut of corn April 27th, 1864."

On the day his son was born (September 13th) he set down the couplet from a hymn: "A charge to keep have I, a God to Glorify."

Here are a few other entries that may be of interest to the reader:

"Hatteras Inlet was cut Sept. 7, 1846."

"John W. Rolinson was appointed magistrate at May Term which was held on the 10th Day, 1857."

"I commence porpoising for Cor. Wainwright November 16, 1885 at $30 per month for myself and $15 per month for boat and I have charge of the cru [crew] and on the 7th day of January we had 300 porpoises."

"John W. Rolinson. My Book.
"Wrote on Cape Hatteras Banks, Hyde County, N. C. August the 29th Day 1845 going to School at Trent to George W. Stowe."

"John W. Rolinson bought at Capt. Murphy vandue one mare at $30, 75 cents March 24th, 1849."

"Notice: I shall attend at my house on Thursday the 4th of this month for the purpose of taking the tax list for the year 1857."

"John W. Rolinson Got in the Double Rule of Three June 10th Day, 1846."

"John W. Rolinson, my Book. Rote at Hatteras Schoolhouse Sept. 7, 1848 going to school to Mr. James Creed."

"Brother Dixon the preacher in charge of Hatteras sircuit departed this life at Barney Peel's. Elder Closs preached his funeral. Text [indecipherable]." [undated]

FIFTY-THREE WORDS—SIX LIVES

Here is set down the report of Captain Benjamin B. Dailey on the rescue of the six members of the crew of the *Ephraim Williams*, December 19, 1884:

Vessel abreast of LSS [live saving station] Big Kinnakeet. Top tide sea running high. It seemed almost impossible to get to sea but seeing no one else making any effort to save the crew after waiting about 30 minutes I ordered my boat off carriage. I told the men to lash everything in the Boat and strip themselves for sea. My No. 1* man came to me & said his wife was dying & wanted him to come home. I asked Capt. P. H. Etheridge, keeper of L.S. Station Creed's Hill if he would go with me. He said yes. I put the boat in & after a hard struggle we got to sea. We boarded or at least went near the Bark & after some hard work we got the crew off in our Boat. We made for the shore after coming through a heavy sea. We landed alright.

---

*I have been unable to identify this man. The Station's roster carried it but when I saw it, in 1938, the name had been crossed out heavily with ink. None on the Island has been able to remember who was No. 1 Surfman on that day.—B. D. M.

THE MEDAL OF HONOR FOR LIFESAVING

First Class (Gold)

For the rescue of six members of the crew of the *Ephraim Williams* five miles off Big Kinnakeet Lifesaving Station, December, 1884:

> BENJAMIN B. DAILEY, *Keeper*
> Cape Hatteras Station
> PATRICK H. ETHERIDGE, *Keeper*
> Creed's Hill Station
> Isaac L. Jennette
> Amalek T. Gray
> John Howard Midgett
> Jabez B. Jennette
> Charles E. Fulcher, *Surfmen*
> Cape Hatteras Station

For the rescue of ten of the crew and passengers of the schooner *Priscilla* south of Gull Shoal Station and the recovery of the bodies of four who did not survive, August 18, 1899, the rescue being effected alone and on horseback:

> RASMUS L. MIDGETT, *Surfman*
> Gull Shoal Station

For the rescue of seven members of the crew of the schooner *Sarah J. D. Dawson* off Ocracoke Inlet in an operation that kept the rescue crews at sea in their lifeboats for twenty-eight hours, February 9–10, 1905:

> W. H. GASKILL, *Keeper*
> Kilbie Guthrie
> Walter M. Yoemans
> Tyre Moore
> Joseph L. Lewis
> John A. Guthrie
> James W. Fulcher
> John E. Kirkman
> Calput T. Jarvis, *Surfmen*
>> Lookout Shoals Station

For the rescue of the entire crew, thirty-five men, from the German steamship *Brewster*, foundered on the Outer Diamonds, November 28, 1909:

> E. H. PEELE, *Keeper*
>> Creed's Hill Station
> BAXTER B. MILLER, *Surfman*
>> Acting Keeper
>> Cape Hatteras Station

For the rescue of the crew of the British tanker *Mirlo* off Chicamicomico, August 16, 1918:

> JOHN ALLEN MIDGETT, *Keeper*
> Zion S. Midgett
> Arthur V. Midgett
> Prochorus L. O'Neal
> LeRoy S. Midgett
> Clarence E. Midgett, *Surfmen*
>> Chicamicomico Station

Second Class (Silver)

Medals of the Second Class (awarded when a rescue crew puts itself in jeopardy not classed above and beyond the call of duty) were awarded in these instances:

For their participation in the rescue of the *Brewster* (see above):

> H. S. Miller
> O. O. Midgett
> Isaac L. Jennette
> E. J. Midgett
> V. B. Williams
> W. L. Barnett, *Surfmen*
>   Cape Hatteras Station, and
> D. E. Fulcher
> V. O. Gaskins
> W. H. Austin, *Surfmen*
>   Creed's Hill Station

For the rescue of John H. Dailey (son of Captain B. B. Dailey) when swept overboard in heavy weather on June 15, 1911:

> BAXTER B. MILLER, *Surfman*
>   Cape Hatteras Station

For the rescue of five members of the crew of the trawler *Anna May* sunk on Diamond Shoals, December 9, 1931:

> BERNICE B. BALLANCE, *Keeper*
>   Cape Hatteras Station
> JOHN R. AUSTIN *Keeper*
>   Big Kinnakeet Station
> Monroe Gilliken
> Erskine Oden, *Surfmen*
>   Creed's Hill Station

James M. Ketcham
Frank W. Miller
Baxter Jennette, *Surfmen*
    Cape Hatteras Station, and
Thomas Barnett
Levene W. Midgett
Dallas Williams
R. J. Scarborough
Guy G. Quidley
Tommie G. Meekins
Sumner [Kimball] Scarborough, *Surfmen*
    Hatteras Inlet Station